PRAISE FOR *THE END OF POWER*

"In his new book called *The End of Power*, Moisés Naím goes so far as to say that power is actually decaying. I actually find the argument rather persuasive."
—General Martin Dempsey, Chairman of the Joint Chiefs of Staff

"I particularly enjoyed *The End of Power* by Moisés Naím. . . . It is particularly relevant for big institutions like GE."
—Jeff Immelt, CEO, General Electric

"Moisés Naím's *The End of Power* offers a cautionary tale to would-be Lincolns in the modern era. Naím is a courageous writer who seeks to dissect big subjects in new ways. At a time when critics of overreaching governments, big banks, media moguls and concentrated wealth decry the power of the '1%,' Mr. Naím argues that leaders of all types—political, corporate, military, religious, union—face bigger, more complex problems with weaker hands than in the past." —*Wall Street Journal*

"Analytically sophisticated . . . [a] highly original, inter-disciplinary meditation on the degeneration of international power." —*Washington Post*

"Naím produces a fascinating account of the way states, corporations and traditional interest groups are finding it harder to defend their redoubts . . . (He) makes his case with eloquence." —*Financial Times*

"A timely and timeless book." —*Booklist*

"Having served as editor-in-chief of Foreign Policy and the executive director of the World Bank, Naím knows better than most what power on a global scale looks like. . . . [A] timely, insightful, and eloquent message."
—*Publishers Weekly,* Starred Review

"Foreign Policy editor-in-chief Naím argues that global institutions of power are losing their ability to command respect. Whether considering institutions of government, military, religion or business, the author believes their power to be in the process of decaying. . . . A data-packed, intriguing analysis." —*Kirkus Reviews*

"*The End of Power* will change the way you read the news, the way you think about politics, and the way you look at the world."
—Bill Clinton, 42nd President of the United States of America

"In my own experience as president of Brazil I observed first hand many of the trends that Naím identifies in this book, but he describes them in a way that is as original as it is delightful to read. All those who have power—or want it—should read this book."
—Fernando Henrique Cardoso

"Moisés Naím's extraordinary new book will be of great interest to all those in leadership positions—business executives, politicians, military officers, social activists and even religious leaders. Readers will gain a new understanding of why power has become easier to acquire and harder to exercise. *The End of Power* will spark intense and important debate worldwide."
—George Soros

"After you read *The End of Power* you will see the world through different eyes. Moisés Naím provides a compelling and original perspective on the surprising new ways power is acquired, used, and lost—and how these changes affect our daily lives." —Arianna Huffington

"Moisés Naím is one of the most trenchant observers of the global scene. In *The End of Power*, he offers a fascinating new perspective on why the powerful face more challenges than ever. Probing into the shifting nature of power across a broad range of human endeavors, from business to politics to the military, Naím makes eye-opening connections between phenomena not usually linked, and forces us to re-think both how our world has changed and how we need to respond." —Francis Fukuyama

THE END OF

POWER

FROM BOARDROOMS
TO BATTLEFIELDS
AND CHURCHES
TO STATES,
WHY BEING
IN CHARGE
ISN'T WHAT IT
USED TO BE

MOISÉS NAÍM

BASIC BOOKS

A MEMBER OF THE PERSEUS BOOKS GROUP

New York

Hardcover first published in 2013 by Basic Books,
A Member of the Perseus Books Group

Paperback first published in 2014 by Basic Books

Books published by Basic Books are available at special discounts for bulk purchases
in the United States by corporations, institutions, and other organizations. For more
information, please contact the Special Markets Department at the Perseus Books
Group, 2300 Chestnut Street, Suite 200, Philadelphia, PA 19103, or call (800) 810-4145,
ext. 5000, or e-mail special.markets@perseusbooks.com.

Designed by Trish Wilkinson
Set in 11.5 point Minion Pro

The Library of Congress has cataloged the hardcover edition as follows:

Naím, Moisés.
    The end of power : from boardrooms to battlefields and churches to states, why
being in charge isn't what it used to be / Moisés Naím.
        pages cm
    Includes bibliographical references and index.
    ISBN 978-0-465-03156-6 (hardcover : alk. paper)—ISBN 978-0-465-03781-0 (e-book)
1. Power (Social sciences) 2. Organization. I. Title.
    HN49.P6N35 2013
    303.3–dc23
                                                                    2012049642

ISBN 978-0-465-06569-1 (paperback)

10 9 8 7 6 5 4 3 2 1

To Susana, Adriana, Claudia, Andres, Jonathan, and Andrew

CONTENTS

PREFACE

How This Book Came About: A Personal Note

POWER MAY FEEL ABSTRACT, BUT FOR THOSE WHO ARE MOST ATTUNED TO it—namely, the powerful themselves—its flow and ebb can have a visceral edge. After all, those in positions of great power are best positioned to spot limits on their effectiveness and to feel frustration over the gap between the power they expect their rank to convey and the power they actually have. In my own small way, I experienced such constraints back in February 1989. At the time I had been named, at age thirty-six, the minister of development in the then-democratic government of my home country, Venezuela. Soon after we took office in a landslide election victory, we faced riots in Caracas—triggered by the anxiety over our plans to cut subsidies and raise fuel prices—that paralyzed the city with violence, fear, and chaos. Suddenly, and despite our victory and apparent mandate, the economic reform program that we had championed acquired a very different meaning. Instead of symbolizing hope and prosperity, it was now seen as the source of street violence, increased poverty, and deeper inequality.

But the most profound insight I had at that time was one I would not fully comprehend until years later. It dwelt in the enormous gap between the perception and the reality of my power. In principle, as one of the main economic ministers, I wielded tremendous power. But in practice, I had only a limited ability to deploy resources, to mobilize individuals and organizations, and, more generally, to make things happen. My colleagues and even the president had the same feeling, though we were loath to acknowledge that our government was a hobbled giant. I was tempted to chalk this up to Venezuela itself: surely our sense of powerlessness had to do with our country's notoriously weak and malfunctioning institutions. Such weakness could not be universal.

Yet later I would appreciate that it was universal indeed, or nearly so, among those with the experience of power. Fernando Henrique Cardoso—the respected former president of Brazil and founding father of that country's success—summed it up for me. "I was always surprised at how powerful people thought I was," he told me when I interviewed him for this book. "Even well-informed, politically sophisticated individuals would come to my office and ask me to do things that showed they assumed I had far more power than I really did. I always thought to myself, if only they knew how limited the power of any president is nowadays. When I meet with other heads of state, we often share very similar recollections in this respect. The gap between our real power and what people expect from us is the source of the most difficult pressure any head of state has to manage."

I heard something similar from Joschka Fischer, one of Germany's most popular politicians and a former vice chancellor and foreign minister. "Since I was young, I was fascinated and allured by power," Fischer told me. "One of my biggest shocks was the discovery that all the imposing government palaces and other trappings of government were in fact empty places. The imperial architecture of governmental palaces masks how limited the power of those who work there really is."

Over time, I would glean similar observations not just from heads of state and government ministers but also from business leaders and the heads of foundations and major organizations in many fields. And it soon became clear that something more was going on—that it wasn't simply that the powerful were bemoaning the gap between their perceived and actual power. Power itself was coming under attack in an unprecedented way. Every year since 1990, I have attended the World Economic Forum's annual meeting in Davos, frequented by the world's most powerful people in business, government, politics, the media, nongovernmental organizations, science, religion, and culture. In fact, I have been lucky enough to attend and speak at almost all of the most exclusive power-fests in the world, including the Bilderberg Conference, the annual meeting of media and entertainment tycoons in Sun Valley, and the annual meetings of the International Monetary Fund. My conversations each year with fellow participants confirmed my hunch: the powerful are experiencing increasingly greater limits on their power. The reactions to my probing always pointed in the same direction: power is becoming more feeble, transient, and constrained.

But this is not a call to feel sorry for those in power. Powerful people bemoaning their powerlessness is certainly no reason for hand-wringing in our winner-take-all world. Rather, my aim is to delineate the impact of the decay of power. In the pages ahead I explore this process of decay—its causes, manifestations, and consequences—in terms of the ways it affects not just the 1 percent at the top but, more importantly, the vast and growing middle class as well as those who seek merely to make it through another day.

Moisés Naím
March 2013

CHAPTER ONE

THE DECAY OF POWER

THIS IS A BOOK ABOUT POWER.

Specifically it is about how power—the capacity to get others to do, or to stop doing, something—is undergoing a historic and world-changing transformation.

Power is spreading, and long-established, big players are increasingly being challenged by newer and smaller ones. And those who have power are more constrained in the ways they can use it.

We often misunderstand or altogether overlook the magnitude, nature, and consequences of this transformation. It is tempting to focus exclusively on the impact of the Internet and other new technologies, on the direction of power shifts from one player to another, or on the question of whether the "soft" power of culture is displacing the "hard" power of armies. But those perspectives are incomplete. Indeed, they can obscure our understanding of the fundamental forces that are changing how power is acquired, used, kept, and lost.

We know that power is shifting from brawn to brains, from north to south and west to east, from old corporate behemoths to agile start-ups, from entrenched dictators to people in town squares and cyberspace. But to say that power is shifting from one continent or country to another, or that it is dispersing among many new players, is not enough. Power is undergoing a far more fundamental mutation that has not been sufficiently recognized and understood. Even as rival states, companies, political parties, social movements, and institutions or individual leaders fight for power as they have done throughout the ages, power itself—what they are fighting so desperately to get and keep—is slipping away.

Power is *decaying*.

To put it simply, power no longer buys as much as it did in the past. In the twenty-first century, power is easier to get, harder to use—and easier to lose. From boardrooms and combat zones to cyberspace, battles for power are as intense as ever, but they are yielding diminishing returns. Their fierceness masks the increasingly evanescent nature of power itself. Understanding how power is losing its value—and facing up to the hard challenges this poses—is the key to making sense of one of the most important trends reshaping the world in the twenty-first century.

This is not to say that power has disappeared or that there aren't still people who possess it in abundance. The president of the United States or China, the CEO of J. P. Morgan or Shell Oil, the executive editor of the *New York Times,* the head of the International Monetary Fund, and the pope continue to wield immense power. But less so than their predecessors. The previous holders of these jobs not only dealt with fewer challengers and competitors, but they also had fewer constraints—in the form of citizen activism, global markets, and media scrutiny—on using the power they had. As a result, today's power players often pay a steeper and more immediate price for their mistakes than did their predecessors. Their response to that new reality, in turn, is reshaping the behavior of those over whom they have power, setting in motion a chain reaction that touches every aspect of human interaction.

The decay of power is changing the world.

The goal of this book is to prove these bold assertions.

HAVE YOU HEARD OF JAMES BLACK JR.?

The forces driving the decay of power are manifold, intertwined, and unprecedented. To see why, turn your mind from Clausewitz, the Fortune 500 rankings, and the top 1 percent of the US population that accounts for a disproportionately large chunk of the nation's income and consider the case of James Black Jr., a chess player from a working-class family in the Bedford-Stuyvesant neighborhood of Brooklyn, New York.

By the time he was twelve, Black had become a Master at chess, a ranking achieved by fewer than 2 percent of the 77,000 members of the United States Chess Federation—and only 13 of those Masters were under fourteen.[1] The year was 2011, and Black has a good shot at becoming a Grandmaster—a ranking awarded by the World Chess Federation based on the player's performance in tournaments with titled players. Grandmaster is the highest title a chess player can attain. Once obtained, the title is held for life.[2]

When Black became a Master, he was following in the footsteps of America's youngest Grandmaster ever: Ray Robson of Florida, who attained that status in October 2009, two weeks before his fifteenth birthday.[3]

Black taught himself the game on a cheap plastic set he bought at Kmart and quickly moved on to chess books and computer programs. His idol is Mikhail Tal, a Russian world chess champion of the 1950s. What motivates Black, in addition to his enjoyment of the game, is the way it lets him wield power. As he told a reporter: "I like to dictate what the other player has to do"—as clear a statement of the innate urge for power as one can find.[4]

But the achievements of James Black and Ray Robson are no longer exceptional. They are part of a global trend, a new phenomenon that has swept through the long-closed world of competitive chess. Players are learning the game and achieving mastery at much younger ages. There are more Grandmasters now than ever before: 1,200-plus today versus 88 in 1972. And as newcomers defeat established champions with increasing frequency, the average tenure of the world's top players is trending down. Moreover, today's Grandmasters hail from far more diverse backgrounds than did their predecessors. As the writer D. T. Max observed: "In 1991, the year the Soviet Union broke up, the top nine players in the world were from the U.S.S.R. By then, Soviet-trained players had held the world championship for all but three of the past forty-three years."[5]

Not anymore. More competitors are now capable of climbing to the top of the chess leagues, and they come from a wide variety of nations and neighborhoods. But once they reach the top, they have a hard time staying there. As Mig Greengard, a chess blogger, observed: "You've got two hundred guys walking the planet who, with a little tailwind, are playing strongly enough to beat the world champion."[6] In other words, among today's Grandmasters, power itself is no longer what it used to be.

What explains these changes in the world's chess hierarchy? In part (but only in part): the digital revolution.

For some time now, chess players have had access to computer programs that enable them to simulate millions of games played by the world's best players. They can also use the software to work out the implications of every possible move; for instance, competitors can replay any game, examine moves under various scenarios, and study specific players' tendencies. Thus the Internet has both broadened the horizons of chess players around the world and—as James Black's story attests—opened new possibilities for players of any age and socioeconomic background. Countless chess sites deliver data and competitive game opportunities to anyone with a Web connection.[7]

But this story isn't just about technology. Take, for example, the case of the young Norwegian champion Magnus Carlsen, another chess phenom who in 2010 became the world's No. 1 player, at age nineteen. According to D. T. Max, who profiled him for *The New Yorker,* Carlsen's success had more to do with his unorthodox and surprising strategies (relying in part on his prodigious memory) than with computer-based training: "Because Carlsen has spent less time than most of his cohort training with computers, he is less prone to play the way they do. He relies more on his own judgment. This makes him tricky for opponents who have relied on software and databases for counsel."[8]

The demolition of the power structure of world chess also stems from changes in the global economy, in politics, and in demographic and migratory patterns. Open borders and cheaper travel have given more players the chance to play tournaments anywhere in the world. Higher education standards and the spread of literacy, numeracy, and child healthcare have created a bigger pool of potential Grandmasters. And today, for the first time in history, more people live in cities than in farms—a development that, along with the prolonged period of economic growth enjoyed by many poor countries since the 1990s, has opened new possibilities for millions of families for whom the game of chess was an unaffordable or even unknown luxury. But it is not easy to become a world-class chess player if you live on an isolated farm in a poor country with no electricity, or lack a computer, or spend many hours each day procuring food—or carrying water to your home. Before the Internet can deliver its empowering magic, many other conditions must be in place.

From the Chess Board . . . to Everything Around Us

Chess is a classic metaphor for power, of course. But what has happened to chess is the erosion, and in some cases the disappearance, of barriers that previously kept the world of champions small, tight-knit, and stable. The obstacles to understanding tactics and developing mastery, as well as all the other barriers that limit access to the top, have become less forbidding.

What has happened to chess is also happening to power in general. The tumbling down of barriers is transforming local politics and geopolitics, the competition for consumers and for believers in the great religions, and the rivalries among nongovernmental organizations, intellectual institutions, ideologies, and schools of philosophical thought and science. Wherever power matters, power is also decaying.

Some signs of this transformation are breathtakingly clear; others are unearthed by expert analysis and academic research.

Let's begin with geopolitics. Sovereign states have quadrupled in number since the 1940s; moreover, they now compete, fight, or negotiate not just with each other but also with numerous transnational and nonstate organizations. In fact, the 2011 birth of South Sudan, the world's newest nation, was effectively midwifed by dozens of nongovernmental organizations, especially evangelical Christian groups such as Samaritan's Purse, run by Franklin Graham, one of the sons of American mega-preacher Billy Graham.

Indeed, when nation-states go to war these days, big military power delivers less than it once did. Wars are not only increasingly asymmetric, pitting large military forces against smaller, nontraditional ones such as insurgents, separatist movements, and militias. They are also increasingly being won by the militarily weaker side. According to a remarkable Harvard study, in the asymmetric wars that broke out between 1800 and 1849, the weaker side (in terms of soldiers and weapons) achieved its strategic goals in 12 percent of cases. But in the wars that erupted between 1950 and 1998, the weak side prevailed more often: 55 percent of the time. For a variety of reasons, the outcome of modern asymmetric conflicts is more likely to be determined by the interplay of opposing political and military strategies than by blunt military force. Thus, a large, advanced army by itself no longer ensures that a country will achieve its strategic goals. One important factor behind this shift is the increasing ability of the weaker party to inflict casualties on its opponent at lower cost to itself. The use of improvised explosive devices (IEDs) in Afghanistan and Iraq is a case in point. One Marine general in Afghanistan estimated that IEDs caused 80 percent of casualties in his unit, and during some years in Iraq, IEDs were responsible for almost two-thirds of the casualties suffered by coalition forces. This level of lethality prevails despite considerable investment by the Pentagon in countermeasures, including the $17 billion it spent to purchase 50,000 radio frequency jammers aimed at neutralizing the primitive remote-controlled devices (cellphones, garage door openers) used to detonate the bombs.[9]

Dictators and party bosses, too, are finding their power diminished and their numbers depleted. In 1977, a total of eighty-nine countries were ruled by autocrats; by 2011, the number had dwindled to 22.[10] Today, more than half the world's population lives in democracies. The tremors of the Arab Spring were felt in every corner of the world where clean elections are not held regularly and one person or ruling clique is trying to hold on to power indefinitely. Even in nondemocracies where political parties are allowed, minority parties have three times more representation now than in the 1980s. And everywhere, party bosses are back on their heels, as they contend with candidates and leaders emerging from realms outside the proverbial smoke-filled back rooms. About half of the major parties in established democracies now use primaries or some other representative method to give the rank-and-file more of a say in choosing their standard-bearers. From Chicago to Milan and New Delhi to Brasilia, the bosses of political machines will readily tell you that they have lost the ability to deliver the votes and decisions that their predecessors took for granted.

The business world is also being touched by this trend. It is indubitable that income is concentrating, the wealthy are accumulating enormous riches, and some are using money to gain political power. But that trend, as alarming as it is unacceptable, is not the only force shaping the workings of power among corporate leaders and wealthy investors.

Indeed, even the vaunted 1 percent in the United States are not immune to sudden shifts in wealth, power, and status. For all the rise in income inequality, the Great Recession also had a corrective effect, disproportionately affecting the incomes of the rich. According to Emmanuel Saez, a Berkeley economics professor, it caused a 36.3 percent drop in the incomes of the top 1 percent of earners in the United States, compared to an 11.6 percent drop for the remaining 99 percent.[11] Steven Kaplan at the University of Chicago's Booth School of Business has calculated that the proportion of income accounted for by the top 1 percent fell from its peak of 23.5 percent of income in 2007 to 17.6 percent in 2009 and, as Saez's data show, it kept falling in following years. Indeed, as Robert Frank reported in the *Wall Street Journal,* "The super-high earners have the biggest crashes. The number of Americans making $1 million or more fell 40 percent between 2007 and 2009, to 236,883, while their combined incomes fell by nearly 50 percent—far greater than the less than 2 percent drop in total incomes of those making $50,000 or less, according to Internal Revenue Service figures."[12] None of this, of course, means that the concentration of income and wealth in many advanced democracies, and especially the United States, has not dramatically increased. It has—and quite sharply. But this reality should not obscure the fact that some wealthy individuals and families have also been hit by the economic crisis and as a result have experienced significant declines in their fortunes and economic power.

Moreover, personal income and wealth are not the only sources of power. The leaders at the helm of large corporations often wield more power than the "simply" rich. Corporate heads nowadays earn much more than before, but tenure at the top has become as tenuous as that of a chess champion. In 1992, a US Fortune 500 CEO had a 36 percent chance of retaining his or her job for the next five years; in 1998, that chance was down to 25 percent. By 2005, the average tenure of an American CEO had dwindled to six years. And the trend is global. In 2011, 14.4 percent of CEOs of the world's 2,500 biggest listed companies left their jobs. Even in Japan, famous for its relative corporate stasis, forced succession among the heads of large corporations quadrupled in 2008.[13]

The same goes for the corporations themselves. In 1980, a US corporation in the top fifth of its industry had only a 10 percent risk of falling out of that tier in five years. Two decades later, that likelihood had risen to 25 percent. Now, a simple count of the US and global top five hundred companies that did not exist ten years ago shows how relative newcomers are displacing traditional corporate behemoths. In finance, banks are losing power and influence to newer and nimbler hedge funds: in the second half of 2010, in the midst of a sharp economic downturn, the top ten hedge funds—most of them unknown to the general public—earned more than the world's largest six banks combined. Even the largest of these funds, which manage unfathomable amounts of money and earn huge profits, operates with only a few hundred employees.

Meanwhile, corporations have become much more vulnerable to "brand disasters" that hit their reputations, revenues, and valuations. One study found that the five-year risk of such a disaster for companies that own the most prestigious global brands has risen in the last two decades from 20 percent to a staggering 82 percent. BP, Tiger Woods, and Rupert Murdoch's News Corporation all saw their fortunes shrink almost overnight as a result of events that scarred their reputations.

In yet another manifestation of the diffusion of power in business, members of a new species, "poor-country multinationals" (i.e., those that come from less developed countries), have displaced or taken over some of the largest companies in the world. Investments originating in developing countries went from $12 billion in 1991 to $210 billion in 2010. The world's largest steel company, ArcelorMittal, has its roots in Mittal Steel, an Indian company created as recently as in 1989.[14] When Americans sip their iconic Budweiser, they are in fact enjoying a beer produced by a company engendered by a 2004 merger of Brazilian and Belgian breweries that in turn managed to gain control of Anheuser-Busch in 2008, thus forming the world's largest beer company. Its CEO, Carlos Brito, is from Brazil.

These trends extend beyond traditional power arenas—war, politics, business—into philanthropy, religion, culture, and the personal power of individuals. The number of new billionaires set a record in 2010, and each year some names disappear from the list while previously unknown individuals hailing from the four corners of the world take their places.

No longer the province of a few major foundations and public and international organizations, philanthropy has exploded into a constellation of small foundations and new modes of giving that in many cases directly match contributors with beneficiaries, bypassing the classic model of charities. International giving by US individuals and institutions quadrupled in the 1990s and doubled again from 1998 to 2007, when it reached $39.6 billion—a sum more than 50 percent larger than the World Bank's annual commitments. In the United States, the number of foundations increased from 40,000 in 1975 to more than 76,000 in 2012. Actors, athletes, and other A-list habitués ranging from Oprah Winfrey and Bill Clinton to Angelina Jolie and Bono have supercharged celebrity giving. And of course the new mega-foundations endowed by Bill and Melinda Gates, Warren Buffet, and George Soros are upending traditional ways of doing business in the big-foundation world. Thousands of newly wealthy technology tycoons and hedge fund managers are also entering the world of "giving" much sooner and making available larger amounts of money than had previously been the norm. "Venture philanthropy" has led to a new industry designed to advise, support, and channel such money. The United States Agency for International Development (USAID), the World Bank, and the Ford Foundation not only face more competitors who have harnessed the Internet and other technology to their advantage, but more public scrutiny and conditions from activists, recipients, and host governments.

Similarly, the long-entrenched power of the major organized religions is decaying at a remarkably rapid pace. For instance, Pentecostal churches are advancing in countries that were once strongholds for the Vatican and mainline Protestant churches. In Brazil, Pentecostals and charismatics made up only 5 percent of the population in 1960—compared to 49 percent in

2006. (They comprise 11 percent in South Korea, 23 percent in the United States, 26 percent in Nigeria, 30 percent in Chile, 34 percent in South Africa, 44 percent in the Philippines, 56 percent in Kenya, and 60 percent in Guatemala.) Pentecostal churches are typically small and tailored to local believers, but some have expanded and crossed borders; examples include Brazil's Igreja Universal do Reino de Deus (IURD), which boasts 4 million members, and Nigeria's Redeemed Christian Church of God (RCCG). One Nigerian pastor has a 40,000-member church in Kiev, Ukraine. Meanwhile, what experts call "organic churches"—that is, grassroots, hands-on, non-hierarchical churches that spring up in communities—are challenging Catholicism and the Church of England from within. And Islam, not centralized to begin with, is continuing to splinter as scholars and imams offer conflicting interpretations from televised platforms.

Add to all this the similar trends being observed in labor, education, art, science—even professional sports—and the picture fills in. It is a picture of power scattered among an increasing number of newer, smaller players from diverse and unexpected origins, much as we see in chess. And these players are using a very different playbook from the one on which traditional players have long relied.

I KNOW THAT ARGUING THAT POWER IS BECOMING MORE FRAIL AND vulnerable goes against the widespread perception to the contrary—the perception that we are living at a time when power is becoming more concentrated and that those who have it are stronger and more entrenched than ever before. Indeed, many people think that power is like money: having it increases the chances of having even more of it. From this perspective, the self-perpetuating cycle of concentration of power and wealth can be considered a central driver of human history. And, surely, the world is full of people and institutions that have immense power and are not about to lose it. But the pages ahead will show that looking at the world through this prism hides very important aspects of the way things are changing.

As we shall see, there is much more going on than a simple shift in power from one coterie of influential players to another. The transformation of power is more total and more complicated. Power itself has become more available—and, indeed, in today's world more people have power. Yet its horizons have contracted, and once attained it has become harder to use. And there is an explanation for this.

WHAT CHANGED?

Power becomes entrenched as a result of barriers that shield incumbents from rivals. Such barriers not only prevent new competitors from growing into significant challengers but also reinforce the dominance of entrenched players. They are inherent in everything from the rules that govern elections to the arsenals of armies and police forces, to capital, exclusive access to resources, advertising budgets, proprietary technology, alluring brands, and even the moral authority of religious leaders or the personal charisma of some politicians.

Over the course of the last three decades, however, barriers to power have weakened at a very fast pace. They are now more easily undermined, overwhelmed, and circumvented. As our discussion of domestic and international politics, business, war, religion, and other areas will show, the causes underlying this phenomenon are related not only to demographic and economic transformations and the spread of information technologies but also to political changes and profound shifts in expectations, values, and social norms. Such information technologies (including but not limited to the Internet) play a meaningful role in shaping access to power and its use. But the more *fundamental* explanation as to why barriers to power have become more feeble has to do with the transformations in such diverse factors as rapid economic growth in many poor countries, migratory patterns, medicine and healthcare, education, and even attitudes and cultural mores—in short, with changes in the scope, state, and potential of human lives.

After all, what most distinguishes our lives today from those of our ancestors is not the tools we use or the rules that govern our societies. It is the fact that we are far more numerous on the planet; we live longer; we are in better health; we are more literate and educated; an unprecedented number of us are less desperate for food and have more time and money for other pursuits; and when we are not satisfied with our present location, it is now easier and cheaper than ever to move and try somewhere else. As our proximity and density have increased along with the duration and richness of our lives, our contacts with one another have also increased, enhancing our aspirations and our opportunities. Of course, health, education, and prosperity are far from universal today. Poverty, inequality, war, disease, and social and economic suffering persist. But overall statistics regarding life spans, literacy, infant mortality, nutrition, income levels, educational attainment, and human development demonstrate a world that has profoundly changed—along with perceptions and attitudes—in ways that directly affect the terms by which power is gained, kept, and lost.

The next three chapters will develop this idea in detail. Chapter 2 presents a clear and practical way of thinking about power that is applicable to every field. It discusses the various ways in which power may be exercised, makes sense of the differences between aspects of power such as influence, persuasion, coercion, and authority, and shows how power takes shelter behind barriers that allow it to expand and concentrate—until those same barriers are eroded and no longer fulfill their shielding function. Chapter 3 explains how power got big in so many different realms. Why, I ask, has power become equated in practice with the size of the organizations that back it? Why did large, hierarchical, and centralized organizations become the dominant vehicles through which power was—and still largely is—exercised? This coupling of power with the size of the organization that has it reached its apogee during the twentieth century. And it is an outlook that still dominates today's debates and conversation, even though the facts have now plainly changed.

Chapter 4 shows in detail how the big changes in our lives have created new challenges that make it more difficult to set up and defend the barriers to power that keep rivals at bay. These changes stem from three revolutionary transformations that define our time: the *More* revolution, which is characterized by increases in everything from the number of countries to population size, standards of living, literacy rates, and quantity of products on the market; the *Mobility* revolution, which has set people, goods, money, ideas, and values moving at hitherto unimagined rates toward every corner of the planet (including those that were once remote and inaccessible); and the *Mentality* revolution, which reflects the major changes in mindsets, expectations, and aspirations that have accompanied these shifts.

Some aspects of these three revolutions will be familiar to the reader, but what is not familiar, and has not been examined in depth, is how each of them is making power easier to get and harder to use or keep. Chapter 4 shows exactly how these profound and simultaneous revolutions are pushing down the barriers to power and increasing the difficulty of wielding it effectively. The result has been to severely hamper large, centralized modern organizations whose sizeable assets no longer guarantee dominance and in some cases may even have become disadvantages. Indeed, the circumstances under which different forms of power are expressed—including coercion, obligation, persuasion, and inducement—have changed in ways that limit to some degree, or roll back altogether, the advantages of size.

THE DECAY OF POWER:
IS IT NEW? IS IT TRUE? SO WHAT?

The changes we'll explore have benefited innovators and new entrants in many fields—including, unfortunately, pirates, terrorists, insurgents, hackers, traffickers, counterfeiters, and cyber-criminals.[15] They have produced opportunities for pro-democracy activists—as well as for fringe political parties with narrow or extreme agendas—and opened alternative paths to political influence that bypass or break down the formal and rigid internal structure of the political establishment, both in democratic countries and in repressive ones. Few could have anticipated that, when a small band of Malaysian activists decided in the summer of 2011 to "occupy" Dataran square in Kuala Lumpur, thus emulating the *Indignados* ("the indignant ones") camping in Madrid's Puerta del Sol, a similar movement would spring up to occupy Wall Street and spark similar initiatives in 2,600 cities around the world.

Although the concrete political changes produced by the "Occupy" movements have thus far been meager, their impact is worthy of notice. As noted 1960s chronicler Todd Gitlin observed, "The sort of sea changes in public conversation that took three years to develop during the long-gone sixties—about brutal war, unsatisfying affluence, debased politics, and the suppressed democratic promise—took three weeks in 2011."[16] In terms of speed, impact, and new forms of horizontal organization, the Occupy movements also revealed the erosion of the monopoly that traditional political parties once had over the channels through which members of society transmitted their grievances, hopes, and demands. In the Middle East, the Arab Spring that began in 2010 does not show any signs of abating and is instead continuing to spread—with reverberations felt by authoritarian regimes the world over.

And as noted earlier, much the same is happening in the business world. Small and obscure companies from countries with barely opened markets have been able to leapfrog and sometimes take over massive global enterprises and prestige brands built over decades by grand captains of industry.

In geopolitics, small players—whether "minor" countries or nonstate entities—have acquired new opportunities to veto, interfere in, redirect, and generally stymie the concerted efforts of "big powers" and multilateral organizations such as the International Monetary Fund (IMF). To name just a few instances: Poland's vetoing of the EU's low-carbon policy, the attempts by Turkey and Brazil to derail the big powers' negotiations with Iran over its nuclear program, Wikileaks' disclosure of US diplomatic secrets, the Gates Foundation's contesting of the World Health Organization leadership in the fight against malaria, and spoilers of various stripes and sizes in global negotiations on trade, climate change, and numerous other issues.

These newly and increasingly relevant "small players" are vastly different from one another, as are the fields they compete in. But they have in common the fact that they no longer require size, scope, history, or entrenched tradition to make their mark. They represent the rise of a new kind of power—call it *micropower*—that previously had little scope for success. Today, this book argues, what is changing the world has less to do with the competition between megaplayers than with the rise of *micropowers* and their ability to challenge the *megaplayers*.

The decay of power does not mean the extinction of those megaplayers. Big government, big armies, big business, and big universities will be constrained and confined as never before, but they will certainly stay relevant and their actions and decisions will carry great weight. But not as much as before. Not as much as they would like. And not as much as they expected. And though it may seem to be an unalloyed good that the powerful are less powerful than before (after all, power corrupts, doesn't it?), their demotion can also generate instability, disorder, and paralysis in the face of complex problems.

The coming chapters will also show how the decay of power has accelerated, despite such seemingly contradictory trends as the "big is back" and "too big to fail" bailouts at the end of the last decade, the constant increases in the military budgets of the United States and China, and the growing disparities in income and wealth throughout the world. Indeed, the decay of power is a more important and far-reaching issue than the superficial trends and developments that currently clog debates among policymakers and analysts.

In particular, this book takes aim at two of the big conventional conversations about power. One is the fixation with the Internet as the explanation for changes in power, especially in politics and business. The other is the obsession with the changing of the guard in geopolitics, whereby the decline of some nations (particularly the United States) and the rise of others (notably China) is presented as the dominant world-transforming trend of our time.

The decay of power is not driven by the Internet specifically or by information technology more generally. The Internet and other tools are undeniably transforming politics, activism, business, and, of course, power. But too often, this fundamental role is exaggerated and misunderstood. New information technologies are tools—and to have an impact, tools need users, who in turn need goals, direction, and motivation. Facebook, Twitter, and text messages were fundamental in empowering the protesters in the Arab Spring. But the protesters and the circumstances that motivated them to take to the streets are driven by circumstances at home and abroad that have nothing to do with the new information tools at their disposal. Millions of people participated in the demonstrations that brought down Hosni Mubarak in Egypt—but at its peak, the Facebook page credited with helping to spur protests there had only 350,000 members. Indeed, a recent study of Twitter traffic during the Egyptian and Libyan uprisings found that more than 75 percent of people who clicked on embedded Twitter links related to those struggles were from outside the Arab world.[17] Another study, by the US Institute of Peace, which also examined patterns of Twitter use during the Arab Spring, concluded that new media "did not appear to play a significant role in either in-country collective action or regional diffusion" of the uprising.[18]

First and foremost among the drivers of protest was the demographic reality of young people in countries like Tunisia, Egypt, and Syria—people who are healthier and better-educated than ever before but also unemployed and deeply frustrated. Moreover, the same information technologies that empower average citizens have ushered in new avenues for surveillance, repression, and corporate control—helping Iran, for example, identify and imprison participants in its stillborn "Green Revolution." It would be wrongheaded either to deny the critical role played by information technologies, especially social media, in the changes we are witnessing or to explain them only as the result of the widespread adoption of these technologies.

THE DECAY OF POWER IS ALSO NOT TO BE CONFUSED WITH ANY OF the "fashionable" power shifts that analysts and commentators have dissected ever since the decline of America and the rise of China became axiomatic as the key geopolitical transformation of our era—one celebrated, decried, or cautioned against, with various degrees of nuance, depending on the author's point of view. Assessing the concomitant decline of Europe and rise of the BRICS (Brazil, Russia, India, China, and South Africa) bloc and "the rest" has become the great parlor game among professional and amateur globe-twirlers. But while rivalries among nations are in flux (they always have been), the fixation with who is declining and who is rising is a grand and perilous distraction. This is a distraction because each new batch of winners is making an unpleasant discovery: namely, that those who hold power in the future will find their latitude constrained and their effectiveness limited in ways that they probably did not anticipate and that their predecessors did not experience.

Moreover, the cumulative effect of these changes has accelerated the corrosion of moral authority and legitimacy writ large. The well-documented decline of trust in the professions and in public institutions is one manifestation of that trend. Not only are society's leaders seen as more vulnerable, but those over whom they once held uncontested sway are more aware of different possibilities and more attuned to their own personal fulfillment. Today, we ask not what we can do for our country but what our country, employer, fast-food purveyor, or favorite airline can do for us.

Failure to look beyond the battles of the moment and see the larger decay of power carries a great cost. It contributes to confusion and prevents progress on the key and complex issues that demand our urgent attention, from the contagion of financial crises, unemployment, and poverty to resource depletion and climate change. We live in a time when, paradoxically, we are more aware of these issues and understand them better than ever before, yet we seem unable to tackle them decisively and effectively. The decay of power is the reason why.

BUT WHAT IS POWER?

A book about power requires a definition of power—and, just as important, a reason to take on this primordial yet in some ways most elusive of topics.

Power has focused behavior and driven competition since the dawn of society. For Aristotle, power along with wealth and friendships were the three components that added up to a person's happiness. The premise that humans naturally seek power at a personal level, and that rulers seek to consolidate and expand their realm, is a matter of near-consensus in philosophy. In the sixteenth century Niccolo Machiavelli wrote in *The Prince,* his primer on statecraft, that the acquisition of territory and political control "is in truth very natural and common, and men always do so when they can."[19] In the seventeenth century, the English philosopher Thomas Hobbes took the issue a step further in *Leviathan,* his classic treatise on human nature and society: "I put for a general inclination of all mankind a perpetual and restless desire of power after power, that ceaseth only after death," Hobbes wrote.[20] Two and a half centuries later, in 1885, Friedrich Nietzsche would write, in the voice of the heroic title character of *Thus Spake Zarathustra*: "Wherever I found a living thing, there found I Will to Power; and even in the will of the servant found I the will to be master."[21]

This is not to say that human life boils down to power alone. Surely love, sex, faith, and other urges and emotions also have their part to play. But just as surely, power is a quest that has forever motivated people. And just as it has always done, power structures society and helps govern relationships and orchestrate the interactions between people and within and among communities and nations. Power plays out in every field in which we contend, compete, or organize: international politics and war, domestic politics, business, scientific inquiry, religion, social action such as philanthropy and activism, and social and cultural relations of all kinds. Arguably, power also plays out in our most intimate love and family relations, as well as in our language and even through our dreams. Those last dimensions are beyond the focus of this book, but that does not mean they have been insulated from the trends that I seek to explain.

The approach here is practical. The aim is to understand what it takes to get power, to keep it, and to lose it. This requires a working definition, and here is one: *Power is the ability to direct or prevent the current or future actions of other groups and individuals.* Or, put differently, power is what we exercise over others that leads them to behave in ways they would not otherwise have behaved.

This practical way of looking at power is neither new nor controversial. Although power is an inherently complex topic, many of the practical definitions that social scientists have used are similar to the one spelled out here. For instance, my approach echoes a classic and much-referenced paper written in 1957 by the political scientist Robert Dahl, "The Concept of Power." In Dahl's phrasing: "A has power over B to the extent that he can get B to do something that B would not otherwise do." Different ways of exercising power, and different expressions of power such as influence, persuasion, coercion, and authority—which the next chapter will address—occur within this context: one party getting or failing to get the other to act in a certain way.[22]

Power may well be an essential motivation that all of us carry in our inner being, as the philosophers tell us; but as a force in action, it is inherently relational. It is not enough to measure power using proxies, such as who has the largest army, the richest treasury, the biggest population, or the most abundant resources. No one walks around with a fixed and quantifiable amount of power, because in reality any person or institution's power varies from situation to situation. For power to operate requires an interaction or exchange between two or more parties: master and servant, ruler and citizen, boss and employee, parent and child, teacher and student, or a complex combination of individuals, parties, armies, companies, institutions, even nations. Just as the players move from situation to situation, the ability of each one to direct or prevent the actions of the others—in other words, their power—also shifts. The less the players and their attributes change, the more stable the particular distribution of power becomes. But when the number, identity, motivations, abilities, and attributes of the players change, the power distribution will change as well.

This is not just an abstract point. What I mean is that power has a social function. Its role is not just to enforce domination or to create winners and losers: it also organizes communities, societies, marketplaces, and the world. Hobbes explained this well. Because the urge for power is primal, he argued, it follows that humans are inherently conflictual and competitive. Left to express that nature without the presence of power to inhibit and direct them, they would fight until there was nothing left to fight for. But if they obeyed a "common power," they could put their efforts toward building society, not destroying it. "During the time men live without a common power to keep them all in awe, they are in that condition which is called war," Hobbes wrote, "and such a war as is of every man against every man."[23]

THE DECAY OF POWER: WHAT'S AT STAKE?

The fall of barriers to power is opening the door to new players of the kind that have transformed chess—and, as the chapters ahead will detail, are now transforming other major fields of human competition.

Those new players are the micropowers mentioned earlier. Their power is of a new kind: not the massive, overwhelming, and often coercive power of large and expert organizations but the counterpower that comes from being able to oppose and constrain what those big players can do.

It is a power that comes from innovation and initiative, yes, but also from the newly expanded scope for techniques like vetoes, foot-dragging, diversions, and interference. The classic tactics of the wartime insurgent are now available and effective in many other fields. This means that they can open new horizons not just to progressive innovators but also to extremists, separatists, and people who are not committed to the general good. And the profusion of all these players, as is already evident and accelerating, should raise some very grave concerns about what stands to happen if the decay of power continues ignored and unchecked.

We all know that too much concentration of power results in social harm, not least in those realms that ostensibly focus on doing good—witness the scandals that have afflicted the Catholic Church. And what happens when power is radically scattered, diffuse, and decayed? The philosophers already knew the answer: chaos and anarchy. The war of all against all that Hobbes anticipated is the antithesis of social well-being. And the decay of power risks producing just this scenario. A world where players have enough power to block everyone else's initiatives but no one has the power to impose its preferred course of action is a world where decisions are not taken, taken too late, or watered down to the point of ineffectiveness. Without the predictability and stability that come with generally accepted rules and authorities, even the most free-spirited creators of art, music, and literature will lack the ability to lead fulfilling lives, beginning with the ability to subsist in some consistent, systematic way off the fruits of their own labor (i.e., with some form of intellectual property protection). Decades of knowledge and experience accumulated by political parties, corporations, churches, militaries, and cultural institutions face the threat of dissipation. And the more slippery power becomes, the more our lives become governed by short-term incentives and fears, and the less we can chart our actions and plan for the future.

The combination of such risks can lead to alienation. Powerful institutions have been with us for so long, and the barriers to power traditionally have been so high, that we've composed the meaning of our lives—our choices about what to do, what to accept, what to challenge—within their parameters. If we become too alienated, the decay of power may turn destructive.

We urgently need to understand and address the nature and consequences of such decay. Indeed, although the aforementioned risks fall short of outright anarchy, they are clearly already interfering with our ability to address some of the great issues of our time. From climate change to nuclear proliferation, economic crises, resource depletion, pandemics, the persistent poverty of the "bottom billion," terrorism, trafficking, cybercrime, and more, the world faces increasingly complex challenges that require the participation of ever more diverse parties and players to solve. The decay of power is an exhilarating trend in the sense that it has made space for new ventures, new companies, and, all over the world, new voices and more opportunities. But its consequences for stability are fraught with danger. How can we continue the welcome advances of plural voices and opinions, initiative and innovation, without at the same time driving ourselves into a crippling paralysis that could undo this progress very quickly? Understanding the decay of power is the first step toward finding our way forward in a world that is being reborn.

Chapter Two

Making Sense of Power

How It Works and How to Keep It

YOUR ALARM GOES OFF AT 6:45 A.M., A HALF-HOUR EARLIER THAN normal, because your boss insisted that you attend a meeting you think is worthless. You would have argued, but next week is your annual review, and you didn't want to jeopardize your promotion. An ad plays on your clock radio for the new Toyota Prius: "It gets the best mileage of any car in America." You're sick of paying so much every week to fill up your tank. The Joneses next door have a Prius; why not you? Except that you don't have the money for a down payment. At breakfast with your daughter, you notice that she—despite your offer last week to allow her to listen to music on her headphones if she would eat granola instead of Cocoa Puffs—is sitting there with headphones on and eating . . . Cocoa Puffs. You and your wife argue over who will leave work early and pick up your daughter from school. You win. But you feel guilty and agree to walk the dog as a conciliatory concession. You go outside with the dog. It's raining. He refuses to move. And there's absolutely nothing you can do to budge him.

As we make the many big and small decisions that come up in daily life, as citizens, employees, consumers, investors, or members of a household or family, we must constantly bear in mind the scope—and the limits—of our own power. Whether the challenge is getting a raise or a promotion, doing our job in a certain way, pushing an elected official to vote for a bill we favor, planning a vacation with a spouse, or getting a child to eat right, we are always, consciously or not, gauging our power: assessing our capacity to get others to behave as we want. We bridle at the power of others and its irritating and inconveniencing effects: how our boss, the government, the police, the bank, or our telephone or cable provider induces us to behave in a certain way, to do certain things, or to quit doing others. And yet we often seek power, sometimes in very self-conscious ways.

Sometimes, the exercise of power is so brutal and definitive that it has an enduring half-life. Even though Saddam Hussein and Moammar Qaddafi are gone, their victims doubtless still shudder at the mention of their names—an experience commonly shared by survivors of brutal crimes long after the perpetrators have been caught. Past or present, we *feel* the presence of power, even when it is subtly used or merely displayed.

Yet whatever the extent to which power is part of our daily lives and on our minds, it eludes our understanding. Except in extreme cases when we are crudely compelled by the menace of handcuffs, fines, demotions, shaming, beatings, or other penalties, we tend to experience power more as emotional coercion than as corporeal force. Precisely because power is primordial, elemental, in our daily lives, we rarely stop to address it analytically—to identify exactly where it resides, how it works, how far it can go, and what stops it from going further.

There is a very good reason for this: power is hard to measure. In fact, strictly speaking, it is impossible to measure. You cannot tally it up and rank it. You can rank only what appear to be its agents, sources, and manifestations. Who has the most money in the bank? Which company can buy another one, or which has the largest assets on its balance sheet? Which army has the most soldiers or tanks or fighter jets? Which political party won the most votes in the last election or controls more seats in parliament? These things can all be measured and recorded. But they do not measure power. They are only proxies. As gauges of power, they are unreliable, and even when tallied up they do not tell the whole story about how powerful someone or something is.

Still, power pervades everything from the system of nations to markets and politics—indeed, any situation in which people or organizations compete or individuals interact. Wherever competition takes place, a distribution of power exists, and it is always relevant to human experience. Though not the only motivation behind such experience, the quest for power is surely one of the most important.

So how can we usefully talk about power? If we are to understand how power is obtained, used, or lost, we need a way to discuss it that is not vague, grandiose, or misleading. Unfortunately, most of our conversations about power never actually make it past those pitfalls.

How to Talk About Power

There is a way to talk productively about power. Yes, power itself is partly material and partly psychological, partly tangible and partly something that affects our imagination. As a commodity or force, power is hard to pin down and quantify. But as a *dynamic* that shapes a specific situation, it can be evaluated, and its limits and latitude assessed.

Take, for example, the ritualized group portrait of the heads of state and government who gather at a summit of the Group of Eight influential countries. Here are the president of the United States, the chancellor of Germany, the president of France, the prime minister of Japan, the prime minister of Italy, and others of their rank. Each of them is "in power." In that respect, they are peers. And indeed, each of them has a great deal of power. Does it come from the prestige of their office, its history, and the ritual that accompanies it? From their victory in an election? From their command over a large civil service and military? From their ability to direct, with a stroke of a pen, the spending of billions of dollars raised by taxes on the labor and commerce of their citizens? Obviously, it is a mix of all these factors and others too. That is power as a force—palpable, but hard to disaggregate and quantify.

Now, with the same photo in mind, imagine the latitude and limits that these leaders enjoy or confront in different situations. What happened during the summit meeting itself? What issues were discussed, what agreements were negotiated, and, in each case, whose will prevailed? Did the American president, often labeled "the most powerful man in the world," win every time? What coalitions formed, and who made what concessions? Then imagine each leader returning to his or her country and addressing the domestic agenda of the moment: budget cuts, labor conflicts, crime, immigration, corruption scandals, military deployments, and whatever else might be going on in that particular region. Some of these leaders command strong parliamentary majorities; others depend on fragile coalitions. Some, through their office, have great scope to rule by executive order or decree; others do not. Some enjoy great personal prestige or high approval ratings; others are beset by scandal or politically vulnerable. Their effective power—the practical translation into action of the power of their position—depends on all these circumstances and varies from issue to issue.

Even if we can't quantify power, we can be quite clear about how it *works*. Power operates in relation to others. The more accurately we define the players and the stakes, the more sharply power comes into focus: no longer an ill-defined force, it can now be seen as an arbiter of a menu of actions, of possibilities for shaping and changing a situation, with a defined scope and real limits. And if we understand how power works, then we can understand what makes it work well, and thus sustain itself and increase; and also what makes it fail, and thus disperse, decline, or even evaporate. In a given situation, to what extent is power fettered or constrained? What ability does each player have to change the situation? By examining competition or conflict in these practical, operational terms, we can begin to understand where events are headed.

Nowadays, as we will see in the pages ahead, the accumulation and exercise of power are headed into uncharted waters.

How Power Works

In Chapter 1, I offered a practical definition: *Power is the ability to direct or prevent the current or future actions of other groups and individuals.* This definition has the benefit of clarity, and better still, it avoids misleading proxies such as size, resources, weapons, and number of supporters. But it does need elaboration. After all, the actions of others can be directed or prevented in many ways. In practice, power is expressed through four different means. Call them the *channels* of power.

- *The Muscle:* The first channel of power is the most obvious and familiar. Force—or threat of force—is the blunt instrument through which power is exercised in certain extreme situations. The muscle can take the form of a conquering army, a police force with its handcuffs and jail cells, a bully in a schoolyard, a knife to the neck, a nuclear arsenal to deter attack, or someone's ability to bankrupt your company, fire you from your job, or expel you from your church. It can also dwell in the exclusive control of some essential resource that can be proffered or denied (money, oil, voters). The presence of muscle is not always bad. We all celebrate a police force that catches criminals even if doing so at times requires the use of force. The legitimate use of violence is a right that citizens grant the state in exchange for protection and stability. But whether in the service of tyrants or enlightened leaders, muscle ultimately relies on coercion. You obey it because if you don't, the consequences will be worse than those of obeying.

- *The Code:* Why do Catholics attend Mass, Jews observe the Sabbath, and Muslims pray five times a day? Why do many societies ask elders to mediate conflicts and consider their decisions just and wise? What causes people to follow the Golden Rule and refrain from harming others even when no law or punishment exists to deter them? The answers can be found in morals, tradition, cultural mores, social expectations, religious beliefs, and values handed down through generations or taught to children in school. We live in a universe of codes that we sometimes follow and sometimes do not. And we allow others to direct our behavior through their invocation of such codes. That channel of power does not employ coercion; instead, it activates our sense of moral duty. Perhaps the best example is the Ten Commandments: through them, a higher and unquestioned power unequivocally tells us how to behave.

- *The Pitch:* You hear a lot about the power of advertising. It gets the credit when people switch from McDonald's to Burger King or when Honda's sales surge as those of Volkswagen dwindle. Billions of dollars go into advertisements in television and radio programs, on billboards and websites, and in magazines, video games, and every other possible vehicle for the express purpose of getting people to do something they would not otherwise have done: purchase the product. The pitch requires neither force nor a moral code. Instead, it gets us to change our thinking, our perception; it persuades us that some product or service is worth selecting over the alternatives. The pitch is just the capacity to persuade others to see the situation in a way that leads them to advance the persuader's goals or interests. Real estate agents who induce potential buyers to value the advantages of living in a specific neighborhood are not applying force, exerting moral suasion, or changing the structure of the situation (by lowering the price, for example). They are changing the clients' behavior by altering their *perception* of the situation.

- *The Reward:* How many times have you heard someone say "I wouldn't do that even if you paid me to"? But typically the opposite is true: people accept payment to do things they would not otherwise do. Any individual who can provide coveted rewards has a major advantage in getting others to behave in ways aligned to his interests. He can change the structure of the situation. Whether in the form of an offer of fuel oil to North Korea in exchange for letting its nuclear reactors get inspected, the addition of hundreds of millions of dollars to the foreign aid budget to buy another country's support, or a bidding war for a top banker, singer, professor, or surgeon, the deployment of material benefits to induce behavior is perhaps power's most common use.

These four channels—*muscle, code, pitch,* and *reward*—are what social scientists call ideal-types: they are analytically distinct and extreme renderings of the category they seek to represent. But in practice—or, more precisely, in the exercise of power in specific situations—they tend to mix and combine and are seldom so clear-cut. Consider, for instance, the power of religion, which operates through multiple channels. Dogma or moral code, whether enshrined in age-old scripture or propounded by a latter-day preacher or guru, is a big part of what earns an organized faith its adherents—along with their commitment of time and belief, their presence at services, their tithes, and their labor. But when churches, temples, and mosques compete for members, they often do so on the basis of a pitch—as in advertising. Indeed, many institutions of faith stage elaborate campaigns managed by highly specialized advertising firms. And they offer rewards as well—not just the immaterial reward of promised salvation but tangible here-and-now benefits such as access to the congregation's job bank, child care, singles' nights, or access to a network of members in prominent positions. In some societies, religious participation itself is enforced by means of muscle; consider, for instance, the laws in certain countries that require certain forms of behavior and punishing others, enforce the length of women's abayas or men's beards, or excommunicate physicians who perform abortions.

Nonetheless, each of the four channels—muscle, code, pitch, and reward—operates in a distinct way. And understanding those differences offers a glimpse of the atomic structure of power.

My formulation of these four channels adheres to the compelling framework first presented by a distinguished scholar of business and management from South Africa: Ian MacMillan of the Wharton School of Business at the University of Pennsylvania (see Figure 2.1). In *Strategy Formulation: Political Concepts,* published in 1978, MacMillan sought to educate business students about the complexities of power and negotiation. He observed that in any power interaction, one party manipulates a situation in a way that affects the actions of another party.[1] But various kinds of manipulation are available depending on the answers to two questions:

- First, does the manipulation change the *structure* of the existing situation, or does it instead change the second party's *assessment* of the situation?
- Second, does the manipulation offer the second party an *improvement,* or does it instead lead the second party to accept a result that is not an improvement?

The relative role of *muscle* (coercion), *code* (obligation), *pitch* (persuasion), and *reward* (inducement) determines the answers to those questions in any given real-world situation.

FIGURE 2.1. MACMILLAN'S TAXONOMY OF POWER

	Outcome seen as improvement	*Outcome seen as nonimprovement*
Change incentives	**Inducement via reward:** Increase the salary, lower a price	**Coercion via muscle:** Law enforcement, repression, violence
Change preferences	**Persuasion via pitch:** Advertising, campaigning	**Obligation via code:** Religious or traditional duty, moral suasion

SOURCE: Adapted from Ian MacMillan, *Strategy Formulation: Political Concepts,* 1978.

Professor MacMillan's approach has three big advantages. First, it goes straight to the practical side of power—its effect on real-life situations, decisions, and behavior. In his assessment of power, MacMillan is not blinded by the image of the leaders posing for the photograph on the red carpet, projecting the pomp of their office. Instead, he asks (a) what tools are available to each leader—and to his or her opponents and allies—in addressing a particular challenge, and (b) what scope and what limits exist for changing the situation.

Second, because his approach is strategic and focuses on power as a dynamic, it is applicable—beyond geopolitics, military analysis, or corporate rivalry—to just about any other domain. A scholar of business, MacMillan devised his framework in the context of his field—business and management—and thus goes on to examine power dynamics within firms. But there is no reason why his approach cannot be applied to other fields—which is what I do in this book.

A third big advantage of this way of looking at power is that it lets us distinguish among concepts such as power, might, force, authority, and influence. For instance, people commonly confuse the difference between power and influence. Here, MacMillan's conceptual framework is very helpful. Both power and influence can change the behavior of others or, more specifically, make others do something or stop them from doing it. But *influence* seeks to change the *perception* of the situation, not the situation itself.[2] So the MacMillan framework helps show that influence is a subset of power, in the sense that power includes not only actions that change the situation but also actions that alter the way the situation is perceived. Influence is a form of power, but power can obviously be exercised through means other than influence.

To illustrate: Extolling the virtues of a neighborhood in order to change a buyer's perception of a deal's value in a way that leads to a closing is different from reaching that goal by lowering the house's price. A real estate agent who changes a buyer's perception has the *influence* to do so, whereas an owner who drops the price to sell the house has the *power* to change the structure of the deal.

WHY POWER SHIFTS—OR STAYS STEADY

Think of power in terms of the ability of different players to affect the outcome of a bargaining situation. Any competition or conflict—whether a war, a battle for market share, diplomatic talks, recruitment of believers by rival churches, even a discussion of who washes the dishes after dinner—hinges on a distribution of power. That distribution reflects the ability of the competing parties to rely on some combination of muscle, code, pitch, and reward to get others to act in the way they desire. Sometimes a distribution of power stays steady, even for a long time. The classic nineteenth-century "balance of power" in Europe was a case in point: the continent avoided all-out war, and the boundaries of nations and empires changed little or only by agreement. So, too, was the heyday of the Cold War: the United States and Soviet Union, using plenty of muscle and also plenty of reward, built and maintained global spheres of influence that, despite local conflicts here and there, stayed remarkably consistent.

The structure of the markets for cola beverages (Coke and Pepsi), operating systems (PC and Mac), and long-haul passenger aircraft (Boeing and Airbus), each with a couple of dominant players and a few also-rans, is another example of a distribution of power that is quite steady—or at least not volatile. But as soon as a new party rapidly gains the ability to project muscle more effectively, invokes tradition or moral code in a more alluring way, presents a more persuasive pitch, or offers a larger reward, power will shift and reorganize the landscape, potentially in drastic ways. That's when things become interesting—when opportunities crop up, industries transform, political systems are upended, and cultures evolve. Indeed, when enough of these changes happen simultaneously, daily life changes for all of us.

But what causes the distribution of power to change? It can happen with the advent of a talented, disruptive newcomer like Alexander the Great or Steve Jobs, or that of a transforming innovation like the stirrup, the printing press, the integrated circuit, or YouTube. It can happen through warfare, of course. And natural disasters may well be a cause: Hurricane Katrina, for example, led to the marginalization of New Orleans's once all-powerful local school boards and the rise of the city's new charter-school movement. Don't discount dumb luck or accident, either: a previously unshakeable incumbent may make a strategic mistake or personal blunder that leads to a precipitous downfall. Think Tiger Woods or David Patreus. Sometimes, illness and age simply take their toll and alter the distribution of power at the top of a company, a government, an army, or a sport.

On the other hand, not every smart innovation gets traction. Not every well-run new business with a desirable product and careful plan acquires the financing or sales opportunities it needs to make its mark. Some giant corporations or institutions prove vulnerable to nimble new competitors; others seem to ward them off as if swatting flies. It will never be possible to predict every shift in power. The collapse of the Soviet Union, the eruption of the Arab Spring, the decline of erstwhile newspaper giants like the *Washington Post,* and the sudden emergence of Twitter as an information provider attest to the impossibility of knowing what power shifts await around the corner.

THE IMPORTANCE OF BARRIERS TO POWER

Although predicting specific power shifts is a fool's errand, understanding the trends that alter either the distribution of power or its very nature is not. The key is to understand the barriers to power in a specific arena. What technology, law, weapon, fortune, or unique asset makes it hard for others to gain the power enjoyed by incumbents? When such barriers go up and stay up, incumbents become entrenched and consolidate their control. When they go down or stay down, new players gain an edge and can challenge the existing power structure. The more drastic the erosion of any given barrier to power, the more unusual or unexpected the new players, and the faster they may attain prominence. *Identify the barriers to power and whether they are coming up or going down, and you can solve a large part of the puzzle of power.*

Monopolies, single-party systems, military dictatorships, societies that officially favor a particular race or religious faith, marketplaces swamped with advertising for a dominant product, cartels like OPEC, political systems like the American one in which two parties effectively control the electoral process and small ones cannot get a foothold—all of these are situations where the barriers to power are high, at least for now. But some citadels can be stormed—either because their defenses are not as strong as they seem, because they are unprepared for new types of attackers, or, for that matter, because the treasures they protected have lost value in the first place. In such instances the trade routes now bypass them, and they are no longer of interest to marauding armies.

For example, the founders of Google did not set out to erode the dominance of the *New York Times* or other powerful media companies, but that is in fact what they accomplished. Insurgents who use improvised explosive devices in Afghanistan, or bands of Somali pirates who use rickety boats and AK-47s to hijack large ships in the Gulf of Aden, are circumventing the barriers that ensured the dominance of technologically sophisticated armies and navies. The result has been not so much a shift in the power of such armies and navies as a challenge to the very nature of that power.

Barriers to power can differentiate situations that look similar on the surface. A small group of firms might be able to control most of the market share in a particular industry because only they possess the required resources, an attractive product, or a unique technology. Alternatively, they might have successfully lobbied or paid off politicians to create rules and regulations that make it harder, or impossible, for rivals to enter the market. Proprietary technology, access to resources, regulatory protections, and a corrupt insider connection are four very different kinds of advantage. Obviously, power shifts occur when the control of certain scarce resources becomes more critical to competition in a given market, substitutes are found that make it less of a barrier for others, or a new technology makes it easier for many other competitors to enter the market.

While such shifts represent a well-known idea in the world of business, this idea has been less frequently applied to politics and to rivalries between nation-states, churches, or philanthropists. Consider, for example, a parliamentary system in which a number of small parties have seats and may be involved in forming a governing coalition. Is there a threshold, as in Germany, such that a party needs to have earned 5 percent of the total national vote to be represented in parliament at all? Is there instead a rule whereby a party must score a minimum proportion of the vote in several different regions? Or look at the competition among top universities. Is accreditation difficult, or do employers and graduate schools no longer care as much about the accreditation of the schools whose graduates they recruit?

Barriers to power might take the form of rules and regulations that prove easy or hard to rewrite or circumvent. They might take the form of costs—of key assets, resources, labor, marketing—that increase or go down. They might take the form of access to growth opportunities—new customers, workers, capital sources, religious believers. The details will vary by field. But as a rule of thumb, the more numerous and stringent the regulations, the higher the costs of replicating the incumbents' advantages; and the more restricted or rare the key assets, the higher the barriers that prevent new players from gaining a toehold, let alone forging a sustained advantage for themselves.

THE BLUEPRINT: EXPLAINING MARKET POWER

The concept of barriers to power is rooted in economics. Specifically, I have adapted the idea of *barriers to entry*—an analytic construct that economists use to understand the distribution, behavior, and prospects of firms in an industry—and applied it to the distribution of power. It is fair to expand the concept this way: after all, the idea of barriers to entry is used in economics to explain a particular kind of power—*market power*.

As we know, the ideal state in economics is perfect competition. Under perfect competition, many different firms make perfectly interchangeable goods and customers are interested in purchasing all the products they make. There are no transaction costs, just the costs of inputs, and all firms have access to the same information. Perfect competition describes an environment in which no single firm can influence on its own the price of goods in its marketplace.

The reality is very different, of course. Two companies, Airbus and Boeing, command the market for big long-haul planes, and a small number of additional manufacturers make smaller jets. But innumerable companies manufacture shirts or socks. It is exceedingly difficult for a new aircraft maker to enter the market. Assemble a few tailors or seamstresses in a workshop, however, and you can produce shirts. A small new shirtmaker may be able to compete with the big names, or at least find a niche in which it can prosper. A brand-new aircraft manufacturer faces less attractive odds.

Industries with stable and narrow structures, where incumbents hold sway and new rivals struggle, feature a great deal of market power. In plain language, this means the ability to ignore competition and still make a profit. In a perfectly competitive market, if you sell above the marginal cost (the cost of producing one additional unit, which is assumed to be the same for all producers in that industry), no one will buy, as all the other competitors will underprice you. The more market power a company possesses, the more it can set its prices without worrying about rivals. The more market power prevails among the companies in a given sector or marketplace, the more entrenched the pecking order. The difference in corporate "league tables" between a sector like personal care and hygiene—where the rankings of firms such as Procter and Gamble, Colgate-Palmolive, and other top companies have barely changed in several decades, and the personal-computer industry, where the rankings have been in utter flux—often has a great deal to do with market power.

Market power is ultimately exclusionary, and thus anti-competitive. But even for the companies that already enjoy a position inside the citadel, protected by barriers that limit the entry of newcomers, an easy life or even survival may be far from guaranteed. Existing rivals may gain market power and turn against them, leveraging their market dominance to buy them out or drive them to bankruptcy. Collusion and exclusion are common among companies that operate in sectors or nations where open competition is stifled and market power reigns. Entrepreneurs like to extol competition, but a chief executive of a dominant firm will be far more concerned with preserving its market power.

These considerations often usefully apply to the power dynamics among competitors in other areas—that is, to actors that are not businesses in search of maximum profit. Ahead we apply this set of ideas to illustrate what is happening to the equivalents of "market power" in military conflict, party politics, and other activities.

BARRIERS TO ENTRY: A KEY TO MARKET POWER

What are the sources of market power? In the business world, what causes certain firms to achieve dominance and remain unchallenged for a long time? Why do some sectors give rise to monopolies, duopolies, or a small number of firms that are able to coordinate their pricing or approaches to regulation, while others remain hospitable to myriad small companies that compete furiously? Why does the configuration of firms in some industries get relatively frozen over time, while in others it changes constantly?

For specialists in industrial organization, who seek to understand how companies gain advantages over their rivals, the factors that make it difficult for a new player to enter a given sector and compete successfully are crucial. And for our purposes, they can illuminate how power is obtained, retained, used, and lost, whether in a market or elsewhere.

Some barriers to entry stem from underlying conditions. They have to do with an industry's technical characteristics: manufacturing aluminum, for instance, requires massive, expensive-to-build, energy-consuming smelters. The underlying conditions may also reflect how much the industry is tied to a particular geographic location. For instance, does it require natural resources that are found only in a few places? Or does the product need to be processed or packaged close to where it will be sold, as in the case of cement, or can it be frozen, as with shrimp from China or lamb from New Zealand or vegetables from Mexico, and shipped around the world? Is a very specialized set of human skills required, such as a PhD in physics or mastery of a particular computer programming language? All of these questions point to requirements that explain why it is easier to open, say, a restaurant, a lawn-mowing company, or an office-cleaning firm than to enter the steel business, where you not only need capital, expensive equipment, a large factory, and expensive and specific inputs but also might incur big transportation costs.

Other barriers to entry result from laws, licenses, and trademarks; examples include bar membership for lawyers, a doctor's license to practice medicine, and the zoning, sanitation, facilities inspection, liquor license, and other hurdles one might face when trying to open a restaurant. Such barriers—whether they stem from scale, access to key resources, access to specialized technology, or legal and regulatory requirements—are *structural barriers* that confront any firm wishing to compete in the market. Even for firms already operating in that particular market, these barriers are hard to change—although firms that have grown large and powerful are often able to influence their regulatory environment.

Alongside these more permanent structural barriers are *strategic barriers* to entry. Incumbents create strategic barriers to prevent new rivals from emerging and to prevent existing rivals from growing. Examples include exclusive marketing agreements (e.g., the one between AT&T and Apple when iPhones were first launched), long-term contracts that tie suppliers to sellers (e.g., oil producers and oil refiners), collusion and price-fixing (e.g., the infamous effort in the 1990s by Archer Daniels Midland and other firms to fix the price of animal-feed additives), and lobbying politicians to extract unique governmental advantages (e.g., a license to run a casino as a monopoly in a certain area). They also include advertising, special promotions, product placement, frequent-user discounts, and similar marketing tools that make entry difficult for would-be competitors. Indeed, it's hard to break in, even with the most exciting product, when you need an enormously expensive advertising budget to let potential customers know that your product exists and an even larger one to persuade them to actually try it.[3]

FROM BARRIERS TO ENTRY TO BARRIERS TO POWER

So it is no surprise that quite a bit of competitive ardor, not just in business but in other fields as well, goes into building up or breaking down the barriers to power—that is, affecting the game by changing its rules and requirements. This is especially true in politics, where parties and candidates often expend tremendous energy in battles over drawing up congressional districts (the infamous practice known in the United States as gerrymandering), or over mandating gender parity in parliament and on candidate slates, as in Argentina and Bangladesh, where a quota of seats in parliament is reserved for women. In India, where Dalits (once known as the caste of "untouchables") have reserved seats in parliament and regional assemblies, intense political and legal battles have raged over extending these benefits to the so-called Other Backward Classes (OBCs). In many countries, leaders with autocratic tendencies have sought to exclude political rivals while preserving a veneer of democracy by pushing through amendments to election law that just happen to disqualify those rivals on technicalities. Battles over corporate contributions in politics, political advertising, disclosure, and access to airwaves are often much more virulent than battles over policy. Parties that vehemently disagree on major policy questions might find themselves in lockstep defending rules that give them, together, the lion's share of seats. After all, a lost election can always be won back, but new rules change the game.[4]

Ultimately, barriers to power are the obstacles that stop new players from deploying enough of the muscle, the code, the pitch, and the reward, or some combination thereof, to gain a competitive hold; and, conversely, that allow incumbent companies, parties, armies, churches, foundations, universities, newspapers, and unions (or whatever other type of organization is involved) to maintain their dominance.

For many decades, even centuries, barriers to power sheltered massive armies, corporations, governments, parties, and social and cultural institutions. Now, those barriers are crumbling, eroding, leaking, or being rendered otherwise irrelevant. To appreciate just how profound this transformation is, and how much it reverses the tide of history, we need to review why and how power got big in the first place. The next chapter explains how, by the twentieth century, the world got to the point where—according to the conventional wisdom—power required size, and no better, more effective, and more sustainable way existed to exercise power than through large centralized and hierarchical organizations.

CHAPTER THREE

HOW POWER GOT BIG

An Assumption's Unquestioned Rise

TAKE YOUR PICK AS TO WHEN THE STORY BEGINS. WAS IT 1648, WHEN the Peace of Westphalia ushered in the modern nation-state, in place of the post-medieval order of city-states and overlapping principalities? Was it 1745, when a French aristocrat and commercial administrator named Vincent de Gournay is said to have coined the term *bureaucracy?* Or perhaps it was 1882, when a constellation of small oil firms in the United States were melded into the gigantic Standard Oil—amid the rise of new large-scale industries, and foreshadowing a great wave of mergers one decade later that would end the heyday of small, local, family-firm capitalism and install a new order based on giant corporations?

At any rate, by the start of the twentieth century, these and other great advances—all generally understood to reflect human progress, science, and ingenuity—were cementing a broadly held consensus about how to accumulate, retain, and exercise power. And by roughly mid-century, *big* had triumphed; no longer could individuals, artisans, family firms, city-states, or loose-knit bands of like-minded people hold their own against the overwhelming advantages of large organizations. Power now required size, scale, and a strong, centralized, hierarchical organization.

Whether the body in question was General Motors, the Catholic Church, or the Red Army, how to organize to get and keep maximum power was a practical question with an obvious answer: get big.

To understand how the idea of big took hold, we must start with some whirlwind history. In particular, we must spend some time getting to know the American dean of business history, the German father of modern sociology, and the British economist who won the Nobel Prize for explaining why, in business, bigger was often better. Taken together, their respective works illuminate not only how the creation of modern bureaucracy enabled the efficient exercise of power but also how the world's most successful corporations—as well as charities, churches, armies, political parties, and universities—have used the bureaucratic exercise of power to keep down rivals and advance their own interests.

Historians have identified the germ of modern bureaucracy in systems of government dating to ancient China, Egypt, and Rome. In both their military and administrative practices, the Romans invested heavily in large-scale, complex, centralized organization. Much later, Napoleon Bonaparte and others in Europe, absorbing the lessons of the Enlightenment, would commit to centralized and professionalized administration as the progressive and rational way to run a government. Drawing on that model and adapting American and European examples, Meiji-era Japan assembled a professional bureaucracy—including, above all, its Ministry of Industry, established in 1870—to reengineer its society and catch up with the West. By World War I the nation-state with a unitary government and civil service was the template for the world, including colonies. In India, for example, the British rulers set up the Indian Civil Service, which would carry on after independence as the prestigious Indian Administrative Service, a much-sought-after career path among the educated elite. Whether free-market or socialist, governed by a single party or robustly democratic, nations around the world in the twentieth century shared a commitment to a large central administration—that is, to a bureaucracy.

The same thing happened in economic life. Pushed by technology, the demands of large-scale industry, and new regulations, smaller companies gave way to large, multi-unit, hierarchically and administratively run firms, a species that had not existed before 1840. During what scholars call the first great merger movement in America—a decade-long period from 1895 to 1904—no fewer than 1,800 small firms disappeared in a wave of consolidation. The familiar names of many major brands date back to that era. General Electric was founded, out of a merger, in 1892. Coca-Cola was founded the same year, and Pepsi in 1902. The American Telephone and Telegraph Company (ancestor of AT&T) was founded in 1885; Westinghouse, in 1886; General Motors, in 1908; and so on. By 1904, seventy-eight corporations controlled more than half the production in their particular industry, and twenty-eight firms controlled more than four-fifths.[1] Commenting on the upheaval these new organizations represented, a dyspeptic

Henry Adams observed that "the Trusts and Corporations stood for the larger part of the new power that had been created since 1840, and were obnoxious because of their vigorous and unscrupulous energy. They were revolutionary, troubling all the old conventions and values, as the screws of ocean steamers must trouble a school of herring."[2]

This "managerial revolution," as the great business historian Alfred Chandler termed it, was also spreading from what he called its American "seed-bed" to the rest of the capitalist world. German industry was increasingly dominated by large firms such as AEG, Bayer, BASF, Siemens, and Krupp—many of them born in the mid-nineteenth century—that were themselves combining into larger formal and informal trusts. In Japan, with a helping hand from the government, the fledgling *zaibatsu* were expanding into new industries such as textiles, steel, shipbuilding, and railroads. Chandler persuasively argued that the more elaborate use of steam power in manufacturing during the nineteenth century as well as the popularization of electricity and innovations in management led to a *second industrial revolution* that spawned much larger companies than those that had emerged during the industrial revolution of the previous century. These new industrial plants used vastly more capital, workers, and managers. As a result, growth in scale became the precondition for business success and big became synonymous with corporate power. In his seminal work (aptly titled *The Visible Hand*), Chandler argued that the visible hand of powerful managers replaced the invisible hand of market forces as the main driver of modern business.[3] The power and the decisions of these professional managers who led giant companies, or giant divisions within companies, shaped economic activities and outcomes as much as if not more than the prices determined by market exchanges.

The ascent and dominance of these large industrial companies led Chandler to identify three distinct models of capitalism, each associated with one of the three leading bastions of capitalism at the time of this second industrial revolution: (a) the "personal capitalism" found in *Great Britain*, (b) the competitive (or managerial) one common in the *United States*, and (c) *Germany*'s "cooperative capitalism."[4] In Chandler's view, even successful large industrial firms in Britain were impaired by the familial nature of the dominant entrepreneurial dynasty that owned and managed them; they lacked the drive, agility, and ambition of their American counterparts. In contrast, the separation of ownership and management that Chandler called "managerial capitalism" enabled American companies to adopt new organizational forms—notably, the multi-divisional, or "M," structure (M-form)—that were far superior for raising and allocating capital, attracting talent, and innovating and investing in production and marketing. The M-form, which entailed a confederation of semi-independent product or geographical groups within a central headquarters, allowed more efficient handling of large-sized operations and created faster-growing corporations. In turn, the propensity of German companies to cooperate with labor unions led to a system that Chandler labeled "cooperative capitalism," which eventually became known as "codetermination." German firms strived to include more stakeholders in the companies' governance structure beyond shareholders and top managers.

Although these three systems differed in many ways, they had one paramount similarity: in each case, corporate power resided in large-sized companies. Size led to power and vice versa.

Whether we call it Big Business, Big Government, or Big Labor, this triumph of large, centralized organizations validated and reinforced the increasingly common assumption that big was best, and that achieving power in any relevant domain was a task best suited to a certain kind of modern and rational organization that was most effective when centralized and large. And if this idea had the force of received wisdom, one key reason was that it found compelling intellectual backing in economics, sociology, and political science. All such backing proceeded, fundamentally, from the seminal work of a remarkable social scientist: Max Weber.

MAX WEBER, OR WHY SIZE MADE SENSE

Max Weber was more than a German sociologist. He was one of the most remarkable intellectuals of his time, a prodigious scholar of economics, history, religion, culture, and more. He wrote on Western economic and legal history; studies of Indian, Chinese, and Jewish religion; public administration; the life of the city; and, finally, a massive tome, *Economy and Society,* published in 1922, two years after his death. He was also, as the political scientist and sociologist Alan Wolfe observed, "the leading scholar of questions of power and authority in the twentieth century,"[5] and it is in that capacity that we draw on him here. Indeed, Weber and his theories about bureaucracy are critical to understanding how power can actually be used.

Born in 1864, Weber came of age in Germany as it was unifying out of an assemblage of regional principalities, under the impetus of the Prussian chancellor Otto von Bismarck, and turning into a modern industrial nation. Weber, though an intellectual, took part in this modernization in multiple roles—not just as an academic but also as an adviser to the Berlin stock exchange, a consultant to political reform groups, and a reserve officer in the Kaiser's army.[6] He first came to public attention with his controversial study of the plight of German agricultural laborers being displaced by Polish migrants, in which he argued that large German estates should be broken up into plots that could be given to workers to encourage them to stay in the area. Subsequently having taken a position at Freiburg University, he again courted controversy with proposals that Germany follow a path of "liberal imperialism" to build up the political and institutional structures needed for a modern state.[7]

In 1898, after a fiery family argument that precipitated his father's death, Weber had a breakdown and developed a form of nervous exhaustion that often left him unable to teach. It was during his recovery from one such bout, in 1903, that he was invited by Hugo Münsterberg, a Harvard professor of applied psychology, to join a gathering of international scholars that was assembling in St. Louis, Missouri. Weber accepted, drawn by the lure of the United States and what he considered to be its relatively undeveloped economic and political forms, the chance to delve deeper into Puritanism (his most influential work, *The Protestant Ethic and the Spirit of Capitalism*, would appear shortly), and a fat honorarium. As the German historian Wolfgang Mommsen later put it, the trip would prove to be "pivotally important to his social and political thought."[8]

Visiting the United States in 1904, Weber expanded his lecture invitation into a grand observation and data-gathering tour across much of the country; he would spend more than 180 hours on trains over a period of nearly three months, visiting New York; St. Louis; Chicago; Muskogee, Oklahoma (to see Indian country); Mt. Airy, North Carolina (where he had relatives); and sundry other destinations (meeting with William James, for example, in Cambridge, Massachusetts). Weber was coming from a modern country to one even more so. Indeed, as Weber viewed America, it represented "the last time in the long-lasting history of mankind that so favourable conditions for a free and grand development will exist."[9] America was the most intensely capitalist society Weber had seen, and he recognized that it presaged the future. The skyscrapers of New York and Chicago appeared to him as "fortresses of capital," and he was awed by the Brooklyn Bridge and by both cities' trains, trams, and elevators.

But Weber also found much to lament in the United States. He was shocked at labor conditions, the lack of workplace safety, the endemic corruption of city officials and labor leaders, and the insufficient ability of civil servants to regulate the whole mess and keep up with the dynamic economy. In Chicago, which he called "one of the most unbelievable cities," he wandered through stockyards, tenements, and streets, watching its residents at work and play, cataloguing the ethnic pecking order (Germans were waiters, Italians were ditch-diggers, and the Irish were politicians), and observing local customs. The city was, he observed, "like a human being with its skin peeled off and whose intestines are seen at work."[10] Capitalist development was moving rapidly, he further noted; everything "opposed to the culture of capitalism is going to be demolished with irresistible force."[11]

What Weber saw in America confirmed and strengthened his ideas about organization, power, and authority—and he would go on to produce a massive body of work that would earn him the reputation of "father of modern social science." Weber's theory of power, laid out in *Economy and Society,* began with authority—the basis on which "domination" was justified and exercised. Drawing on his encyclopedic command of global history, Weber argued that, in the past, much authority had been "traditional"—that is, inherited by its holders and accepted by the holders' subjects. A second source for authority had been "charismatic," in which an individual leader was seen by followers to possess a special gift. But the third form of authority—and the one suited to modern times—is "bureaucratic" and "rational" authority, grounded in laws and wielded by an administrative structure capable of enforcing clear and consistent rules. It rests, Weber wrote, on the "belief in the validity of legal statute and functional competence based on rationally created rules."

And so, Weber believed, the key to wielding power in modern society is bureaucratic organization. Bureaucracy to Weber was far from the dirty word it has become today. It described the most advanced form of organization humans had achieved and the one best suited for progress in a capitalist society. Weber enumerated bureaucratic organizations' fundamental characteristics: specific jobs with detailed rights, obligations, responsibilities, and scope of authority as well as a clear system of supervision, subordination, and unity of command. Such organizations also relied heavily on written communications and documents, and on the training of personnel according to each job's requirements and the skills it needed. Importantly, the inner workings of bureaucratic organizations were based on the application of consistent and comprehensive rules for everyone regardless of socioeconomic status or family, religious, or political links. Therefore, recruitments, responsibilities, and promotions were based on competence and experience—not, as in the past, on the basis of family connections or personal relationships.[12]

Germany had been at the forefront of European efforts to create a modern civil service, beginning with Prussia in the seventeenth and eighteenth centuries. In Weber's day, that process intensified, with parallel developments in other countries that reduced the scope for patronage. The UK's Civil Service Commission, established in 1855, is one such example; another is the US Civil Service Commission created in 1883 to control entry into the Federal service. And 1874 saw the first step toward an international civil service, with the formation of the Universal Postal Union.

On his American journey, Weber also witnessed a parallel revolution in methods and bureaucratic organization among the new pioneers in business. In Chicago's stockyards, whose packing plants were at the forefront of assembly-line mechanization and specialization of tasks that allowed management to substitute unskilled labor for craft workers, Weber was agog over "the tremendous intensity of work."[13] Yet even amid the "wholesale slaughter and oceans of blood," his observer's mind was engaged:

> From the moment when the unsuspecting bovine enters the slaughtering area, is hit by a hammer and collapses, whereupon it is immediately gripped by an iron clamp, is hoisted up, and starts on its journey, it is in constant motion—past ever-new workers who eviscerate and skin it, etc., but are always (in the rhythm of work) tied to the machine that pulls the animal past them. . . . There one can follow the pig from the sty to the sausage and the can.[14]

For managers, large-scale industrial production in an increasingly international market required the advantages of bureaucratic specialization and hierarchy, or, as Weber listed them: "precision, speed, unambiguity, knowledge of the files, continuity, discretion, strict subordination, reduction of friction and of material and personal costs."[15] What was good for cutting-edge government was also good for cutting-edge commerce. "Normally," Weber wrote, "the very large, modern capitalist enterprises are themselves unequalled models of strict bureaucratic organization."[16]

Deploying a range of examples, Weber would ultimately show that rational, professionalized, hierarchical, and centralized structures were ascendant in every domain, from successful political parties to trade unions, "ecclesiastical structures," and great universities. "It does not matter for the character of bureaucracy whether its authority is called 'private' or 'public,'"

Weber wrote. "Where the bureaucratization of administration has been completely carried through," he concluded, "a form of power relation is established that is practically unshatterable."[17]

How the World Went Weberian

One of the catalysts for the spread of bureaucratization was the outbreak of World War I, a conflict that Weber initially supported but came to bitterly regret. The mass mobilization of millions of men and millions of tons of materiel required managerial innovations on the battlefield and the home front. Given the stationary nature of trench warfare, for example, the supply of ammunition became arguably the most critical constraint on operations. As just one facet of the organizational challenge this represented, consider the French production of 75-millimeter artillery shells. Prewar planners set a production goal of twelve thousand shells per day. Shortly after the outbreak of hostilities, they increased it to a hundred thousand per day—still only half the level that production eventually reached to meet demand. By 1918, more than 1.7 million men, women, and youths (including prisoners of war, mutilated veterans, and conscripted foreigners) were working in French munitions plants alone. As the historian William McNeill observed, "Innumerable bureaucratic structures that had previously acted more or less independently of one another in a context of market relationships coalesced into what amounted to a single national firm for waging war"—a process that played out in every combatant nation.[18]

Weber died of a lung infection two years after the war ended. But everything that happened for decades after his death only confirmed his insight about the fundamental superiority of large-scale, bureaucratic systems. Weber had been keen to show the effectiveness of such systems in organizations beyond the military and business, and this indeed proved to be the case. The managerial model soon took hold in philanthropy, for example, as the same great industrialists who pioneered modern business created foundations that would dominate charitable work for a century. By 1916, there were more than forty thousand millionaires in the United States, up from just one hundred in the 1870s. Tycoons like John D. Rockefeller and Andrew Carnegie teamed up with social reformers to endow universities and create free-standing institutes such as the Rockefeller Institute for Medical Research, which became a model for similar institutions. By 1915, the United States had twenty-seven general-purpose foundations, a uniquely

American innovation, with in-house experts conducting independent research on a variety of social problems and putting programs in place to ameliorate them. By 1930, that number had swelled to more than two hundred. The rise of independent endowed foundations was accompanied by the advent of mass philanthropy, especially in areas such as public health, where reformers harnessed community giving for broad social goals. In 1905, for example, no more than five thousand Americans were donating time and money to the fight against tuberculosis, a scourge that accounted for up to 11 percent of all US deaths. By 1915, led by organizations such as the National Association for the Study and Prevention of Tuberculosis (created in 1904), there were as many as five hundred thousand donors, many of them involved in the popular "Christmas seals" campaign, a Danish innovation popularized in the United States by the reformer Jacob Riis.[19]

What does all this have to do with power? Everything. It is not enough to control large, power-endowing resources like money, weapons, or followers. Such resources are a necessary precondition of power; but without an effective way of managing them, the power they create is less effective, more transient, or both. Weber's central message was that without a reliable, well-functioning organization, or, to use his term, without a bureaucracy, power could not be effectively wielded.

If Weber helped us understand the rationale and workings of bureaucracy in the exercise of power, the British economist Ronald Coase helped us understand the economic advantages that they conferred on companies. In 1937, Coase produced a conceptual breakthrough that explained why large organizations were not just rational according to a certain theory of profit-maximizing behavior but, indeed, often proved more efficient than the alternatives. It was no coincidence that, while still an undergraduate, in 1931–1932, Coase carried out the research for his seminal paper, "The Nature of the Firm," in the United States. Earlier he had flirted with socialism, and he became intrigued by the similarities in organization between American and Soviet firms and, in particular, by the question of why large industry, where power was highly centralized, had emerged on both sides of the ideological divide.[20]

Coase's explanation—which would help earn him the Nobel Prize in economics decades later—was both simple and revolutionary. He observed that modern firms faced numerous costs that were lower when the firm brought the functions in-house than they would have been when dealing at arms' length with another enterprise. Included among such costs are those for drafting and enforcing sales contracts—expenses that Coase initially called "marketing costs" and later redubbed "transaction costs." Specifically, transaction costs helped explain why some firms grew by vertically integrating—that is, by buying their suppliers or distributors—while others didn't. Large oil producers, for example, prefer to own the refineries where their oil is processed, as this tends to be less risky and more efficient than relying on a commercial relationship with independent refiners whose actions the oil companies can't control. In contrast, a large garment retailer like Zara and computer companies like Apple or Dell are less compelled to own the manufacturing facilities that make their products. They subcontract ("outsource") the manufacturing to another firm and concentrate on the technology, design, and marketing and retailing of their products. The propensity to operate through a vertically integrated firm is driven by the structure of the market of buyers and sellers active in the different stages of the industry and by the kinds of investments needed to enter the business. In short, transaction costs determine the contours, growth patterns, and, ultimately, the very nature of firms.[21] Although Coase's insight became an important underpinning of economics in general, its main initial impact was in the field of industrial organization, which focuses on factors that stimulate or hinder competition among firms.

The idea that transaction costs determine the size and even the nature of an organization can be applied to many other fields beyond industry to explain why not just modern corporations but also government agencies, armies, and churches became large and centralized. In all such cases, it has been rational and efficient to do so. High transaction costs create strong incentives to bring critical activities controlled by others inside the organization, thereby growing it. And by the same token, the more the pattern of transaction costs made it rational for organizations to grow large by integrating vertically, the more daunting an obstacle this growth represented for new rivals trying to gain a foothold. It is harder for a new rival to challenge an existing company that also controls the main source of raw materials, for example, or has internalized the main distribution channels or retail chain. The same applies to situations in which one army has exclusive control over the procurement of its weapons and technology and a second army is forced to depend on another nation's arms industry. Thus, the transaction costs that some organizations are able to minimize by "internalizing" or controlling the provider or the distributors constitute one more barrier to potential new rivals and a barrier to gaining power more generally—and scale boosted by vertical integration provides a high protective barrier for incumbents inasmuch as newer, smaller players have a lesser chance to compete and succeed. It is worth noting that until the 1980s many governments were tempted to "integrate" vertically and own and operate airlines, smelters, cement factories, and banks. Indeed, governments' quest for efficiency and autonomy often masked other motivations such as public sector employment creation and opportunities for patronage, corruption, regional development, and so on.

Though not commonly thought of as such, transaction costs are indeed determinants of an organization's size and, often, of its power. And as discussed below, since the nature of transaction costs is changing and their impact is dwindling, the barriers that used to shield the powerful from their challengers are falling. And this is not happening only in the realm of business competition.

THE MYTH OF THE POWER ELITE?

In process and outcome, World War II reinforced the equation of size with power. The US "arsenal of democracy" that fueled the Allied victory nearly doubled the size of the US economy over the course of the war and nurtured corporate giants that were paragons of mass production. And who were the ultimate winners of this conflict but the United States and the USSR—countries that spanned whole continents, not island-nations like Japan or even Great Britain, beggared by the costs of the fighting into second-class status. At war's end, pent-up American consumer demand, supported by wartime savings and new, generous government programs, allowed big companies to grow even bigger. More broadly and more ominously, as the Good War segued into what John F. Kennedy would call the "long, twilight struggle," the contest for mastery between the capitalist West and the communist East fed huge security establishments on both sides of the Cold War divide, each guided by its own ideology, with bureaucratic imperatives stretching far beyond the purely military into science, education, and culture. As the historian Derek Leebaert put it in *The Fifty-Year Wound,* his wide-ranging tally of the costs of the Cold War, "Emergency played into the penchant for bigness that was a child of earlier industrialization, of the radical insecurity that the Depression inflicted on small organizations, and of the cooperative giantism of World War II: big unions, big corporations, and big government, with little concern for the market."[22]

In short order, the symbolism of size and scale—the idea that the ventures most likely to succeed and endure were in some way the most monumental—passed into popular imagery virtually everywhere. As the world's largest office building (as measured by floor area), the Pentagon, built during World War II, from 1941 to 1943, was a perfect symbol of this principle during the 1950s and '60s. So, too, was the famed buttoned-down culture of IBM, whose attributes of hierarchy and convention were placed in support of the goal of advanced engineering. In 1955, General Motors, one of the early adopters and paradigmatic examples of the M-form management structure, became the first US corporation to net more than $1 billion in a year as well as the largest corporation in the United States, in terms of its revenues as a proportion of gross domestic product (roughly 3 percent); it employed more than five hundred thousand workers in the United States alone, offered consumers eighty-five different models to choose from, and sold about 5 million cars and trucks.[23] Mass-production principles were also being expanded to industries such as homebuilding by businessmen like Bill Levitt, a former Navy construction worker who pioneered suburban development by building affordable middle-class homes by the thousands.

But the apparent triumph of the behemoth organizations that produced this Cold War cornucopia of goods and services also stirred worries. Architecture critics like Lewis Mumford complained that the new Levittowns were monotonous and the houses too spread out to create a real community. Irving Howe, the literary and social commentator, decried the postwar years as the "Age of Conformity," and in 1950 the sociologist David Riesman bemoaned the loss of individualism under institutional pressure in his influential book *The Lonely Crowd*.[24]

And these were not the only concerns raised. As large organizations took hold in every area, apparently cementing their grip on various facets of human life, social critics worried that the hierarchies they established would become permanent, separating an elite that controlled politics and business from everyone else, and concentrating power in a ruling group or class at the same time that the implacable logic of size caused organizations to grow larger and larger, swallowing each other up if need be through mergers or sharing the wealth in cartels and combines. For some, the expansion of government programs from military to social spending, and the growth of the bureaucracies tasked with administering them—again, not just in left or socialist societies—was a similarly worrying trend.

Others viewed the concentration of power as chiefly a product of the capitalist economy.

In one way or another, these fears echoed the beliefs of Karl Marx and Friedrich Engels, who argued in *The Communist Manifesto* (1848) that governments in capitalist society were political extensions of the interests of business owners. "The executive of the state," they wrote, was "nothing more than a committee for managing the affairs of the whole bourgeoisie."[25] Over the following decades, scores of influential followers would advance various arguments that had in common a core theme. Marxists argued that the expansion of capitalism brought with it the reinforcement of class divisions and, through imperialism and the spread of finance capital around the world, the replication of these divisions both within countries and between them.

But the rise of large hierarchical organizations focused a very particular critique that owed a debt to Weber, for its focus, and to Marx, for its argument. In 1951, the Columbia University sociologist C. Wright Mills published a study titled *White Collar: The American Middle Classes.*[26] Like Ronald Coase, Mills was fascinated by the rise of large managerial corporations. He argued that these firms, in their pursuit of scale and efficiency, had created a vast tier of workers who carried out repetitive, mechanistic tasks that stifled their imagination and, ultimately, their ability to fully participate in society. In short, Mills argued, the typical corporate worker was alienated. For many, that alienation was captured in the warning printed on the Hollerith punch cards that, thanks to IBM and other data processing firms, became ubiquitous symbols and agents of bureaucratized life during the 1950s and 1960s: "Do Not Fold, Spindle, or Mutilate."

In 1956 Mills further developed this argument in his most famous work, *The Power Elite.* Here, he identified the ways in which, according to him, power in the United States clustered in the hands of a ruling "caste" that dominated economic, industrial, and political affairs. Yes, Mills argued, American political life was democratic and pluralistic; yet despite this, the concentration of political and economic power put the elite in a stronger position than ever before to retain its supremacy.[27] These ideas made Mills a social critic, but his views were by no means radical for their time. President Dwight Eisenhower would make a similar point only five years later in his farewell speech to the nation, in which he warned against unchecked power and the "undue influence" of the "military-industrial complex."[28]

During the 1960s, the suspicion that modern economic organizations inherently produced inequalities and a permanent elite spread further among sociologists and psychologists. In 1967, a scholar at the University of California at Santa Cruz, G. William Domhoff, published a book titled *Who Rules America?* In it, Domhoff used what he called the "Four Networks" theory to show that American life was controlled by the owners and top managers of large corporations. Domhoff has continued to update the book in new editions, weaving in everything from the Vietnam War to the election of Barack Obama to make his case.[29]

The trope of an entrenched elite or establishment has itself become a foil for those who want to join its ranks, whether politicians who run against Washington or upstart firms seeking to dethrone a larger, more powerful rival. An example of the latter traces back to 1984, when Apple made advertising history with its iconic commercial introducing the Macintosh personal computer: in a tableaux inspired by George Orwell's dystopic novel, a woman pursued by a phalanx of jackbooted police hurls a sledgehammer at a huge screen broadcasting a Big Brotheresque message to row upon row of benumbed automatons, setting them free. The ad was not-so-subtly aimed at IBM, Apple's then-dominant competitor in the personal computer market. Of course, today IBM is out of the PC market, and its market capitalization value is dwarfed by that of Apple, which, in turn, is being criticized for maintaining its own Big Brotheresque grip on its operating system, hardware, stores, and consumer experience. Google, incorporated in 1998 with the informal hacker ethos and corporate motto of "Don't Be Evil," is now one of the world's biggest corporations (as measured by market capitalization) and is seen in some quarters as akin to the Antichrist, single-handedly destroying newspapers, crushing rivals, and violating consumer privacy.

Increasing wealth and income inequality in the United States in the last twenty years, along with the global trend toward massive CEO pay packages and banker bonuses, have fed the perception that those who get to the top stay there, remote and above the cares that afflict lesser mortals. The theorist Christopher Lasch, who died in 1994, called the policies and behaviors in the West that made these trends possible—deregulation and such social choices as private schooling, private security, and so on—the "revolt of the elites." He described this phenomenon as a kind of opting-out of the social system by those wealthy enough to be able to do so. "Have they canceled their allegiance to America?" Lasch asked in a cover essay in *Harper's.*[30]

The idea of a "revolt of the elites" has resonated. Despite fuzziness as to what exactly defines the elite (Wealth? Status measured some other way? Particular professions?), the notion of a resurgent elite further strengthening its hold on government is very much alive. In 2008, days after the massive US bank bailout was announced and a few short weeks after the collapse of Lehman Brothers and the rescue of the insurance giant American International Group (AIG), the critic Naomi Klein described the era as "a revolt of the elites . . . and an incredibly successful one." She argued that both the long neglect of financial regulation and the sudden bailout reflected elite control over policy. And she suggested that a common trend in the concentration of power linked together major countries with seemingly opposed political and economic systems. "I see a drift toward authoritarian capitalism that is shared in [the United States], Russia and China," Klein told an audience in New York. "Not to say that we're all at the same stage—but I see a trend toward a very disturbing mix of big corporate power and big state power cooperating in the interests of the elites."[31] A concomitant belief is that globalization has merely increased the concentration of power in individual industries and economic sectors, with market leaders cementing their hold on the top spots.

Events of recent years have revived the concern that power in many or most countries is ultimately held by an oligarchy—a small number of top players that enjoy disproportionate control over wealth and resources and whose interests are intimately woven, whether in blunt or subtle ways, into government policy. Simon Johnson, an MIT professor and former chief economist of the International Monetary Fund, drew on his experience to argue that everywhere the fund was called on to intervene, it found oligarchies seeking to shelter themselves and off-load the burdens of reform onto other constituencies (or foreign lenders). Oligarchies are a standard feature in emerging markets, Johnson asserted in a 2009 article in *The Atlantic*, but not just there. In fact, he argued, the United States set the lead here, too: "Just as we have the world's most advanced economy, military, and technology, we also have its most advanced oligarchy." He pointed to lobbying, financial deregulation, and the revolving door between Wall Street and Washington and argued in favor of a "breaking of the old elite."[32]

Such analyses inform a more general belief that is so pervasive as to have become almost a collective instinct: "Power and wealth tend to concentrate. The rich will become richer and the poor will stay poor." This rendering of the idea is something of a caricature, yet it is the default assumption underpinning conversations in parliaments, at millions of household dinner tables, in university halls and at after-work gatherings of friends, in erudite books, and in popular TV series. Even among free-market devotees, it is common to find echoes of the Marxist idea that power and wealth tend to concentrate. In the last decade or two, media coverage of the extravagant wealth of Russian oligarchs, oil sheiks, Chinese billionaires, and American hedge-fund managers and Internet entrepreneurs has been enthusiastically provided and consumed. And whenever these tycoons intervene in politics—as with Silvio Berlusconi in Italy, Thaksin Shinawatra in Thailand, or Rupert Murdoch and George Soros globally— or Bill Gates and others try to shape public policies in the United States and around the world, the public is again reminded that money and power reinforce each other, creating an almost impenetrable barrier for rivals.

The received wisdom that economic inequality is fated to endure and even get worse makes all of us, in a little way, Marxists. But what if the model of organization that Weber and his inheritors in economics and sociology found to be the most adapted to competition and management in modern life has become obsolete? What if power is dispersing, coming to dwell in new forms and through new mechanisms in a host of small and previously marginal players, while the power advantage of the big, established, and more bureaucratic incumbents decays? The rise of micropowers throws open such questions, for the first time. It holds out the prospect that power may have become remarkably unmoored from size and scale.

CHAPTER FOUR

HOW POWER LOST ITS EDGE

The More, Mobility, *and* Mentality *Revolutions*

JAVIER SOLANA, THE SPANISH FOREIGN MINISTER WHO IN THE MID-1990s became secretary-general of NATO and then the European Union's foreign policy chief, told me: "Over the last quarter-century—a period that included the Balkans and Iraq and negotiations with Iran, the Israeli-Palestinian issues and numerous other crises—I saw how multiple new forces and factors constrained even the richest and most technologically advanced powers. They—and by that I mean we—could rarely do any longer what we wanted."[1]

Solana is correct. Insurgents, fringe political parties, innovative start-ups, hackers, loosely organized activists, upstart citizen media, leaderless young people in city squares, and charismatic individuals who seem to have "come from nowhere" are shaking up the old order. Not all are savory; but each is contributing to the decay of power of the navies and police forces, television networks, traditional political parties, and large banks.

These are the *micropowers:* small, unknown, or once-negligible actors that have found ways to undermine, fence in, or thwart the megaplayers, the large bureaucratic organizations that previously controlled their fields. Going by past principles, micropowers should be aberrations. Because they lack scale, coordination, resources, or a preexisting reputation, they should not even be making it into the game—or at least, not making it for long before being squashed or absorbed by a dominant rival. But the reverse is true. Indeed, micropowers are denying established players many options that they used to take for granted. In some cases, the micropowers are even winning the contests against the megaplayers.

Do the newly arrived micropowers achieve this by overrunning the competition and driving the big incumbents out of business? Rarely. They are not equipped for vast takeovers. Their advantage is precisely that they are not burdened by the size, scale, asset and resource portfolio, centralization, and hierarchy that the megaplayers have deployed and spent so much time and effort nurturing and managing. The more the micropowers take on these traits, the more they turn into the type of organization that other new micropowers will attack with just as much effectiveness. Instead, successful micropowers capitalize on a new set of advantages and techniques. They wear down, impede, undermine, sabotage, and outflank the megaplayers in ways that the latter, for all their vast resources, find themselves ill-equipped and ill-prepared to resist. And the effectiveness of these techniques to destabilize and displace entrenched behemoths means that power is becoming easier to disrupt and harder to consolidate. The implications are breathtaking. They signal the exhaustion of the Weberian bureaucracy, the system of organization that delivered the benefits and also the tragedies of the twentieth century. *The decoupling of power from size, and thus the decoupling of the capacity to use power effectively from the control of a large Weberian bureaucracy, is changing the world.* And this decoupling invites a disquieting thought: if the future of power lies in disruption and interference, not management and consolidation, can we expect ever to know stability again?

So What Has Changed?

It's hard to identify the moment when the dispersal and decay of power, and the decline of the Weberian bureaucratic ideal, began—much less to do so in the precise way with which, say, the poet Philip Larkin pinpointed the advent of the sexual revolution: "Between the end of the *Chatterley* ban" and the Beatles' first album.[2]

Still, November 9, 1989—the date the Berlin Wall fell—is not a bad place to start. Loosening half a continent from tyranny's grip, unlocking borders, and opening new markets, the end of the Cold War and its animating ideological and existential struggle undermined the rationale for a vast national security state and the commitment of economic, political, and cultural resources that supported it. Whole populations forced to march more or less in lockstep were freed to find their own drummers, an upending of the existing order that found visceral expression in events such as the Christmas 1989 execution of the Ceausescus in Romania and the January 1990 storming of East Germany's Stasi headquarters—the secret-service organization that represented one of the darker pinnacles of postwar bureaucratic achievement. Economies trapped in a mostly closed system were opened to foreign investment and trade championed by a burgeoning herd of multinational corporations. As General William Odom, Ronald Reagan's National Security Agency director, observed: "By creating a security umbrella over Europe and Asia, Americans lowered the business transaction costs in all these regions: North America, Western Europe and Northeast Asia all got richer as a result."[3] Now those lower transaction costs could be extended, and with them also the promise of greater economic freedom.

Slightly more than a year after thousands of Germans took sledgehammers to the Berlin Wall, in December 1990, Tim Berners-Lee, a British computer scientist at the European Organization for Nuclear Research on the Franco-Swiss border, sent the first successful communication between a Hypertext Transfer Protocol and a server via the Internet, thereby creating the World Wide Web. That invention, in turn, sparked a global communications revolution that has left no part of our lives untouched.

The end of the Cold War and the birth of the Internet were certainly factors enabling the rise of today's micropowers, but they were by no means the only important ones. We often find it hard to resist the urge to attribute a period of great flux to a single cause. Take, for instance, the role of text messaging and social media such as Facebook and Twitter in upheavals around the world. A fierce but ultimately sterile debate has occurred between those who argue that social media have sparked new political movements and those who argue that their effect has been overstated. As elements in the struggle for power, social media have helped coordinate demonstrations and inform the outside world about human rights abuses. But savvy repressive regimes like those of Iran and China have also used these tools for surveillance and repression. And when in doubt, a government can simply turn off national Internet access (at least in large measure, as Egypt and Syria did when their dictators were challenged) or establish an elaborate system of filters and controls that reduces the flow of nonapproved online communication (as China has done with its "Great Firewall"). There are plenty of cases and counter-cases that illustrate the arguments of Internet optimists and techno-futurists like Clay Shirky as well as the counter-arguments of skeptics like Evgeny Morozov and Malcolm Gladwell. Thus, to understand why the barriers to power have become porous, we need to look at deeper transformations—to changes that began accumulating and accelerating even before the end of the Cold War or the spinning of the Web. The biggest challenges to power in our time have come from changes in the basics of life—in how we live, where we live, for how long and how well. What has changed is the landscape in which power operates.

This is the terrain of demographics, standards of living, levels of health and education, patterns of migration, families, communities, and, ultimately, our attitudes: the reference points for our aspirations, beliefs, desires, and, indeed, the ways in which we think about ourselves and others. To describe such changes at this deep level and to understand what they are doing to power, we need to break them down into three categories: the *More* revolution, the *Mobility* revolution, and the *Mentality* revolution. The first is swamping the barriers to power; the second is circumventing them; the third is undercutting them.

THE *MORE* REVOLUTION:
OVERWHELMING THE MEANS OF CONTROL

Ours is an age of profusion. There is simply more of everything now. There are more people, countries, cities, political parties, armies; more goods and services, and more companies selling them; more weapons and more medicines; more students and more computers; more preachers and more criminals. The world's economic output has increased fivefold since 1950. Income per capita is three and a half times greater than it was then. Most importantly, there are more people—2 billion more than there were just two decades ago. By 2050, the world's population will be four times larger than it was in 1950. Comprehending the size of this population as well as its age structure, geographical distribution, longevity, health, and aspirations is critical for understanding what has happened to power.

The More revolution is not limited to one quadrant of the globe or to one segment of humanity. It has progressed in the face of all the negative events that make the headlines each day: economic recession, terrorism, earthquakes, repression, civil wars, natural disasters, environmental threats. Without diminishing the urgency and human and planetary toll of these crises, we can assert that the first decade of the twenty-first century was arguably humanity's most successful: as the analyst Charles Kenny put it, our

"Best. Decade. Ever."[4] The data back up this claim. According to the World Bank, between 2005 and 2008, from sub-Saharan Africa to Latin America and from Asia to Eastern Europe, the proportion of people living in extreme poverty (those with incomes under $1.25 day) plunged—the first time that has happened since statistics on global poverty became available. Given that the decade was marked by the onset of the deepest economic crisis since the Great Depression of 1929, this progress is even more surprising. Indeed, in the midst of the crisis, Robert Zoellick, the then-president of the World Bank, expressed serious concern about the financial crash's impact on poverty: the experts, he said, had told him that the number of poor would increase substantially. Fortunately, they were wrong. In fact, the world is expected to reach the Millennium Development Goals on poverty set in 2000 by the United Nations much earlier than expected; one was to cut the world's extreme poverty in half by 2015, a goal met five years earlier.

The explanation is that despite the crisis, the economies of poorer countries continued to expand and create jobs. And it's a trend that began three decades ago: 660 million Chinese have escaped poverty since 1981, for example. In Asia, the percentage of those living in extreme poverty dropped from 77 percent of the population in the 1980s to 14 percent in 1998. This is happening not only in China, India, Brazil, and other successful emerging markets but also in the poorest countries in Africa. The economists Maxim Pinkovskiy and Xavier Sala-i-Martin have shown that between 1970 and 2006, poverty in Africa declined much faster than generally recognized. Their conclusion, based on a rigorous statistical analysis, is that in Africa "poverty reduction is remarkably general: it cannot be explained by a large country, or even by a single set of countries possessing some beneficial geographical or historical characteristic. All classes of countries, including those with disadvantageous geography and history, experienced reductions in poverty. In particular, poverty fell for both landlocked as well as coastal countries; for mineral-rich as well as mineral-poor countries; for countries with favorable or with unfavorable agriculture; for countries regardless of colonial origin; and for countries with below- or above-median slave exports per capita during the African slave trade. In 1998, for the first time since data is available, there are more Africans living above the poverty line than below."[5]

Of course, billions of people still live in unspeakable conditions. And having an income of three or five dollars a day instead of the $1.25 that the World Bank cites as the extreme poverty line still means a life of struggle and deprivation. But it is also a fact that quality of life has increased even for the world's poorest and most vulnerable "bottom billion." Since 2000 child mortality has decreased by more than 17 percent, and child deaths from measles dropped by 60 percent between 1999 and 2005. In developing countries, the number of people in the "undernourished" category decreased from 34 percent in 1970 to 17 percent in 2008.

The rapid economic growth of many poor countries and the consequent decline in poverty have also fueled the growth of a "global middle class." The World Bank reckons that since 2006, twenty-eight formerly "low-income countries" have joined the ranks of what it calls "middle-income" ones. These new middle classes may not be as prosperous as their counterparts in developed countries, but their members now enjoy an unprecedented standard of living. And this is the world's fastest-growing demographic category. As the Brookings Institution's Homi Kharas, one of the most respected researchers on the new global middle class, told me: "The size of the global middle class has doubled from about 1 billion in 1980 to 2 billion in 2012. This segment of society is still growing very fast and could reach 3 billion by 2020. I estimate that by 2017 Asia's middle class will be more numerous than that of North America and Europe combined. By 2021, on present trends, there could be more than 2 billion Asians in middle-class households. In China alone, there could be over 670 million middle-class consumers."[6]

And Kharas is quick to point out that this is happening not just in Asia: "Around the world, fast-growing, poor nations have been constantly adding numbers to their middle classes. I see nothing that indicates that this will not continue in the years ahead despite the occasional bump on the road that may slow down the growth of the middle class in some countries for a while. But globally, the trend is clear."

The world's socioeconomic landscape has been drastically altered in the last three decades. The list of changes—indeed, of achievements—is as long as it is surprising: 84 percent of the world's population is now literate, compared to 75 percent in 1990. University education is up, and even average scores on intelligence tests all over the world are now higher. Meanwhile, combat deaths are down—by more than 40 percent since 2000. Life expectancy in countries most hard-hit by the HIV/AIDS pandemic is starting to rise again. And we are providing for our agricultural needs better than ever: since 2000, cereal production in the developing world has increased twice as fast as population. Even "rare earths"—the seventeen scarce elements used in the manufacture of cellphones and in fuel refining—are not so rare anymore, as new sources and producers enter the market. Perhaps one reason for all this progress is the rapid expansion of the professional community of scientists: in the countries covered by an Organisation for Economic Co-operation and Development (OECD) survey, the number of working scientists grew from 4.3 million in 1999 to 6.3 million in 2009.[7] And that tally does not include several countries with large and growing science communities, most notably India.

Human beings are indeed enjoying longer and healthier lives. According to the United Nations Human Development Index, which combines health, education, and income indicators to give a global measure of well-being, standards of living have risen everywhere in the world since 1970. In fact, you can count on one hand the countries in which it was lower in 2010 than in 1970. And between 2000 and 2010 only *one* country in the world—Zimbabwe—saw its human development index go down. From poverty and child mortality to educational attainment and caloric intake, the key numbers at the end of 2012 were better than they were in 2000. Simply put, billions of people who until recently lived with almost nothing now have more food, more opportunities, and longer lives than ever before.

My aim here is not to sound like Voltaire's Dr. Pangloss, who proclaimed that "all is for the best in the best of all possible worlds." Indeed, every one of the aforementioned advances points to glaring challenges and exceptions that often turn tragic. The progress of the poor countries stands in clear contrast to the recent situation in Europe and the United States, where a middle class that enjoyed decades of growth and prosperity has been losing economic ground and shrinking as a result of the financial crash. Nevertheless, the overall picture of humanity living longer and healthier lives, with basic needs far better addressed than ever, is crucial to understanding today's shifts and redistributions of power—and to putting into perspective more fashionable explanations of current events. Yes, the Arab Spring and other recent social movements have made often spectacular use of modern technologies. But they owe even more to the rapid rise in life expectancy in the Middle East and North Africa since 1980; to the "youth bulge" made up of millions of people under thirty who are educated and healthy, with a long life span ahead of them, yet have no jobs or good prospects; and, of course, to the rise of a politically active middle class. It's no coincidence that the Arab Spring started in Tunisia, the North African country with the best economic performance and the most success in lifting its poor into the middle class. Indeed, an impatient, better-informed middle class that wants progress faster than the government can deliver, and whose intolerance for corruption has transformed it into a potent opposition, is the engine driving many of this decade's political changes. By itself, the growth of population and incomes is not sufficient to transform the exercise of power: power may still concentrate in few hands. But the More revolution is not just about quantity; it is also about qualitative improvements in people's lives. When people are better nourished, healthier, more educated, better informed, and more connected with others, many of the factors that locked power in place are no longer quite so effective.

The key is this: *When people are more numerous and living fuller lives, they become more difficult to regiment and control.*

The exercise of power in any realm involves, fundamentally, the ability to impose and retain control over a country, a marketplace, a constituency, a population of adherents, a network of trade routes, and so on. When the people in that territory—whether potential soldiers, voters, customers, workers, competitors, or believers—are more numerous and in fuller possession of their means and functioning at ever-greater levels of ability, they become more difficult to coordinate and control. The former US national security adviser Zbigniew Brzezinski, reflecting on the drastic changes in the world order since he entered public life, put it bluntly: "It is infinitely easier today to kill a million people than to control them."[8]

For those in power, the More revolution produces thorny dilemmas: How to coerce effectively when the use of force gets more costly and risky? How to assert authority when people's lives are fuller and they feel less dependent and vulnerable? How to influence people and reward them for their loyalty in a universe where they have more choices? The task of governing, organizing, mobilizing, influencing, persuading, disciplining, or repressing a large number of people with generally good standards of living requires different methods than those that worked for a smaller and less developed community.

THE *MOBILITY* REVOLUTION: THE END OF CAPTIVE AUDIENCES

Not only are there more people today, more of whom live fuller and healthier lives: they also move around a lot more. That makes them harder to control. It also changes the distribution of power within and among populations, whether through the rise of ethnic, religious, and professional diasporas or as individual vectors of ideas, capital, and faiths that can be either destabilizing or empowering. The United Nations estimates that there are 214 million migrants across the globe, an increase of 37 percent in the last two decades. In that same period, the number of migrants grew by 41 percent in Europe and by 80 percent in North America. We are experiencing a Mobility revolution, in which more people are moving than at any other time in world history.

Consider, for example, the effect that accelerated global mobility has had on the US labor movement. In 2005, a half-dozen unions defected from the AFL-CIO to form a competitor federation called Change to Win. The breakaway unions included the Service Employees International Union (SEIU) and the garment industry union UniteHere; both count among their ranks a higher proportion of low-wage immigrant workers, whose interests and priorities are different from those in the old-line manufacturing and industrial unions like the Teamsters. The impact of the split spilled over into national politics. As Jason DeParle, a reporter at the *New York Times,* put it: "Change to Win unions played an important (some have argued decisive) role in the early stages of Mr. Obama's first presidential campaign."[9] And in his bid for reelection in 2012, Hispanic voters proved determinant. In this unexpected way, international mobility helped to shape political outcomes in the United States—as it is doing everywhere.

Under the terms of the 2009 Sudanese Referendum Act passed by Sudan's legislature, voters from the Sudanese diaspora, including the 150,000 or so in the United States, were empowered to vote in the 2011 referendum concerning South Sudan's decision to become an independent nation. Some members of Colombia's senate are elected by Colombians living abroad. Political candidates for state governor or president from countries with large emigrant populations—for example, for state governorships in Mexico or for president of Senegal—often travel to Chicago or New York or London, or wherever their compatriots have put down roots, to raise votes and money.

By the same token, immigrants are changing the businesses, religions, and cultures of the countries they settle in. In the United States, the Hispanic population grew from 22 million in 1990 to 51 million in 2011, such that now one of every six Americans is Hispanic; they accounted for more than half of the growth in US population in the past decade. And in Dearborn, Michigan, the world headquarters for the Ford Motor Company, 40 percent of the population is Arab-American; its Muslim members have built the largest mosque in North America. Such enclaves are bound to transform coalitions and voting patterns as well as business strategies and even the competition for members of churches. Political parties, politicians, businesses, and other institutions increasingly face competitors that have deeper roots and a better understanding of this new population. The same is happening in Europe, as governments have proven unable to stem the tide of immigrants from Africa, Asia, and indeed other, less wealthy European countries. An interesting case in point: in 2007, a Nigerian-born man was elected in Portlaoise, Ireland, a commuter town west of Dublin, as that country's first black mayor.

Even efforts to *restrict* this new mobility can have powerful unexpected consequences. Jorge G. Castañeda, a former Mexican secretary of foreign affairs, and Douglas S. Massey, a Princeton sociologist, explain that in response to the harsher treatment and unwelcoming environment for immigrants in some American states, "many Mexican permanent residents made an unexpected choice: Rather than leave the United States because they felt unwelcome, they became citizens—a practice known as 'defensive naturalization.' In the decade before 1996, an average of 29,000 Mexicans were naturalized each year; since 1996, the average has been 125,000 per year, yielding two million new citizens who could then bring in close relatives. At present, nearly two-thirds of legal permanent residents from Mexico enter as relatives of U.S. citizens."[10] These new citizens are, of course, also voters—a fact that is reshaping the election landscape.

Immigrants also send billions of dollars in remittances to their home countries, promoting economic growth and development. Worldwide, they wired, mailed, or carried home $449 billion in 2010. (In 1980 remittances totaled just 37 billion.)[11] Nowadays, remittances are more than five times larger than the world's total foreign aid and larger than the annual total flow of foreign investment to poor countries. In short, workers who live outside their home country—and who are often very poor themselves—send more money to their country than foreign investors, and more than rich countries send as financial aid.[12] Indeed, for many countries, remittances have become the biggest source of hard currency and, in effect, the largest sector of the economy, thereby transforming traditional economic and social structures as well as the business landscape.

PERHAPS THE MOST AGGRESSIVELY POWER-TRANSFORMING ASPECT OF the Mobility revolution is urbanization. What was already the fastest process of urbanization in history is accelerating, especially in Asia. More people have moved, and continue to move, from farms to cities than ever before. In 2007, for the first time in history, more people lived in cities than in rural areas. Richard Dobbs describes the immense scale of this transformation as follows: "The megacity will be home to China's and India's growing middle classes—creating consumer markets larger than today's Japan and Spain, respectively."[13] The US National Intelligence Council reckons that "every year 65 million people are added to the world's urban population, equivalent to adding seven cities the size of Chicago or five the size of London annually."[14] The consequences of this revolution for the distribution of power are just as intense internally; indeed, an increasing number of people are spending and investing in two (or more) countries at the same time. Internal migration—especially population shifts from farms to cities—can be as disruptive to power as is international migration.

Though less broad-based than urbanization, a newer form of mobility is also reshaping the landscape of power: brain circulation. Poor nations tend to lose many of their skilled and better-educated citizens to richer countries, which attract them with the expectation of a better life. This well-known "brain drain" deprives nations of nurses, engineers, scientists, entrepreneurs, and other professionals who have been expensive to train—departures that obviously lessen the countries' endowment of human capital. In recent years, however, increasingly more of these professionals have been returning to their countries of origin and upending business as usual in industries, universities, the media, and politics. AnnaLee Saxenian, the dean of the School of Information at the University of California, Berkeley, has found that Taiwanese, Indian, Israeli, and Chinese immigrants who worked in California's Silicon Valley often became "angel investors" and "venture capitalists" in their old countries, starting up companies and eventually either moving back or traveling often between their old and new countries (that is why Saxenian calls it *brain circulation*). In so doing, they transfer the culture, approaches, and techniques they learned in the United States. Inevitably, in the case of the entrepreneurs, the dynamic, competitive, and disruptive business culture common in entrepreneurial hubs clashes with the monopolistic and traditional ways of doing business often found in developing countries with dominant, family-controlled business conglomerates. This is another example of the surprising ways in which the Mobility revolution is altering the acquisition and exertion of power in traditional but fast-changing societies.[15]

This movement of temporary and permanent migrants is occurring in the context of a vast increase in the movement of goods, services, money, information, and ideas. Short-term travel has quadrupled: in 1980, the number of international tourist arrivals accounted for just 3.5 percent of the world's population, compared to almost 14 percent in 2010.[16] Every year, an estimated 320 million people fly to attend professional meetings, conventions, and international gatherings—and their numbers are steadily growing.[17]

The trade in goods was barely slowed by the recession that started in 2008. In 1990, the world's total exports and imports amounted to 39 percent of the global economy; by 2010, they had risen to 56 percent. And between 2000 and 2009, the total value of merchandise traded across borders nearly doubled, from $6.5 trillion to $12.5 trillion (in current dollars), according to the United Nations; total exports of goods and services in that period jumped from $7.9 trillion to $18.7 trillion, according to the IMF.

Money has also become unprecedentedly mobile. The stock of foreign direct investment measured as a percentage of the world's economy jumped from 6.5 percent in 1980 to a whopping 30 percent in 2010, while the volume of currency that moved internationally *every day* grew sevenfold between 1995 and 2010. In the latter year, more than $4 *trillion* changed hands across international borders daily.[18]

The ability to move information around has vastly expanded as well. How many people do you know who don't own a cellphone? Very few. This answer holds true even in the poorest and most dysfunctional nations. "Somali Mobile Phone Firms Thrive Despite Chaos" was the headline of a 2009 Reuters dispatch from that ravaged country.[19] Somalia epitomizes the concept of "failed states," societies in which citizens lack access to basic services that most of us take for granted. Yet, even there, twenty-first-century mobile telephony is widely available. The expansion of mobile telephony is as surprising for its speed as for its novelty. In 1990, the number of mobile cellular subscriptions per 100 people worldwide was 0.2. By 2010 it had exploded to more than 78 subscribers for every 100 persons.[20] The International Telecommunications Union reports that in 2012 subscriptions to mobile telephony exceeded the 6 billion mark—equivalent to an astonishing 87 percent of the world's population.[21]

And then, of course, there is the Internet. Its expansion and the surprising new ways in which it is used (and abused) don't need much elaboration. In 1990, the number of Internet users was insignificant—a mere 0.1 percent of the worlds' population. That number rose to 30 percent of the population worldwide in 2010 (and to more than 73 percent in developed countries).[22] By 2012, eight-year-old Facebook was on its way to having more than 1 billion users (with more than half of them accessing it via their mobile phones and tablets), Twitter (launched in 2006) had 140 million active users, and Skype—the voice-over-Internet service created in 2003—boasted almost 700 million regular users.[23]

The Twitter and Facebook revolutions in the Middle East and the impact of social media on politics are much discussed, and we examine their role in the decay of power. But in terms of this initial discussion of the Mobility revolution, we should also consider the impact of another tool that does not get the credit it deserves for changing the world: the prepaid phone card. Web users need electricity, a computer, and an Internet service provider, things that most of us take for granted but that are too expensive for most of the world's population. Calling-card users need only a few cents and a pay phone to connect with the rest of the world regardless of how isolated or remote their own location. The growth of calling-card usage and global reach leaves the Internet's growth in the dust. Prepaid phone cards were invented in Italy in 1976 as a response to the shortage of metal coins and to curb pay phone theft and vandalism. The new product took off and in 1977 was also launched in Austria, France, Sweden, and the United Kingdom and, five years later, in Japan (also prompted by a coin shortage). But truly explosive growth took place once prepaid calling cards became popular among the poor of the world. Driven by gains in the poorer countries, industry revenues skyrocketed from $25 million in 1993 to more than $3 billion in 2000.[24] Now prepaid calling cards are giving way to prepaid mobile phones. In fact, prepaid cellphones have displaced those that require a long-term subscription and bound the user to a service provider through an elaborate contract.[25] The less-well-off who choose to leave home for better, or merely some, work far away no longer face as stark a choice between staying close to their families and communities and improving their fortunes.

Two characteristics shared by all of these mobility-enhancing technologies are the speed and extent of the drop in costs of moving goods, money, people, and information. Airline tickets that used to cost thousands of dollars can now be had at a fraction of their prices twenty or thirty years ago, and the cost per mile of transporting a ton of cargo today is ten times lower than in the 1950s. Wiring money from California to Mexico in the late 1990s cost about 15 percent of the sum being transferred; today it is less than 6 percent. Mobile-phone platforms through which money can be transferred from one cellphone to another will make remittances almost cost-free.

And what exactly do all these revolutionary changes in mobility and communication mean for power? The Mobility revolution has a profound effect that can be just as intuitively grasped as that of the More revolution. Exercising power means not only maintaining control and coordination over a real or figurative territory but also policing its borders. That is true for a nation-state, but also for a corporation that dominates a given market, a political party that depends on a geographically bound constituency, or a father who wants to keep his children within reach. Power needs a captive audience. In situations where citizens, voters, investors, workers, parishioners, or customers have few or no alternative outlets, they have little choice but to consent to the terms of the institutions they face. But when borders become porous and the governed—or controlled—population more mobile, entrenched organizations have a harder time retaining their dominance. The most radical example is migration, whereby people simply remove themselves from one distribution of power to another, thus putting themselves in a position they believe will give them better options.

Inevitably, the ease of travel and transportation and the faster, less costly ways of moving information, money, or values make life easier for challengers and harder for incumbents.

THE *MENTALITY* REVOLUTION: TAKING NOTHING FOR GRANTED ANYMORE

In the late 1960s, the Harvard political scientist Samuel Huntington famously argued that a fundamental cause of social and political instability in developing countries—which he preferred to call "rapidly changing societies"—was that people's expectations expanded much faster than the capacity of any government to satisfy them.[26] The More and Mobility revolutions have created a new, vast, and fast-growing middle class whose members are well aware that others have even more prosperity, freedom, or personal fulfillment than they do—and who hope and expect to catch up. This "expectations revolution" and the disconnect it breeds are now global. They affect both rich and poor countries alike; indeed, the overwhelming majority of the world's population lives in what could now be called "rapidly changing societies." The difference, of course, is that whereas in developing countries the middles class is expanding, in most wealthy countries it is shrinking. And both growing and shrinking middle classes fuel political turmoil. The embattled middle classes take to the streets and fight to protect their living standards while the expanding middle classes protest to get more and better goods and services. In Chile, for example, students have been rioting almost routinely since 2009, demanding cheaper and better university education. It doesn't matter that a few decades ago access to higher education was a privilege reserved for a tiny elite and that universities are now flooded with the sons and daughters of the new middle class. For the students and their parents, access to higher education is no longer enough. They want better and cheaper education. And they want it now. The same is happening in China, where protests over the poor quality of new apartment buildings, hospitals, and schools are now common. Here, too, the argument that a few years ago those apartments, hospitals, and schools didn't even exist does not placate the ire of those who want improvements in the quality of the medical and educational services being offered. This is a new mindset—a change in mentality—that has profound consequences for power.

A profound change in expectations and standards has come about, and not just in liberal societies but even in the most hidebound ones. Most people look at the world, their neighbors, employers, clergy, politicians and governments with different eyes than their parents did. To some degree, that has always been the case. But the effect of the More and Mobility revolutions has been to vastly broaden the cognitive, even emotional impact of more access to resources and the ability to move, learn, connect, and communicate more broadly and inexpensively than ever before. Inevitably, this sharpens the intergenerational gaps in mentality—and in worldview.

HOW DOES IT WORK?

Consider divorce, anathema in many traditional societies but today more common everywhere. A study conducted in 2010 found that divorce rates have risen even in the conservative Persian Gulf states, reaching 20 percent in Saudi Arabia, 26 percent in the United Arab Emirates, and 37 percent in Kuwait. In addition, these higher divorce rates were correlated to education. Specifically, the increased number of educated women was putting a strain on conservative marriages, leading to marital conflict and summary divorces pronounced by threatened husbands. In Kuwait, the rate of divorce soared to 47 percent among couples in which both spouses held a university degree. "Women used to accept social sacrifices," Saudi sociologist and report author Mona al-Munajjed said, comparing Gulf society thirty years ago and today. "Now they will not accept that anymore."[27]

The Muslim world is just one rich source of examples of how the Mentality revolution is transforming long-held traditions, from the rise of a fashion and glamour industry aimed at hijabi (veiled or covered) women to the spread of no-interest banking in Western countries where large Muslim immigrant communities have formed. Meanwhile in India, the transformation in attitudes is spreading back from the young generation to their elders: a country where divorce was once considered shameful—and women, in particular, were discouraged from remarrying—now has an increasingly robust matrimonial advertising industry devoted to listings by divorced senior citizens, some as old as their eighties or even nineties, seeking love late in life and without embarrassment. Mature adults are leaving the arranged marriages into which they were inducted when they were teens or young adults. Late in life, they are at last able to rebel against the encoded powers of family, community, society, and religion. They have changed their mentality.

Changes in mentality and attitudes toward power and authority are also taking place among youths—a segment of the population that is now more numerous than ever before. According to the US Intelligence Council, "Today, more than 80 states have populations with a median age of 25 years or less. As a group, these countries have an over-sized impact on world affairs—since the 1970s, roughly 80 percent of all armed civic and ethnic conflict . . . has originated in states with youthful populations. The 'demographic arc of instability' outlined by these youthful populations ranges from clusters in the mid-section of Central America and the Central Andes, covers all of sub-Saharan Africa and stretches across the Middle East into South and Central Asia."[28]

THE PROPENSITY OF THE YOUNG TO QUESTION AUTHORITY AND challenge power is now amplified by the More and Mobility revolutions. Not only are there more people than ever under thirty, but they *have* more—prepaid calling-cards, radios, TVs, cellphones, computers, and access to the Internet as well as to travel and communication possibilities with others like them at home and around the world. They are also more mobile than ever. Aging baby boomers may be a feature of several industrialized societies, but elsewhere it is the young—irreverent, change-seeking, challenging, better informed, mobile, and connected—who comprise the largest demographic group. And as we have seen in North Africa and the Middle East, they can have a powerful impact.

Complicating this picture in some advanced societies are cross-cutting demographic trends driven by immigration. The 2010 US Census revealed that the American population under eighteen would have undergone a decade-long decline had it not been for the inflow of millions of young

Hispanic and Asian immigrants. These young immigrants are an important factor behind an unprecedented transition: in 2012, white babies were a minority of all US births.[29] According to William Frey, a demographer at the Brookings Institution, inasmuch as the share of immigrants in the US population was at its lowest level in the twentieth century from 1946 to 1964,

> boomers had minimal involvement with people from other countries. Today, immigrants are 13 percent of the population, and they are far more diverse. That created an isolation that persists. Among Americans older than 50, 76 percent are white, and the black population, at 10 percent, is the largest minority. Among those younger than 30, 55 percent are whites. Hispanics, Asians and other nonblack minorities account for 31 percent of that age group. Younger people are much more likely to be first- and second-generation Americans of non-European ancestry and able to speak English and other languages.[30]

In short, old folks today not only just don't get it, they can't even speak it. But for those seeking to acquire, wield, or retain power in the United States and Europe, an understanding of the mindsets and expectations of these new constituencies will be essential.

A number of global public opinion surveys are providing a clearer picture of the extent and velocity of these attitudinal changes. Since 1990, the World Values Survey (WVS) has been tracking changes in people's attitudes in over eighty countries containing 85 percent of the world's population. In particular, Ronald Inglehart, the director of the WVS, and several of his co-authors, notably Pippa Norris and Christian Welzel, have documented profound changes in attitudes concerning gender differences, religion, government, and globalization. One of their conclusions about these changes in peoples' mentality is that there is a growing global consensus regarding the importance of individual autonomy and gender equality as well as a corresponding popular intolerance for authoritarianism.[31]

On the other hand, there is ample survey evidence pointing toward an equally profound but more worrisome attitudinal trend: in mature democracies (Europe, the United States, Japan), public confidence in leaders and institutions of democratic governance such as parliaments, political parties, and the judiciary not only is low but shows a secular decline.[32]

Reflecting on this trend, Jessica Mathews, the president of the Carnegie Endowment for International Peace, noted that

[t]he American National Election Studies group has been asking Americans the same question roughly every two years since 1958: "Do you trust the government in Washington to do what is right, all or most of the time?" Until the mid-sixties, 75 percent of Americans answered yes. A slide then began and continued steeply downward for fifteen years, so that by 1980, only 25 percent said yes. In the interim, of course, were the Vietnam War, two assassinations, Watergate and the near-impeachment of the president and the Arab oil embargo. So there were plenty of reasons for people to feel estranged, even antagonistic. But what matters most is that the trust did not recover. For the last three decades, the approval level has bumped around in the region from 20 to 35 percent. The trust percentage fell below half in about 1972. This means that anyone under the age of forty has lived their entire life in a country the majority of whose citizens do not trust their own national government to do what they think is right. Through four long decades, none of the massive changes Americans have voted for in leadership and in ideology have changed that. Think what it means for the healthy functioning of a democracy that two-thirds to three-quarters of its people do not believe that their government does the right thing most of the time.[33]

This drastic shift in attitudes is corroborated by Gallup, which has been tracking public opinion since 1936. For example, it found that in the United States, public approval of labor unions and confidence in Congress, political parties, big business, banks, newspapers, television news, and many other fundamental institutions have been declining. (The military is one of the few institutions that retains the confidence and support of Americans.)[34] Even the US Supreme Court, an institution long held in high esteem by Americans, has suffered a sharp decline in public support—from almost 70 percent approval of those surveyed in 1986 to 40 percent approval in 2012.[35]

It should not be surprising that, as the survey data collected by the Pew Global Attitudes Project confirms, this decline in trust in government and other institutions is not a strictly American phenomenon.[36] In *Critical Citizens,* Harvard's Pippa Norris and an international network of experts concluded that dissatisfaction with the political system and the core institutions of government is a growing and global phenomenon.[37] The economic crisis that erupted in 2008 in the United States and then ravaged Europe has also fueled strong sentiments against the powerful actors that the public blames for the crisis: the government, politicians, banks, and so on.[38]

None of these surveys is exhaustive, yet each shows at least a few of the ways in which attitudes and values are shifting in the wake of—and perhaps sometimes ahead of—political and material changes in people's lives.

The Mentality revolution encompasses profound changes in values, standards, and norms. It reflects the growing importance attributed to transparency and property rights, and to fairness, whether in the treatment of women in society, of ethnic and other minorities, and even of minority shareholders in corporations. Many of these standards and norms have deep philosophical roots. But their spread and prevalence today—though still highly uneven and imperfect—is spectacular. These changes in mentality have been driven by demographic changes and political reforms, by the expansion of democracy and prosperity, by dramatic increases in literacy and access to education—and by the explosion in communications and media.

Globalization, urbanization, changes in family structure, the rise of new industries and opportunities, the spread of English as a global lingua franca—these have had consequences in every sphere, but their effect has been most fundamental at the level of attitudes. Indeed, the signal effect of these changes is the ever-increasing salience of *aspiration* as a motivator of our actions and behaviors. Desiring a better life is a normal human trait, but aspiration toward specific examples and narratives of how life could be better, not some abstract notion of improvement, is what drives people to take action. Economists have shown this to be the case in emigration, for instance: People emigrate not because of absolute deprivation but because of relative deprivation; not because they are poor, but because they are aware that they could be doing better. The more contact we have with one another, the greater the extent to which contact breeds aspiration.

The effects of the Mentality revolution on power have been manifold and complex. The combination of emerging global values and the increase in aspirational behavior poses the strongest challenge of all to the moral basis of power. It helps spread the idea that things do not need to be as they have always been—that there is always, somewhere and somehow, a better way. It breeds skepticism and mistrust of any authority, and an unwillingness to take any distribution of power for granted.

One of the best examples of all three revolutions simultaneously at work is the Indian outsourcing industry. Young, educated Indians who belong to the country's burgeoning middle class have flocked to work at urban call centers and other business process outsourcing (BPO) companies, which in 2011 generated $59 billion in revenue and directly and indirectly employed almost 10 million Indians.[39] As Shehzad Nadeem observed in *Dead Ringers,* his study of the impact of Indian call centers on their workers, "The identities and aspirations of the ICT [information and communications technology] workforce are defined increasingly with reference to the West. . . . Radical in their rejection of old values, conspicuous in their consumption, workers construct an image of the West that is used to benchmark India's progress toward modernity."[40] Although the jobs pay relatively well, they plunge young Indians into a welter of contradictions and competing aspirations—that is, aspirations to succeed in an Indian social and economic context while sublimating their cultural identities with fake accents and names and dealing with abuse and exploitation at the hands of affluent customers in a different continent.

For young urban Indian women in particular, the jobs have provided opportunities and economic benefits that they might otherwise not have had, leading to lasting changes in behavior that are upending cultural norms. Never mind the lurid newspaper article that talked about call centers as "a part of India where freedom knows no bounds, love is a favourite pastime, and sex is recreation." Closer to the mark would be a recent survey by India's Associated Chambers of Commerce that young working married women in Indian cities are increasingly choosing to put off having children in favor of developing their careers.[41]

REVOLUTIONARY CONSEQUENCES: UNDERMINING THE BARRIERS TO POWER

Plenty of events would seem to suggest that things have not changed all that much, that micropowers are an anomaly, and, ultimately, that big power can and will continue to call the shots. Individual tyrants may be gone in places like Egypt and Tunisia, but the power establishment behind them still wields clout. After all, don't the repressive ripostes of the Chinese, Iranian, or Russian governments, the consolidation of big banks, and the pattern of government expansion, bailouts, and even nationalization of major companies in many rich and developing nations show that in the end power still follows the same old rules? Goldman Sachs, the US military, the Chinese Communist Party, and the Catholic Church have not gone away. They still impose their will in myriad ways.

And while some giants have fallen, those that have risen in their place seem to follow the same principles of organization and display the same urge to expand and consolidate. Does it matter that the world's largest steel company is no longer U.S. Steel or one of the European giants but the outgrowth of a once-marginal Indian player, if it has acquired many of the assets, personnel, and customers of some of these old rivals? Is it fair to argue that the emergence of new giants that are operationally similar to the old ones, especially in business, is simply part of the regular working of capitalism?

The answer to both questions is yes and no. The trends we are currently observing can be interpreted—or simply dismissed—as the manifestation of what economist Joseph Schumpeter (and before him Karl Marx) dubbed "creative destruction." In Schumpeter's words: "The opening up of new markets, foreign or domestic, and the organizational development from the craft shop and factory to such concerns as U.S. Steel illustrate the same process of industrial mutation . . . that incessantly revolutionizes the economic structure from within, incessantly destroying the old one, incessantly creating a new one. This process of Creative Destruction is the essential fact about capitalism. It is what capitalism consists in and what every capitalist concern has got to live in."[42]

The shifts in power that we see all around us—which include and transcend the ascent and demise of business enterprises—are certainly consistent with Schumpeter's expectations. They are also in line with the insights of Clayton Christensen, a Harvard Business School professor who coined the term *disruptive innovation,* meaning a change—in technology, service, or product—that creates a new market by relying on a completely new approach. The effects of a disruptive innovation eventually spill over to other related or similar markets and undermine them. The iPad is a good example. Using your cellphone to pay for groceries or to send money to your daughter in another continent are two other good examples.

Yet, whereas Schumpeter focused on the forces of change within the capitalist system in general and Christensen dissected specific markets more narrowly, the argument here is that similar forces are at work in a much broader set of human endeavors. As this chapter tries to make clear, the More, Mobility, and Mentality revolutions represent change of a much greater magnitude and scale.

Each of these revolutions presents a specific challenge to the traditional model of power. In that model, large, centralized, coordinated modern organizations that deployed overwhelming resources, special assets, or crushing force offered the clearest path to getting and keeping power. For centuries, that model proved to be the best-adapted one not just for coercing people but also for exercising power in its subtler dimensions.

As we saw in Chapter 2, power operates through four distinct channels: *muscle,* or blunt coercion, which forces people to do things they would not otherwise choose to do; *code,* the power of moral obligation; *pitch,* the power of persuasion; and *reward,* the power of inducement. Two of these—muscle and reward—alter the incentives and reshape a situation to move people to act in a certain way, while the other two—pitch and code—shift people's assessment of a situation without changing the incentives. Barriers to power must be in place if muscle, code, pitch, and reward are to be effective. And the effect of the More, Mobility, and Mentality revolutions is precisely to reduce these barriers. The chart in Figure 4.1 offers a summary.

FIGURE 4.1. POWER AND THE THREE REVOLUTIONS

	MORE REVOLUTION *Overwhelms the barriers: "Harder to control and coordinate"*	MOBILITY REVOLUTION *Circumvents the barriers: "No more captive audience"*	MENTALITY REVOLUTION *Undermines the barriers: "Take nothing for granted"*
Muscle (actual or potential use of coercion)	Can laws or armies "keep the lid on" when people are more numerous, healthier, and more informed?	Jurisdictions and market boundaries are porous and slippery; frontiers are harder to police.	Automatic deference to authority is no longer the case.
Code (moral and traditional obligation)	Can moral claims keep up with changing material realities and more information?	Aspiration attacks all certainties.	Universal values take precedence over dogma.
Pitch (persuasion, appeal to preferences)	Is a big market an advantage when there are so many promising niches?	There's an awareness of almost infinite alternatives—and a growing ability to get them.	Skepticism and mindsets are more open to change, and there's an increased propensity to switch preferences.
Reward (inducement in exchange for compliance)	How to tailor incentives in a world of so much choice?	How to tailor incentives when people, money, and ideas are on the move?	The cost of loyalty is ever increasing, and there are weaker incentives to accept status quo.

As this chart makes clear, the three revolutions pose challenges to power in all four of its channels—muscle, code, pitch, and reward. Coercion, of course, is the bluntest exercise of power—whether exercised through laws, armies, governments, or monopolies. But as the three revolutions progress, organizations that rely on coercion face ever-increasing costs simply to maintain control over their domains and patrol their boundaries.

The inability of the United States or the European Union to curb illegal immigration or illicit trade is a good example. Walls, fences, border controls, biometric identification documents, detention centers, police raids, asylum hearings, deportations—these are just part of an apparatus of prevention and repression that has thus far proven to be extremely expensive, if not futile. Witness the failure of the United States to curb the inflow of drugs from Latin America despite its long-standing and enormously expensive "War on Drugs."

Moreover, the combination of greater well-being and spreading global values is giving people the space, the desire, and the tools to challenge coercive authorities. Civil liberties, human rights, and economic transparency are increasingly cherished values, and there are more and more advocates, experts, supporters, and platforms available to advance them. My point here is not that coercion is no longer possible but, rather, that it has become more costly and harder to sustain over time.

Power exercised through code, or moral obligation, also faces challenges as the three revolutions advance. Custom and religion have long been relied upon to provide moral order and explain the world. Indeed, for people who live short lives marked by disease and poverty, traditions embedded in families or tightly knit communities help them to cope, share support, and accept harsh realities. But as their material comforts increase and they gain access to more alternatives, they become less dependent on their inherited belief systems and more open to experimentation with new ones.

In times of intense material and behavioral change, appeals to custom or moral obligation are less likely to succeed unless they reflect changing conditions. As an example consider the crisis of the Catholic Church, whose growing inability to recruit priests who accept the vow of celibacy—or to compete with small evangelical churches that can tailor messages to the culture and the concrete needs of specific local communities—makes for a spectacular cautionary tale.

Power also operates through persuasion—for example, the pitch made by an advertising campaign or a real estate broker—and through inducement—by rewarding constituents, employees, or other subjects with packages of benefits that ensure their participation and consent. The three revolutions are changing the landscape for pitch and reward as well.

Imagine a political candidate or party trying to drum up votes for an upcoming election through a combination of messages, advertising, and promises of rewards in the form of constituent services and jobs. The More revolution is creating better-educated and better-informed pools of constituents who are less likely to passively accept government decisions, more prone to scrutinize authorities' behavior, and more active in seeking change and asserting their rights. The Mobility revolution is making the demographics of the constituency more diverse, fragmented, and volatile. In some cases it may even be creating interested players who are able to affect the debate and influence voters from faraway locations—indeed, from a different country. The Mentality revolution breeds increasing skepticism of the political system in general.

A similar dilemma affects employers, advertisers, and anyone else trying to attract support or sales in communities where interests and preferences are fragmenting and becoming more diverse. It may be easier to invent a package of benefits that does a good job of achieving the enthusiastic consent of a smaller group than one that does a mediocre job of attracting a larger population. The more the advantage of size and scale diminishes, the more niche marketing and single-issue politics, for example, stand to benefit. As a result, large corporations are increasingly being compelled by market forces and the actions of smaller rivals to behave as niche players—something that does not come naturally to organizations long accustomed to relying on the overwhelming power of their large scale.

BARRIERS DOWN:
THE OPPORTUNITY FOR MICROPOWERS

In the pages ahead, we will take these concepts into the real world. One reason it can be difficult to talk about power except in the most general philosophic terms is that we are accustomed to think about the dynamics of power very differently depending on whether we focus on military conflict, business competition, international diplomacy, the relationship between husband and wife, father and son, or some other arena. Yet the changes highlighted by the three revolutions affect all of these fields and go beyond any one particular trend-of-the-moment. Indeed, they are more deeply woven into the patterns and expectations of human society today than they were just a few years or decades ago, and they are challenging the conventional wisdom about what it takes to get, use, and keep power. The question of how that challenge is unfolding, and how the dominant players inherited from the twentieth century are responding to it, will occupy the rest of this book.

By no means is big power dead: the big, established players are fighting back, and in many cases they are still prevailing. Dictators, plutocrats, corporate behemoths, and the leaders of the great religions will continue to be an important feature of the global landscape and the defining factor in the lives of billions of people. But these megaplayers are more constrained in what they can do than they used to be in the past, and their hold on power is increasingly less secure. The chapters ahead will show how the micropowers are limiting the choices available to the megaplayers and how in some instances they are forcing them to retreat—or, as was the case during the Arab Spring, even to lose power altogether.

The More, Mobility, and Mentality revolutions are attacking the model of organization so persuasively advocated by Max Weber and his followers in sociology, economics, and other fields, and they are attacking it precisely at the points where it drew its strength. Large organizations were more efficient because they operated with lower costs, thanks to economies of scale; today, however, the costs of maintaining order and control are going up. Large organizations were more effective because they centralized and warehoused scarce resources; today, resources such as commodities, information, human talent, and customers are easier to source and serve, from distances near and far. Large organizations had a sheen of authority, modernity, and sophistication; today, headlines are being made by small newcomers that are challenging the big powers. And as the advantages of the large-scale, rational, coordinated, and centralized model of organization diminish, the opportunities increase for micropowers to make their mark using a different model for success.

But to what extent is power decaying? And with what consequences? In the rest of the book we turn to the specifics of how this process is playing out in domestic politics, war, geopolitics, business, and other fields. Exactly which barriers to power are coming down? What new players have emerged, and how have the powers-that-be fought back?

The reorganization of power, as the barriers have fallen, is far from complete but is already producing fundamental changes.

CHAPTER FIVE

WHY ARE LANDSLIDES, MAJORITIES, AND STRONG MANDATES ENDANGERED SPECIES?

The Decay of Power in National Politics

THE ESSENCE OF POLITICS IS POWER; THE ESSENCE OF POWER IS politics. And since the Ancients, the classic path to power has been the pursuit of politics. Indeed, power is to politicians what sunlight is to plants. What politicians do with their power varies; but the aspiration to power is their essential common trait. As Max Weber put it almost a century ago: "He who is active in politics strives for power, either as a means in serving other ends, ideal or egoistic, or as 'power for power's sake,' that is, in order to enjoy the prestige-feeling that power gives."[1]

But that "prestige-feeling" is a fragile emotion. And these days, its half-life is getting shorter. Consider the last decade in American politics, which political analyst Ron Brownstein has called "The Age of Volatility." Voters gave the Republicans control of both Congress and the White House in 2002 and 2004 and then took it away from them in 2006 and 2008—only to restore control of the House of Representatives to them in 2010 and 2012. Previously, in the five elections from 1996 to 2004, the biggest gain in House seats by any one party was nine; in 2006, the Republicans lost thirty seats, in 2008 the Democrats won twenty-one, and in 2010 the Democrats lost sixty-three. The number of American voters registered as independents now regularly exceeds the number who align with Republicans and Democrats.[2] In 2012, the importance of Hispanics became obvious.

This is not just an American phenomenon. Everywhere, the basis of political power is growing more fragile; gaining a majority of votes no longer guarantees the ability to make decisions, inasmuch as a multitude of "micropowers" can veto, delay, or water them down. Power is seeping away from autocrats and single-party systems whether they embrace reform or not. It is spreading from large and long-established political parties to small ones with narrow agendas or niche constituencies. Even within parties, party bosses who make decisions, pick candidates, and hammer out platforms behind closed doors are giving way to insurgents and outsiders—to new politicians who haven't risen up in the party machine, who never bothered to kiss the ring. People entirely outside the party structure—charismatic individuals, some with wealthy backers from outside the political class, others simply catching a wave of support thanks to new messaging and mobilization tools that don't require parties—are blazing a new path to political power.

Whatever path they followed to get there, politicians in government are finding that their tenure is getting shorter and their power to shape policy is decaying. Politics was always the art of the compromise, but now politics is downright frustrating—sometimes it feels like the art of nothing at all. Gridlock is more common at every level of decision-making in the political system, in all areas of government, and in most countries. Coalitions collapse, elections take place more often, and "mandates" prove ever more elusive. Decentralization and devolution are creating new legislative and executive bodies. In turn, more politicians and elected or appointed officials are emerging from these stronger municipalities and regional assemblies, eating into the power of top politicians in national capitals. Even the judicial branch is contributing: judges are getting friskier and more likely to investigate political leaders, block or reverse their actions, or drag them into corruption inquiries that divert them from passing laws and making policy. Winning an election may still be one of life's great thrills, but the afterglow is diminishing. Even being at the top of an authoritarian government is no longer as safe and powerful a perch as it once was. As Professor Minxin Pei, one of the world's most respected experts on China, told me: "The members of the politburo now openly talk about the old good times when their predecessors at the top of the Chinese Communist Party did not have to worry about bloggers, hackers, transnational criminals, rogue provincial leaders or activists that stage 180,000 public protests each year. When challengers appeared, the old leaders had more power to deal with them. Today's leaders are still very powerful but not as much as those of a few decades back and their powers are constantly declining."[3]

Strong claims, these. After all, the diversity of the world's political systems is intimidating. There are centralized and federal systems and many variants in between, and some countries are part of supranational political systems like the European Union. Dictatorships are single-party, nominally but artificially multi-party, or no-party; they are military or hereditary or underpinned by ethnic or religious majority or minority groups, and so on. Democracies are even more diverse. Presidential and parliamentary systems fragment into numerous subdivisions that hold elections according to different schedules, make room for fewer or more parties, and have complex rules governing participation, representation, election financing, checks and balances, and all the rest. The customs and traditions of political life vary by region; even the respect accorded political leaders and the allure of political careers depend on numerous shifting factors. So how can we generalize and announce that politics is fragmenting and that, everywhere, political power faces more constraints and is increasingly becoming more ephemeral?

Consider, first, the answer from politicians themselves. Every political leader or head of state I've spoken with has cited a growing litany of interfering forces that limit their ability to govern: not just factions within their parties and ruling coalitions, or uncooperative legislators and increasingly free-wheeling judges, but also aggressive bondholders and other agents of global capital markets, international regulators, multilateral institutions, investigative journalists and social media campaigners, and an ever-widening circle of activist groups. As Lena Hjelm-Wallén, Sweden's former deputy prime minister, minister for foreign affairs, minister of education, and, for many years, one of her country's leading politicians, told me: "I never cease to be amazed at how much and how fast political power has changed. I now look back and marvel at the many things we could do in the 1970s and 1980s and that now are almost unimaginable given the many new factors that reduce and slow down the ability of governments and politicians to act."[4]

ESTABLISHED POLITICIANS ARE ALSO BUMPING INTO A NEW CAST OF characters within the corridors of legislative power. In the 2010 parliamentary elections in Brazil, for example, the candidate who won the most votes anywhere in the country (and the second-most-voted congressman in the country's history) was a clown—an actual clown who went by the name of Tiririca and wore his clown costume while he campaigned. His platform was as anti-politician as it gets. "I don't know what a representative in congress does," he told voters in YouTube videos that attracted millions of viewers, "but if you send me there I will tell you." He also explained that his goal was "to help needy people in this country, but especially my family."[5]

Politics in Max Weber's sober view was a "vocation"—a craft to which politicians aspired and which required discipline, a set of character traits, and considerable effort. But as the standard "political class" in country after country loses popular credibility, outsiders such as Tiririca are finding more success. In Italy, the comedian Beppe Grillo, who lambastes politicians of every stripe, writes the most popular blog in the country and fills every stadium in which he appears. "Call him a comedian, a clown or a showman but Beppe Grillo is the juiciest piece of Italian political news for a while," wrote Beppe Severgnini in the *Financial Times* in 2012. In that year's local elections, Grillo's movement polled about 20 percent of the national vote and won several mayoral contests.[6] In Canada, Rob Ford—whose past transgressions gave his opponents fodder for attack signs reading "wife-beating, racist drunk for mayor"—got elected mayor of Toronto in 2010. In Spain, Belén Esteban, a strident television personality who reveals her most intimate secrets on camera, has gathered a cadre of enthusiastic followers that many traditional politicians would like to have.

In the United States, the rise of the Tea Party movement—far from unorganized, but also very far from any traditional political organization— boosted candidates like Christine O'Donnell, who allegedly dabbled in witchcraft and made opposition to masturbation a key part of her agenda. Even when O'Donnell and her fellow Tea-Partier, Nevada Republican Sharron Angle (who at one point suggested that the way to fix Congress was for Americans to resort to "Second Amendment remedies"—i.e., armed insurrection[7]), failed to win their races, their victories in Republican Party primaries in 2010 underscored the waning ability of traditional party leaders to control the nomination process. The Republican party's traditional leaders not only lacked the power to contain the savage rivalry among the presidential contenders for the party's nomination but also could not protect several incumbent senators (notably Indiana's long-serving Richard Lugar) and hand-groomed senatorial candidates (Texas Lieutenant Governor David Dewhurst) from successful 2012 primary challenges by Tea Party upstarts.

Increasingly, political heroes are transcending not only parties but organized politics itself. They accrue power and influence not necessarily to seek and hold a political office but to advance and draw attention to their cause. These are the likes of Alexey Navalny, the Russian lawyer and blogger who has become a focal point for the anti-Putin opposition; Tawakkol Karman, the mother of three who won a Nobel Peace Prize for her efforts to promote freedom and democracy in Yemen; and Wael Ghonim, who emerged as a key leader of Egypt's revolution (and thus, like Karman, is an iconic figure of the overall Arab Spring) from his position as a mid-level executive in the local office of Google.

Of course, as impressive as such stories are, they are just that—stories. To truly chart the ebb and flow of power in politics, and specifically its decay, we need data and hard evidence. This chapter aims to provide proof that in many (and increasingly more) countries, the clearly defined power centers of the past no longer exist. A "cloud" of players has replaced the center, each with some power to shape political or governmental outcomes, but none with enough power to unilaterally determine them. That might sound like healthy democracy and desirable checks and balances, and in some measure this is the case. But in many countries, the fragmentation of the political system is creating a situation where gridlock and the propensity to adopt minimalist decisions at the last minute are severely eroding the quality of public policy and the ability of governments to meet voters' expectations or solve urgent problems.

FROM EMPIRES TO STATES: THE MORE REVOLUTION AND THE PROLIFERATION OF COUNTRIES

Can one date, one moment, change history? Jawaharlal Nehru, India's first prime minister, called it a "tryst with destiny." And indeed the stroke of midnight, ushering in August 15, 1947, did more than just mark political freedom for India and Pakistan. It set in motion the wave of decolonization that transformed the world order from one dominated by empires to one that today has almost two hundred separate and sovereign states. And with that, it set out the new context in which political power would henceforth operate—a context unknown since the era of medieval principalities and city-states, and certainly never before known on the world scale. If world politics today is fragmenting, it is because there are so many countries in the first place, each with a modicum of power. The scattering of empires into separate nations whose existence we now take for granted represents the first level in the political cascade.

Before that moment in 1947, the world counted sixty-seven sovereign states.[8] Two years earlier the United Nations had been founded with an initial roster of fifty-one members (see Figure 5.1). After India, decolonization spread in Asia, reaching Burma, Indonesia, and Malaysia. Then it hit Africa with full force. Within five years after Ghana's independence in 1957, another two dozen African countries had gained freedom as the British and French colonial empires unwound. In almost every year until the early 1980s, at least one new country in Africa, the Caribbean, or Pacific achieved independence.

The colonial empires were gone but the Soviet empire—both the formal structure of the Soviet Union, and the de facto empire of the Eastern Bloc— remained. That would soon change, too, thanks to another "tryst with destiny." November 9, 1989, saw the collapse of the Berlin Wall and launched the breakup of the Soviet Union, Czechoslovakia, and Yugoslavia. In just four years, between 1990 and 1994, the United Nations added twenty-five members. Since then the flow has slowed but not completely stopped. East Timor joined the United Nations in 2002; Montenegro, in 2006. On July 9, 2011, South Sudan became the world's newest sovereign state.

FIGURE 5.1. THE NUMBER OF SOVEREIGN NATIONS HAS QUADRUPLED
SINCE 1945

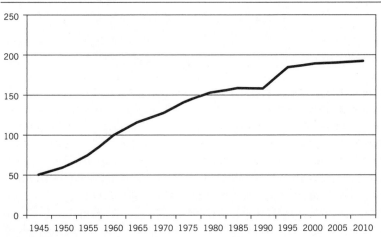

SOURCE: Adapted from "Growth in United Nations Membership, 1945–Present," http://www .un.org/en/members/growth.shtml.

To the twenty-first-century mind, this chain of events may feel familiar. Yet the scope of change we have lived through in just two or three generations has no precedent. The More revolution that we examined in the last chapter is clearly visible in the proliferation of separate states with their own capitals, governments, currencies, armies, parliaments, and other institutions. This proliferation has, in turn, reduced the geographic distance between ordinary people and the seat from which they are governed. Indians look to New Delhi, not to London, for decisions that affect them. Poland's power center is Warsaw, not Moscow.

This change is simple but profound. Capitals are within closer reach, and the Mobility revolution with its easier, cheaper travel and quicker transmission of information facilitates contacts between the governed and their government. But there are also so many more political roles to fill, so many more elected offices and civil service positions and the like. The practice of politics is that much less distant a possibility; the circle of leaders is that much less exclusive a club. With the quadrupling of sovereign states in just over half a century, many barriers of access to meaningful power have become less daunting. We should not minimize the changes caused by this first cascade of power simply because they feel so familiar. But the next level of the cascade—increased fragmentation and dilution of politics within all these separate sovereign countries—contains other surprises.

FROM DESPOTS TO DEMOCRATS

In what came to be known as the Carnation Revolution, the soldiers who swarmed into the streets of Lisbon, Portugal, placed flowers in their gun barrels to reassure the population of their peaceful intentions. And the officers who overthrew President Antonio Salazar on April 25, 1974, proved true to their word. Having ended close to half a century of repressive rule, they held elections the next year that brought to Portugal the democracy that it still enjoys today.

But the impact went much further. After the Carnation Revolution, democracy bloomed in key Mediterranean countries held back by dictatorships from much of the social and economic progress of the rest of postwar Western Europe. Three months after the Lisbon uprising, the junta of colonels that was running Greece fell. In November 1975, Francisco Franco died, and Spain, too, became a democracy. Between 1981 and 1986, all three would join the European Union.

The wave spread. Argentina in 1983, Brazil in 1985, Chile in 1989—all came out from long and traumatic military dictatorships. By the time the Soviet Union fell, South Korea, the Philippines, Taiwan, and South Africa were in the midst of their own democratic transitions. Across Africa, single-party states gave way to multi-party elections in 1990 and after. The Carnation Revolution began what the scholar Samuel Huntington christened the Third Wave of democratization. The first wave had come in the nineteenth century, with the expansion of suffrage and appearance of modern democracies in the United States and Western Europe, only to suffer reverses in the run-up to World War II with the rise of totalitarian ideologies. The second wave came after World War II with the restoration of democracy in Europe, but it proved short-lived as communism and single-party regimes spread in the East Bloc and many newly independent states. The Third Wave has been both durable and far-reaching. The number of democracies in the world is unprecedented. And remarkably, even the remaining autocratic countries are less authoritarian than before, with electoral systems gaining strength and people empowered by new forms of contestation that repressive rulers are poorly geared to suppress. Local crises and setbacks are real, but the global trend is strong: power continues to flow away from autocrats and become more fleeting and dispersed (see Figure 5.2).

FIGURE 5.2. THE PROLIFERATION OF DEMOCRACIES AND THE DECLINE OF AUTOCRACIES: 1950–2011

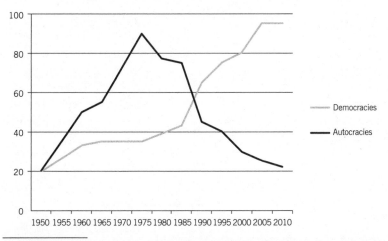

SOURCE: Adapted from Monty G. Marshall, Keith Jaggers, and Ted Robert Gurr, "Political Regime Characteristics and Transitions, 1800–2010," Polity IV Project, http://www.systemicpeace.org /polity4.htm.

The data confirm this transformation: 1977 was the high-water mark
of authoritarian rule, with 90 authoritarian countries. According to the
Polity Project, by 2008 the world included 95 democracies, only 23 autocracies, and 45 cases that ranked somewhere in between.[9] Another respected
source, Freedom House, assessed whether countries are electoral democracies, based on whether they hold elections that are regular, timely, open,
and fair, even if certain other civic and political freedoms may be lacking
(see Figure 5.3 for regional trends). In 2011 it counted 117 of 193 surveyed
countries as electoral democracies. Compare that with 1989, when only 69
of 167 countries made the grade. Put another way, the proportion of democracies in the world increased by just over half in only two decades.

What caused this global transformation? Obviously local factors were
at work, but Huntington noted some big forces as well. Poor economic
management by many authoritarian governments eroded their popular
standing. A rising middle class demanded better public services, greater
participation, and eventually more political freedom. Western governments and activists encouraged dissent and held out rewards for reform,
such as membership in NATO or the EU or access to funds from international financial institutions. A newly activist Catholic Church under Pope
John Paul II empowered opposition in Poland, El Salvador, and the Philippines. Above all, success begat success, a process accelerated by the new

FIGURE 5.3. REGIONAL TRENDS (FREEDOM HOUSE 2010)

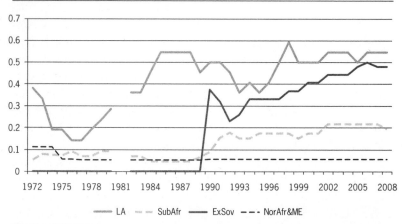

SOURCE: Adapted from Freedom House, *Freedom in the World: Political Rights and Civil Liberties
1970–2008* (New York: Freedom House, 2010).

reach and speed of mass media. As news of democratic triumphs spread from country to country, greater access to media by increasingly literate populations encouraged emulation. In today's digital culture, the force of that factor has exploded. Literacy and education, achievements that epitomize the global More revolution, made political communication across borders much easier and helped fuel political aspiration—the Mentality revolution at work, applied to core values of freedom, self-expression, and the desire for meaningful representation.

There have been exceptions, of course—not just countries where democracy has yet to spread but others where it has experienced reversals. Larry Diamond, a leading scholar in this field, calls the stalling in recent years in countries like Russia, Venezuela, or Bangladesh a "democratic recession." Yet against this is mounting evidence that public attitudes have shifted. In Latin America, for example, despite persistent poverty and inequality, and constant corruption scandals, opinion polls show greater confidence in civilian government than in the military.[10]

Even autocracies are less autocratic today. According to one study of the world's democratic electoral systems, Brunei may be the only country where "electoral politics has failed to put down any meaningful roots at all."[11] With far fewer repressive regimes in the world, one might have expected the holdouts to be places where freedom and political competition are increasingly suppressed. But in fact the opposite is true. How? Elections are central to democracy but they are not the only indicator of political openness. Freedom of the press, civil liberties, checks and balances that limit the power of any single institution (including that of the head of state), and other measures convey a sense of a government's grip on society. And the data show that on average, even as the number of authoritarian regimes has gone down, the democracy scores of countries that remain politically closed have gone up. The sharpest improvement occurred in the early 1990s, suggesting that the same forces that pushed so many countries into the democratic column at that time had profound liberalizing effects in the remaining nondemocratic countries as well.

This might be cold comfort to an activist or dissident thrown in jail. And from Cairo to Moscow, and Caracas to Tunis, for every step forward, one can find cautionary tales or counter-examples that should restrain any outbursts of democratic exuberance. The backlash by powerful governments against new democratic tools and techniques is a topic that is often present in the news, and it should come as no surprise that the megapowers are resisting the trends that are sapping their might. For now, though, what can be said with certainty is that democracies are spreading, and therefore trends within democracies are increasingly harbingers for trends in countries that are not yet fully democratic. Moreover, the numbers and the facts suggest that within democracies—in the intricate mechanics of their voting patterns, parliamentary negotiations, governing coalitions, decentralizations, and regional assemblies—the decay of power has found intense momentum.

From Majorities to Minorities

We are voting more often. A lot more often. This is a major trend of civic life in the last half-century, at least for people who live in the established Western democracies. In a set of eighteen countries that have been consistently democratic since 1960, including the United States, Canada, Japan, Australia, New Zealand, and most of Western Europe, the frequency with which citizens are called to the polls increased in a large majority of cases between 1960 and 2000. Citizens in these countries have thus had more frequent opportunities to select and reject the people who represent them as well as to voice through referenda their preferences in matters of public policy or national priorities. The frequency of elections does not mean that voters are more likely to take part: in many Western countries, abstention rates have gone up in recent years. But those who choose to vote have had more chances to do so—and that means politicians have had to re-earn the public's consent many more times. This constant scrutiny and the burden of recurring electoral contests not only shortens the time horizon that elected officials use to make their decisions or to select the initiatives on which they will invest their time and political capital but also greatly limits their autonomy.

How much more are we voting? A study by Russell Dalton and Mark Gray addressed this question. In the five-year period from 1960 to 1964, the countries they examined held sixty-two nationwide elections (see Figure 5.4). In the five-year period from 1995 to 1999, they held eighty-one such elections. Why the increase? The cause may be related to changes in election rules, the growing use of referenda, or the advent of elections for the new regional assemblies that some countries have created. Members of the EU have held regular elections to the European Parliament (EP). The researchers point out that the data cover days when elections are held, not the quantity of separate polls held on each voting day. In fact, the trend

FIGURE 5.4. TOTAL NUMBER OF ELECTIONS BY YEAR IN SAMPLE OF COUNTRIES AROUND THE WORLD: 1960–2001

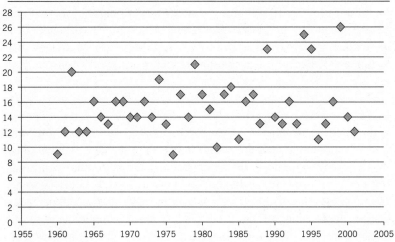

SOURCE: Adapted from Russell Dalton and Mark Gray, "Expanding the Electoral Marketplace," in Bruce E. Cain et al., eds., *Democracy Transformed? Expanding Political Opportunities in Advanced Industrial Democracies* (New York: Oxford University Press, 2003).

may be even stronger than their numbers suggest, because several countries have consolidated multiple elections (e.g., presidential and legislative or legislative and municipal) in a single voting day. The United States, with its strong tradition of fixed national-election days in November every two years, is an exception to this trend—but not because Americans are voting any less frequently. In fact, the two-year renewal cycle of the US House of Representatives is the briefest in all the established democracies, making Americans some of the most called-upon voters in the world.[12]

The world in general is following this trend toward more frequent elections at all levels of government. Matt Golder, a professor at Pennsylvania State University, tracked democratic legislative and presidential elections in 199 countries between 1946 (or the year since they became independent) and the year 2000.[13] He found that during this period the 199 nations held 867 legislative elections and 294 presidential elections. In other words, during these fifty-four years (which included more than a decade in which democracy had not become as prevalent as it later became), somewhere in the world there were, on average, two important elections *every month.*

As Bill Sweeney, the president of the International Foundation for Electoral Systems (IFES), a nonprofit organization that is the world's most important provider of technical assistance to election officials, told me: "The demand for our services is booming. Almost everywhere, elections are becoming more frequent and we can feel the hunger for systems and techniques that ensure more transparent and fraud-free elections."[14]

MORE FREQUENT VOTES ARE JUST ONE WAY IN WHICH POLITICAL leaders are experiencing greater limits on their latitude of action. Another is the stunning decline of the electoral majority. Nowadays, minorities rule. In 2012, among the thirty-four members of the "rich nations club," the Organisation for Economic Co-operation and Development, only four featured a government that also had an absolute majority in parliament.[15] In India, thirty-five parties shared seats in the 2009 election; no party has won an absolute majority since 1984. In fact, absolute majorities are globally on the wane. In electoral democracies, minority parties have won on average more than 50 percent of the seats in parliament throughout the postwar period; in 2008, minority parties controlled 55 percent of seats on average. But even in countries that are not deemed democracies, minority parties are increasing their clout. In those countries, minority parties held fewer than 10 percent of seats three decades ago; now their average share has risen to nearly 30 percent.[16]

So when politicians claim a "mandate" these days, they are more often than not engaging in wishful thinking. The type of clear-cut election victory that could justify this terminology is simply too rare. Political scientists point out that even in the United States, where the two-party system would seem to produce clear winners and losers, only one recent presidential election—Ronald Reagan's reelection in 1984, defeating Walter Mondale—qualified as a landslide. Reagan not only swept all but one state and the District of Columbia and their electoral votes but also won a massive share of actual votes, with 59 percent—a margin that no US candidate since then has equaled or beaten.[17] This sort of victory is even less likely in systems with three, four, five, or more major parties and many small ones splitting allegiances.

Accordingly, the noble art of governing now depends more heavily on a much dirtier, hands-on skill: forming and maintaining a coalition. And the horse-trading that coalitions require gives small parties more clout to demand particular policy concessions or ministerial positions. In a scattered election landscape, it's good to be a small party. In fact, parties on the fringes—those with extreme views or a single-issue focus, or that cater to a regional base—can wield more power without needing to dilute their stance to attract middle-of-the-road voters. The chauvinist libertarian Northern League in Italy, the far-right party of Israeli foreign minister Avigdor Lieberman, the would-be secessionists of the Flemish Popular Party in Belgium, and the various Communist parties in the national parliament and regional assemblies in India have all enjoyed outsized influence in coalitions with other partners who oppose their message but have no choice but to bring them aboard. In December 2011, for example, fierce opposition from two parties in India's Congress Party–led coalition forced Prime Minister Manmohan Singh to set aside plans to let foreign supermarkets own 51 percent of their ventures—a humiliating climb-down.

Wrangling over coalitions reveals the compromises that an election's "winner" has to take on from the outset. In May 2010, elections in the United Kingdom produced a hung parliament, leading to the formation of a coalition between David Cameron's Conservative Party and Nicholas Clegg's Liberal Democrats—two parties with sharp differences on immigration and European integration, among other issues. Both parties made notable concessions as a consequence. But sometimes coalition-building may prove to be an elusive goal. The Netherlands spent four months without a government in 2010. Belgium had it even worse. In 1988, its politicians set a national record when it took them 150 days to form a coalition. That seemed bad enough, but in 2007–2008, beset by worsening tensions between its Dutch-speaking Flemish and its French-speaking Walloon regions, the country went for nine and a half months with no government, while extremist factions agitated for the Flemish region's outright secession. That government resigned in April 2010, followed by another prolonged stalemate. In February 2011, Belgium beat out Cambodia to set a world record for the period a country went without a government; finally, on December 6, 2011, after 541 days of deadlock, it swore in a new prime minister. Tellingly for the diminishing power of politicians, despite this absurd and presumably crippling crisis of government, the economy and society kept chugging along and performed as well as other European neighbors; in fact, it was only a downgrade of Belgium's credit rating by Standard & Poor's that pressured the opposing parties toward a solution.[18]

Recent research into other aspects of government formation, duration, and termination yield further evidence regarding the decay of power. One fascinating source is provided by Scandinavian researchers who have compiled detailed information on the governments of seventeen European democracies, stretching back to the end of World War II or, in some cases, to the time when countries in the survey (e.g., Greece, Spain, and Portugal) finally became democratic. The data include Germany, France, the United Kingdom, and the other European heavy-hitters. Even though these research findings cannot be generalized to, say, India or Brazil or South Africa, they still offer compelling headlines about how politics in democracies is fracturing today. Some examples follow.

The Advantage Enjoyed by Incumbents Is Disappearing

It's generally the case that though incumbent parties and coalitions have built-in advantages such as patronage and visibility, they are likely to lose some votes, if only because their sympathizers may have lost enthusiasm while their opponents have a record to criticize. In recent years, the incidence of this phenomenon has increased: an analysis of seventeen established democracies in Europe showed that in every decade since the 1940s, the average loss of votes by incumbents facing reelection has risen. In the 1950s, incumbents had lost on average 1.08 percent of the vote; by the 1980s, the average loss was 3.44 percent; and in the 1990s, it almost doubled again, to 6.28 percent. In the 1950s, thirty-five cabinets in the countries surveyed won reelection whereas thirty-seven lost; in the 1990s, only eleven cabinets won reelection whereas forty-six lost. Hanne Marthe Narud and Henry Valen, the political scientists who carried out this analysis, also pointed out that the trend was as strong in established democracies such as the United Kingdom or the Netherlands as it was in new democracies such as Greece or Portugal; in other words, the trend was impervious to the length of democratic experience and tradition.[19]

Governments Are Falling More Quickly

There is also evidence that since World War II, governing coalitions or cabinets have increasingly tended to end due to political infighting before their term is up. Political scientists distinguish between two kinds of cabinet termination. One is technical—that is, pertaining to constitutional reasons particular to the country in question or to situations in which elections are due by law or a prime minister dies and must be replaced. The other kind of cabinet termination is discretionary—in other words, due to political volatility, as when a cabinet resigns due to political dissension or loses a vote of confidence in parliament. According to a study based on the same data set of seventeen parliamentary democracies in Europe since 1945, there were more discretionary terminations than technical terminations in the 1970s and 1980s (72.9 percent and 64.7 percent, respectively) than in previous decades. In the 1990s the proportions balanced out, however, with an equal number of technical and discretionary terminations.[20]

Not surprisingly, in the first decade of the twenty-first century this trend toward discretionary terminations accelerated. Since the financial crisis erupted in 2008, governments fell, cabinets collapsed, coalitions frayed, ministers were fired, and once-untouchable party bosses were forced to resign. As economic problems raged throughout Europe, the inability of the powerful to tame the crisis became dramatically apparent.

EVEN OUTSIDE PARLIAMENTARY SYSTEMS, EVIDENCE ABOUNDS OF the constraints that now undermine the seeming mandate of an election victory. In the United States, one source of increasing frustration for each presidential administration is how long nominees take to get confirmed by the Senate. As New York University scholar Paul Light has observed, "A nomination and confirmation process lasting more than six months was nearly unheard of between 1964 and 1984." In that same period, only 5 percent of appointees waited more than six months between being contacted in advance of nomination and actually getting confirmed. By today's glacial standards, that past performance is unbelievably speedy. Between 1984 and 1999, Light found, 30 percent of appointees needed more than six months to get confirmed. On the other hand, quick confirmations—those taking just one to two months—occurred in 50 percent of the cases between 1964 and 1984 but only 15 percent of the cases between 1984 and 1999. In the following decade, as political polarization became more acute, this trend would only get worse.

FROM PARTIES TO FACTIONS

Party bosses chomping on cigars and trading patronage favors as they set out their platforms and policies and candidates—the image looms large in political mythology, but it is further and further removed from reality. Exhibit A is the shifting fortunes of the Republican Party in the United States. Not so long ago, the GOP epitomized buttoned-down business conservatism and the discipline that came with it—characteristics that it succeeded in maintaining in the face of concerted, and sometimes successful, agitation by social-conservative-issue groups. The rise of the Tea Party has proved to be more of an organizational challenge. Tellingly, the Tea Party is not a party at all but a loose amalgam of organizations and factions and affinity groups and individuals motivated by the ideas (themselves fluid) that they associate with the "Tea Party" concept and brand. Some Tea Party candidates and groups have garnered funding from powerful business interests that have considerable experience influencing American politics (e.g., David and Charles Koch, the billionaires who run Koch Industries, the second-largest private company in the United States). Other Tea Party components resemble nothing more than grassroots direct-democracy activist movements in a long-standing tradition of American political participation. These disparate elements come together in a way that no traditional political party, with its committees and rules and small circle of elite power-brokers, could hope to contain. It took only months from the emergence of the Tea Party in 2009 for it to reshape Republican and, with it, American politics, driving primary victories for rank outsiders and others not preferred by the party establishment. Indeed, in the 2008 election, the Tea Party did not exist; four years later, the contenders for the 2012 Republican presidential nomination all eagerly sought its mantle.

The Tea Party is a very American phenomenon, whether as a reflection of the American infatuation with direct democracy, as a vehicle for injecting money into politics, or as the latest vessel for small-government populism. But its rapid emergence out of nowhere has corollaries. In Europe, the Pirate Party movement, which draws on a hacker ethos of free information and greater civil liberties, has expanded from its origins in Sweden in 2006 to Austria, Denmark, Finland, Germany, Ireland, the Netherlands, Poland, and Spain. Its platform, the so-called Uppsala Declaration promulgated in 2009, focuses on liberalizing copyright and patent laws, promoting transparency and freedom of speech, and mobilizing the youth vote. Not only did it win 7.1 percent of the vote in Sweden's European Parliament elections and two of Sweden's EP seats, but in September 2011 it won representation in a state parliament by securing 9 percent of the vote in Berlin. Among the parties it outstripped were a key partner in Angela Merkel's ruling coalition, the long-established Free Democratic Party—which didn't even rise above the 5 percent threshold needed for state representation.[21] In 2012 the Pirate Party achieved another milestone when a member of its Swiss branch won the election for mayor of the city of Eichberg.[22]

Another kind of campaign insurgency was carried out by Ségolène Royal in France's 2007 presidential election. Running to lead the Socialist Party against Nicolas Sarkozy, Royal opposed all of the party's traditional "barons" with their deep support networks among party cadres and high elected officials.

So how did Royal get to be the candidate? Through a Tea Party–like movement—and, as in America, through the use of primaries to determine the candidate. Primaries are a recent tool in democracies: in America, where they are most familiar, they really only became generalized in the late 1960s, and elsewhere they are even more recent than that. They are also increasingly common. For the 2007 election in France, the Socialist Party held a primary open to all party members—and Royal's camp launched a massive campaign to sign up new members in time to take part. Through this device along with a website and political messaging that separated Royal from the party apparatus, she won a crushing 61 percent in the primary—although in the general election she lost.

The French Socialists, not content with this innovation, decided to take it a step further in 2011 as they prepared for the 2012 elections. This time they decided to hold primaries open to all voters, not just to their own party members. To participate, the voter needed only to sign his or her approval of a basic statement of agreement with the values of the Left—hardly a binding and enforceable arrangement. And at least one candidate signed up who was himself not a member of the party. In other words, there was no longer much that was party-like about this party's way of selecting the candidate to oppose the incumbent president. François Hollande, who had lived with Ségolène Royal since the 1970s and with whom had four children, won the Socialist Party's nomination and defeated Nicolas Sarkozy in the presidential election. By then Hollande and Royal were separated and the new president moved to the Élysée Palace with his companion, journalist Valérie Trierweiler.

The Tea Party on one side of the political spectrum and French Socialists on the other are just two examples of an international trend: across the advanced democracies, major parties are feeling the distance between leaders selected behind closed doors and those who can mobilize voters. With minority parties on the rise, the need to adapt has become urgent. In many countries, parties that for decades expected to have a share or a turn in power have opened up the way they choose their standard-bearer. Using one method or another, they are expanding the "selectorate"—a term that designates the field of people who get a say in selecting a party leader.[23]

The spread of primaries is a telling sign of that change. Tallying fifty major parties from eighteen parliamentary democracies, Ofer Kenig, head of the political parties' research group at the Israel Democracy Institute, noted in 2009 that twenty-four gave their ordinary members "a significant role" in choosing the leader. The others divided between selection by members of parliament and selection by some appointed committee.[24]

As noted, primaries are spreading elsewhere as well.[25] In Latin America, an estimated 40 percent of the presidential elections since the political transitions away from military rule in the 1980s have included at least one major candidate selected through a primary. One survey of political parties in Latin America found that more than half had used some kind of primary or primary-like internal election by 2000. Another study found that the lowest levels of confidence in political parties in Latin America were in countries, such as Bolivia and Ecuador, where no candidates had ever been selected by primaries. Overall, political scientists have found that even though open primaries—the kind that bring in the biggest "selectorate"— are in place in only a limited number of countries, a clear international trend points in their direction. And California, long a bellwether for national trends in the United States, has tilted the balance further in favor of voter over party preferences: it agreed by popular referendum in 2011 to have all primary candidates appear on a single ballot, with the top two vote-getters moving on to the general election regardless of party.

As if US party bosses didn't have already enough problems keeping their power and enforcing discipline, along came the Super-PACs, a new vehicle engendered in 2010 by the Supreme Court through its Citizens United decision eliminating limits to campaign contributions and empowering private corporations as political actors. These Super-Political Action Committees are not allowed to coordinate with the candidates they support, but in the 2012 campaign it became obvious that each of the presidential candidates (even each of the Republican party contenders for the nomination) had one or more Super-PACs which were massively funding initiatives that promoted them or attacked their rivals. Super-PACs are both a new form of substantial political power based on access to large quantities of money and an example of yet another form of fragmentation of that power. Their defenders see them as merely a healthy addition to the arsenal of those who want to bring more competition to politics. Joel M. Gora, a law professor who helped advocacy groups in their efforts to resist donor disclosure requirements, says that many of the regulations allowing access to Super-PACs are simply part of an "incumbent protection racket." As he argues, "These laws are restricting outsiders, whether liberal or left-wing outsiders or conservative and right-wing outsiders."[26] In fact, businessman Leo Linbeck III launched a Super-PAC in

2012 whose only aim was to dislodge entrenched incumbents, whom he believes are no longer responsive to voters. As the *Washington Post*'s Paul Kane reported, "While most PACs aim to boost the chances of a favored candidate or to bring down an ideological opponent, the super PAC has a decidedly different goal: to oust incumbents. Of both parties. And why not? . . . [Linbeck's Super-Pac] helped defeat two veteran Republicans and two long-time Democrats, knocking out almost 65 years of combined House experience."[27] And although Linbeck's funds were limited and his Super-PAC was running out of money, its spokesman victoriously noted that "[w]e've demonstrated that our concept works."[28]

Super-PACs may be a distinctly American phenomenon, but worldwide, money is clearly becoming as potent a political driver of political outcomes as ideology once was. Still, as the cases of Silvio Berlusconi in Italy, Thaksin Shinawatra in Thailand, Ben Ali in Tunisia, and many others show, money alone is far from enough these days to seal the many holes through which power seeps away.

FROM CAPITALS TO REGIONS

More countries. More democracies. More pressure to share power even in nations with authoritarian regimes while democracies offer more choices both inside and outside political parties. More frequent elections, more referenda, more scrutiny, and more contenders. All of these trends point to the same direction: the redistribution and scattering of power from established players to more competitors.

Add one more global trend to all these: power is also shifting from capitals and the executive branch to state and local governments.[29]

Take the United Kingdom, for example. Its political system is famously stable. Conservatives and Labour take turns in office, with Liberal Democrats holding a sliver in the center. When neither of the main parties has a majority, producing a "hung parliament," as in 2010, a coalition with the Liberal Democrats puts either party over the top. That negotiation, while serious, is far less complicated than it would have been if it took a coalition of five or six parties to form a majority in parliament.

In Britain, those three parties control the bulk of the House of Commons, and election rules make it difficult for anyone else to break through. And so how do we explain the presence of the multiple parties we've heard about in recent years? The UK Independence Party, the British National Party, the Scottish National Party, Sinn Fein, the Ulster Unionists, the Plaid

Cymru—the British political landscape is much more varied than the traditional picture would suggest. Some regional, some extreme, these parties
have found elected office—and the media attention and credibility that ac-
company it—in the past two decades. How? Thanks to new elected bodies.
In 1998, the vast political reform known as *devolution* transferred some
statutory powers from the UK parliament to the Scottish, Welsh, and
Northern Ireland assemblies. In addition, membership in the EU brought
participation in the European Parliament elections, where proportional
representation opened the door for small parties to win seats. The UK Independence Party, which is skeptical of the benefits of EU membership, owes
its rise to having taken part in European Parliament elections. And the
far-right, xenophobic British National Party won two European Parliament
seats in 2009—a small victory in numbers, but a huge breakthrough in
credibility for an outfit that the political mainstream considered a pariah.

Britain is not alone. In Spain, the two main parties, Partido Popular
(PP) and the Partido Socialista Obrero Español (PSOE), have alternated
power since the onset of democracy in 1978. But, like Britain, Spain also
has important regional parties, and the Provincial governments (Catalo-
nia and the Basque country, among others) have been very successful in
gaining more autonomy at the expense of the power of the national government in Madrid. In Italy, the same is true with the Lega del Nord and
other regional political groups.

The EU parliament has opened avenues of participation for small parties in all twenty-seven member-states. Whether the parliament has real
powers does not matter as much as the path that it offers to legitimacy and
viability at home. Meanwhile, devolution is an international trend. Italy
set up elected regional councils as early as 1970. France followed suit with
regional assemblies in 1982. Belgium turned itself into a federal system
with regional assemblies in 1993. Finland, Ireland, New Zealand, and Norway all introduced some kind of new elected body at the subnational level
between the 1970s and the 1990s. In some countries, the number of municipalities with elected officials has increased: Bolivia doubled its municipalities in 1994 and increased the scope of their authority.

Here again, the increasingly established democracies of Latin America
are contributing to the growing pace of decentralization. The number of
countries in Latin America in which the local government executive authorities (mayors) are directly elected by the population, as opposed to
appointed by the central authorities, increased from three in 1980 to seventeen in 1995.[30] A study by the Interamerican Development Bank found that

subnational governments in the region went from handling 8 percent to 15 percent of public expenditure in a fifteen-year period that began in 1990. In the most decentralized countries, the proportion was much higher: around 40 percent of expenditure in Argentina, Brazil, and Colombia. Major decentralization programs are also under way in countries like the Philippines, Indonesia, and Estonia.[31]

Meanwhile, several federal systems have divided existing states into two, creating new local executive and legislative bodies. Since 2000, India has added the states of Chhattisgarh, Uttarakhand, and Jharkhand and proposed another, Telangana. Nigeria has nearly doubled its number of states, from nineteen in 1976 to thirty-six today. Even Canada has divided its Northwest Territories, creating the province of Nunavut.

New forums mean new opportunities. Across Europe, an array of left-wing, right-wing, ecologist, regionalist, single-issue, and, in some cases, downright eccentric parties like the Pirate Party International have taken advantage of new arenas to gain respectability and take votes away from the traditional players. A vote for them is no longer wasted; their small sizes or outlier stances are no longer an obstacle to relevance. These "fringe" parties can spoil, distract, retard, and even veto the decisions of the larger parties and their coalitions. The small "pirate" parties have always existed, but nowadays there are more of them and their ability to limit the choices of the megaplayers is felt in most of the world's democracies.

More power for local and regional authorities has also changed the prospects and public profiles of mayors and regional governors, sometimes boosting their national political careers and sometimes creating alternatives that bypass the capital altogether. The de facto foreign policy that some cities and regions now carry out goes well beyond the conventional trade promotion delegations and sister-city ceremonies.

Some scholars argue that many cities and regions are now so successfully unmoored from central governments that a modern version of the medieval order of city-states is coming into being.[32]

FROM GOVERNORS TO LAWYERS

The pattern and the players were familiar. For more than seventy years, a civilian and military elite held sway in Thailand, first through military rule and then, after 1970, in a fragile electoral framework upended periodically by coups and military transition governments of various durations. Despite the instability, Thailand achieved fast economic growth in the 1980s

and 1990s. Military-owned banks and manufacturers and civilian busi-
nessmen prospered through coups and constitutions. Billionaire and former policeman Thaksin Shinawatra became prime minister in 2001 on a
populist platform, and won reelection in 2005. Soon accusations of mal-
feasance and corruption began to swirl. A two-year political crisis ensued.
It featured botched elections, a coup, and elections again in 2007, with the
eventual result that Thaksin's sister became prime minister.

Amid this turbulence, a new political player was asserting itself: the judiciary. Beginning in 2006, rulings by Thailand's top courts increasingly
set the direction for national politics. The courts dissolved Thaksin's party
and several others, banned various leaders from politics, and at one point
disqualified a prime minister for taking payments to appear on a television cooking show. In December 2008, the Constitutional Court dissolved
the ruling party for the rather more serious cause of electoral fraud, ending three months of popular unrest and opening the way for a new coalition government.

The Thai courts had cover. The original 2006 intervention came from a
tribunal originally set up by the Thai military. And not long before that,
the king of Thailand—a figure with considerable moral authority—had
made a speech in which he urged the courts to act wisely. Still, the emergence of the courts in political life altered long-established traditions and
gave protesters and activists a new forum to make their case. In India, the
Supreme Court has stepped into the vacuum created by Prime Minister
Manmohan Singh's unwieldy and ineffective coalition, investigating illegal
mining, overturning appointments, even determining the retirement age
of the army's chief. As one Indian commentator was quoted as saying, "India has become a banana republic in which the banana is peeled by the
supreme court."[33]

A functioning judiciary is one thing. Courts that solve political disputes
or step in to remove governments are another thing altogether. Even in
countries with respected judicial systems, the precedents are few. But those
that exist are spectacular. One was the litigation in the Florida and US Supreme Courts in 2000 that resulted in George W. Bush's winning the US
presidency on a legal ruling. Another was the Mani Pulite ("Clean Hands")
investigation by a panel of Italian judges, led by Antonio di Pietro, beginning in 1992. It revealed a system of corruption so extensive that it became
known as *tangentopoli,* or "bribesville." In a few months the investigation
ensnared party heads, former ministers, and regional officials along with
many industrialists.

Eventually, the probe implicated so many figures in Italy's traditionally dominant parties, including the Christian Democrats and the Socialists, that in subsequent elections these parties faded into irrelevance. In 1994 the Christian Democrats, who had supplied Italy with most of its prime ministers since World War II, disbanded altogether, splintering into other parties. The same year, the Socialist Party—whose leader, Bettino Craxi, had been prime minister in the 1980s but became a principal target of the investigation—dissolved itself as well after 102 years in existence. Mani Pulite did not rid Italy of corruption. But it completely transformed the Italian political landscape, exploding the old party system and setting the stage for new groups on the right (Silvio Berlusconi's Forza Italia), left (the Democrats), and regional and other parties. Judges again became important protagonists during the long reign of Silvio Berlusconi over Italian politics, as he became entangled in one scandal after another. These made him a frequent target of judicial inquiries until his final fall from power in 2011.

Such investigations have turned celebrity judges into new players in political life. Antonio di Pietro, the judge at the center of the probe, eventually resigned from the bench and went into politics himself at the helm of a small party. Baltasar Garzon, the Spanish judge who has led numerous high-profile investigations at home and overseas, has targeted Spanish politicians, bankers, and the Basque militant organization ETA as well as US officials, Al Qaeda, and former Argentine military rulers. His most famous case was his demand for extradition of Chile's former dictator Augusto Pinochet, resulting in Pinochet's lengthy detainment in Britain in 1998–1999. (Garzon would himself be indicted and then suspended for exceeding his authority with an aggressive investigation into atrocities committed by the regime of Francisco Franco.) The formation of the International Criminal Court in The Hague and the establishment of international tribunals on war crimes have made international public figures of magistrates like South Africa's Richard Goldstone and Canada's Louise Arbour. Their level of prominence and power on the world stage easily outstrips that attained by some of their predecessors during the two Allied war crimes tribunals following World War II.

In the landscape of domestic politics, the increasing power of judges varies enormously from one country to another, but in general terms it has imposed new constraints on the exercise of power by government leaders and political parties. True, with many judicial systems only dubiously independent, the increased frequency of legal rulings in politics is no guarantee of wise oversight. In Pakistan, for example, many suspect that the country's military has used the Supreme Court to keep its civilian government in check. It is not necessarily a democratic development—the accountability of judges varies greatly—but it is nonetheless a real part of the decay of political power.

From Leaders to Laymen

Who are our leaders? There was a time when leaders were inextricably entwined with the apparatus of governments and parties. Even revolutionaries aspired to high office. Lately, however, many of our heroes have arrived at their fame via the digital world—using technology to spread messages and influence outcomes in ways that would previously have required the infrastructure of parties, nongovernmental organizations (NGOs), or the traditional press. The Beijing writer and activist Liu Xiaobo spearheaded the online manifesto Charter 08 calling for China to incorporate universal democratic and human rights values into its modernizations and reforms—and he was summarily arrested and imprisoned, winning the Nobel Peace Prize the following year while in jail for his "subversive" activities.

Egypt's Wael Ghonim, finding the local opposition parties weak and unreliable, organized a movement through Facebook to demand government accountability. In Colombia, an engineer named Oscar Morales started a Facebook group called "One Million Voices Against FARC" to protest the rebel group's widespread attacks on civilians, leading to massive rallies and pressure that resulted in the release of hostages. The Twitter activists of Moldova helped spark that country's political transition. Kenyan lawyer Ory Okolloh and a blogger called "M" launched a watchdog site in 2006 on Kenya's corrupt political scene.[34] Iranian-American Kelly Golnoush Niknejad started TehranBureau.com to gather and spread news directly from fellow Iranians during the popular uprising after the 2009 presidential elections, with foreign journalists banned from the country.[35] Sami Ben Gharbia, a blogger and civil society activist, helped incite anti-regime demonstrations in Tunisia by using his group blog to spread devastating tales of corruption contained in the US diplomatic cables released through WikiLeaks.

These new actors are enriching the scope of political discourse around the world. They operate outside the channels and beyond the control of traditional political organizations, both government- and party-related. They are ubiquitous and, when facing repression, they can also be highly elusive. But technology is simply the tool. The bigger picture is a cascading diffusion of power that has put individuals in an unprecedented position not only to bypass political institutions developed over decades but also to influence, persuade, or constrain "real" politicians more directly and more effectively than any classical political theorist could have imagined.

HEDGE FUNDS AND HACKTIVISTS

Left in a room together, John Paulson and Julian Assange might soon be at each other's throats. Paulson runs Paulson & Co, one of the world's largest hedge funds. Assange is the founder of WikiLeaks, the Web-based organization that specializes in divulging the secret information of governments and corporations. And yet they have one very significant thing in common: both symbolize a new breed of actors who are transforming national politics by limiting the power of governments.

With their ability to move billions of dollars at the speed of light away from a country whose economic policies they distrust, hedge funds are just one of the many financial institutions whose decisions constrain the power of governments. *New York Times* columnist and author Thomas Friedman calls the constraints imposed by these players "the Golden Straitjacket":

> To fit into the Golden Straitjacket a country must either adopt, or be seen as moving toward, the following golden rules: making the private sector the primary engine of its economic growth, maintaining a low rate of inflation and price stability, shrinking the size of its state bureaucracy, maintaining as close to a balanced budget as possible, if not a surplus, eliminating and lowering tariffs on imported goods, removing restrictions on foreign investment, getting rid of quotas and domestic monopolies, increasing exports, privatizing state-owned industries and utilities, deregulating capital markets, making its currency convertible, opening its industries, stock and bond markets to direct foreign ownership and investment, deregulating its economy to promote as much domestic competition as possible, eliminating government corruption, subsidies and kickbacks as much as possible, opening its banking and telecommunications systems to private ownership and competition and allowing its citizens to choose from an array of competing pension options and foreign-run pension and mutual funds. When you stitch all of these pieces together you have the Golden Straitjacket. . . . As your country puts on the Golden Straitjacket, two things tend to happen:

your economy grows and your politics shrinks. That is, on the economic front the Golden Straitjacket usually fosters more growth and higher average incomes—through more trade, foreign investment, privatization and more efficient use of resources under the pressure of global competition. *But on the political front, the Golden Straitjacket narrows the political and economic policy choices of those in power to relatively tight parameters.* . . . Governments—be they led by Democrats or Republicans, Conservatives or Labourites, Gaullists or Socialists, Christian Democrats or Social Democrats—that deviate too far from the core rules will see their investors stampede away, interest rates rise and stock market valuations fall.[36]

The havoc wreaked by the financial crisis in Europe is an extreme example of the power of bond markets and global financiers to impose conditions on governments and, as was the case of Greece, even to help bring them down when they resist the economic reforms demanded by financial markets.

But as discussed in the previous section, a new class of political activists unmoored from political parties and other traditional political organizations have also become the bane of governments. Today these activists are known as *hacktivists* (a term coined in 1996 by *Omega,* a member of a group of Internet hackers who called themselves *The Cult of the Dead Cow*). Hacktivism, defined as "the use of legal and/or illegal digital tools in pursuit of political ends,"[37] forces governments to play an endless hi-tech game of cat and mouse—a game that includes and transcends efforts to penetrate and compromise computer networks. It also includes the use of a wide variety of information and communications technologies (ICTs) that Stanford professor Larry Diamond calls "Liberation Technologies." As Diamond points out in his book by the same name:

> Several years ago, as I was completing a work on the worldwide struggle for democracy, I became struck by the growing use of the Internet, the blogosphere, social media, and mobile phones to expose and challenge the abuses of authoritarian regimes; to provide alternative channels through which information and communication could flow outside the censorship and controls imposed by dictatorships; to monitor elections; and to mobilize people to protest. By 2007—which now seems like a generation ago in terms of the speed with which these technologies have developed—digital ICTs had already registered some stunning

successes. The new technologies had enabled Philippine civil society to fill the streets to drive a corrupt president (Joseph Estrada) from power; facilitated the rapid mass mobilizations against authoritarianism mounted by the Orange Revolution in Ukraine and the Cedar Revolution in Lebanon, respectively; documented the rigging of the 2007 elections in Nigeria; exposed (via satellite photography) the staggering inequality embodied in the vast palace complexes of Bahrain's royal family; and forced the suspension of an environmentally threatening chemical plant in Xiamen, China, through the viral spread of hundreds of thousands of impassioned mobile-phone text messages. I called the ICTs that these citizens were using "liberation technologies" because of their demonstrated potential to empower citizens to confront, contain, and hold accountable authoritarian regimes—and even to liberate societies from autocracy.[38]

THE POLITICAL CENTRIFUGE

If you are a career politician forged in the classic mindset of that craft, the combined effect of six decades of fragmentation in national political life has been devastating. The "prestige-feeling" that Max Weber identified as a politician's deep craving is fading for the stark reason that the underlying power of political office is ebbing away.

More nations, more governments, more political institutions and organizations reflect and shape our opinions, choices, and actions than ever before. Migration and urbanization have created new political, social, cultural, and professional networks, concentrating them in urban nodes invested with new and growing power. Global norms have achieved a new reach, and individual aspirations and expectations have been turbocharged by social media, fiber optics, satellite dishes, and smartphones. It is as if a political centrifuge had taken the elements that constituted politics as we knew it and scattered them across a new and broader frame. Here are a few of its key effects.

Disintermediating Parties

For centuries, politics operated on the premise that it channels the interests of the masses (expressed through votes, or asserted by rulers) into coherent outcomes. Representative government meant the channeling of the public will up from the neighborhood or town level, through regions or provinces, and, ultimately, to the sovereign state. Political parties, or organized groups within a single party, together with unions and civic associations, promised to represent ordinary people and convey their views up these channels.

Parties no longer perform this crucial role. Why? Because the channels are much shorter and more straightforward than they used to be. As Lena Hjelm-Wallén, Sweden's former deputy prime minister and foreign minister, told me, with a combination of exasperation and resignation in her voice: "People are mobilized more by single issues that affect them, rather than by the abstract, overarching ideologies espoused by parties."[39] New forums and platforms direct public support to political leaders or deliver back benefits and accountability without the need for a political party to serve as go-between. In a landscape of fragmented votes and parliaments, dominant political parties have lost much of their appeal. Joining, voting for, or even forming a new small party carries much less cost than before. Crucially, supporting one of these new parties carries less of an opportunity cost as well; in other words, we now forsake less by voting or supporting a small party instead of a big one, or by participating in the political process through other methods altogether. Large, well-established political parties continue to be the main vehicle for gaining the control of government in a democracy. But they are increasingly being undermined and bypassed by new forms of political organization and participation.

Constraining Government

At every level the decay of power has limited autonomy of action. Even in presidential systems, the increased incidence of factional politics can make it harder to move legislation through the parliament. But the constraints on government come from outside the standard political system as well. The list of players with the ability to blow the whistle, remove key support, or successfully put forward a damaging storyline that holds up government action extends from bond holders and international activists to bloggers and celebrities. As Ricardo Lagos, the former president of Chile, told me: "The more power that NGOs have to pursue uni-dimensional goals, the less power the government has to govern. In effect, many NGOs are single-issue interest groups that are more politically nimble, media savvy and internationally agile than most governments. Their proliferation ties the government machinery down and greatly limits the range of options. I experienced this myself when I was president and I see it in my travels when I talk to other heads of state and cabinet ministers. Overall, NGOs are good for society but their tunnel vision and the pressures they have to show results to their constituents and funders can make them very rigid."[40] In the past, governments could seek to reshape the political landscape—whether to satisfy public demand or, instead, to repress it—by altering election rules, passing constitutional amendments, or imposing emergency laws. They can still attempt these measures, but more and more, they must contend with scrutiny and action that comes from outside conventional politics.

Introducing Hypercompetition

With the scattering of political power has come a blurring of lines among categories of political player: political parties (major and minor, mainstream and extreme), advocacy groups, press, voters. Elected officials and government offices now are likely to produce their own media material or communicate directly with voters online. Single-issue interest groups now throw up their own candidates rather than participating in the political process at arm's length. With barriers to participation lower than they have ever been, the field of rivals has grown. An aspiring politician must consider alliances and anticipate attacks from a shape-shifting milieu of parties, activists, funders, opinion makers, citizen journalists, watchdogs, and advocates of all sorts.

Empowering Individuals

The expanding role for individuals—nonpoliticians, nonprofessionals— may be the most exciting and challenging effect of the political centrifuge. It results from the collapse of the organizational and cultural barriers that separated people in the profession of politics from those outside. The declining relevance of major political parties and the proliferation of direct, plug-and-play ways to jump into the political discourse have made those barriers obsolete. This development invokes the promise of direct democracy, on the model of the Athenian agora or Swiss canton meetings taken into the digital age. By the same token, it invites great disruption, and examples abound already of the ability of a malevolent individual or outside group to distract or stymie the political process.

SO BRAZIL'S PRESIDENT FERNANDO HENRIQUE CARDOSO, GERMANY'S Vice Chancellor Joschka Fischer, Sweden's Lena Hjelm-Wallén, and Chile's Ricardo Lagos are not just complaining gratuitously from a position of power and privilege. The power of their lofty government jobs is indeed ebbing, and not to the benefit of a particular rival politician or organization that they can counter, buy off, or shut down. It is not leaching from their personalities or platforms in ways they could correct by changing policy stances or hiring new advisers. Rather, it is draining from their office—from the high positions of power and prestige that have always been, for a political career, the ultimate reward. Again, power is not just shifting. It is also decaying and, in some cases, evaporating.

The political centrifuge challenges authoritarian regimes, rendering their enemies more elusive and throwing up new challengers and contenders. But its effects challenge democracies as well. To many advocates, democracy is a destination—and the decay of the power of authoritarian governments has helped push a great many countries toward that goal. But the effects of the decay do not stop there. The deep economic, technological, and cultural forces behind it empower a wide range of ideas and sentiments, not all of which are democratic in spirit. Regional separatism, xenophobia, anti-immigrant campaigns, and religious fundamentalisms all stand to benefit from the decay of power. The one common effect of the political centrifuge in every location is to complicate the political landscape and erase old patterns and habits. The one certainty is that it will continue to do so.

CHAPTER SIX

PENTAGONS VERSUS PIRATES

The Decaying Power of Large Armies

AL QAEDA SPENT ABOUT $500,000 TO PRODUCE 9/11, WHEREAS THE direct losses of that day's destruction plus the costs of the American response to the attacks were $3.3 trillion. In other words, for every dollar Al Qaeda spent planning and executing the attacks, the United States spent $7 million.[1] The costs of 9/11 equal one-fifth of the US national debt. In 2006, Hezbollah fired a precision-guided cruise missile at an Israeli ship during the Lebanon War. The missile struck, and almost sank, the *Hanit* ("Spear"), a corvette of the Israeli Navy equipped with missile defense systems. The cost of the Israeli ship was $260 million; the reported price of the missile, a mere $60,000.[2] In 2011, Somali pirates imposed costs of between $6.6 billion and $6.9 billion on the world. They launched a record 237 attacks—up from 212 in 2010—despite ongoing patrols by a multinational fleet that included some of the most technologically advanced warships ever built.[3]

Terrorists, insurgents, pirates, guerrillas, freedom fighters, and criminals are nothing new. But to adapt a Churchillian turn of phrase: never in the field of human conflict have so few had the potential to do so much damage to so many at so little cost. Thus, also in the realm of armed conflicts, the micropowers, while seldom winning, are making life harder for the megaplayers—the world's large and expensive defense establishments.

The growing ability of small, nimble combatant groups to advance their interests while inflicting significant damage on much larger, well-established military foes is one way in which the exercise of power through force has changed; another is the diminished ability and willingness of states with traditional militaries to make full use of the huge destructive powers they have at their command. While it is clear that today's micro-powers cannot go toe-to-toe with the world's military powers, they are increasingly able to "deny" victory to the larger, more technologically advanced players in an asymmetric conflict—and that speaks to a fundamental change in how power operates.

John Arquilla is one of the most respected thinkers in the field of modern warfare. He believes the world has entered "an era of perpetual irregular warfare." He writes: "The great captains of traditional forms of conflict have little to tell us about this. Nor can the classical principles of war provide much help, in particular the notion of the sheer power of mass, which has lived on until now in the form of Colin Powell's doctrine of 'overwhelming force' and other concepts like 'shock and awe.' Such ideas were already faltering at the time of the Vietnam War; today it is clear that attempts to retool them against insurgent and terrorist networks will prove just as problematic."[4]

When it comes to the display and use of power, military force represents the ultimate means. Whereas politics seeks to persuade, war—or the threat of war—aims to coerce. Military might, measured by the size of an army, along with its equipment and technical prowess, is the show-stopping stand-in for more complex ideas of power. Armed force is the blunt fact that remains when you strip away the niceties of diplomacy, cultural influence, and "soft power." And when in doubt, according to the conventional wisdom, the balance of power tilts toward the fuller arsenal. As the journalist Damon Runyon put it (in another context), "The race is not always to the swift, nor the battle to the strong, but that's how the smart money bets."[5] Or as Joseph Stalin once famously asked when told he should help Catholics in Russia in order to curry favor with the pope: "The Pope? How many divisions has *he* got?" (Upon hearing of Stalin's question, Pope Pius XII sternly rebutted, "You can tell my son Joseph that he will meet my divisions in heaven.")[6]

Even though World War II is almost seven decades behind us, and the arms race of the Cold War two decades gone, military planners are still betting on the doctrine of superior firepower. They continue to assume that a large and technologically advanced military is essential for security and might.

Exhibit A is the United States. In 2012, its defense budget was over $700 billion,[7] accounting for almost half the world's military spending. Related expenses from other US agencies increased the total to about $1 trillion. America's largest military rivals, China and Russia, accounted for only 8 percent and 5 percent of world military spending, respectively—even though their spending (especially that of China) is growing very rapidly. Relative to GDP, only about twenty-five countries, most of them in the Middle East, spent more on their military. Even with the cuts in defense spending that the United States is planning to make in the next decade, the expenditures will be enormous. By 2017, when the planned cuts take fuller effect, the US defense budget will still be six times what China now spends and more than the next ten countries combined.[8] Under this slightly reduced budget, for example, the United States will still field eleven aircraft carriers and maintain all three legs of its nuclear triad (long-range bombers, intercontinental ballistic missiles, and missile-carrying submarines).[9]

Whenever the United States has engaged in conventional war in the last two decades, its forces have easily triumphed. But these conventional wars have been few: just the first Gulf War, in 1991, and arguably the second, although the Iraqi military barely fought back. In 2008, US defense secretary Robert Gates observed that of all the many deployments of US forces over more than four decades, only one—the first Gulf War—was "a more or less traditional conventional conflict." The others, from Grenada and Lebanon to Somalia, Kosovo, Iraq, and Afghanistan, involved counter-insurgency, anti-terrorism, or political or humanitarian intervention rather than a sustained duel of command-and-control armies. That trend applies to the world at large. During the 1950s an average of six international conflicts were fought each year, compared to an average of less than one per year in the first decade of this millennium.[10] And over the last 60 years, there has not been a single war between the major powers.[11]

This doesn't mean that wars are not being fought. Although the number of state-based armed conflicts around the world dropped by 40 percent between 1992 and 2003 (this includes not just wars between states but wars waged by states against nonstate groups), it has since increased.[12] And following a decline since 2003, nonstate armed conflicts—defined by the Human Security Report Project as "the use of armed force between two organized groups, neither of which is the government of a state"— ticked sharply upward in 2008.

Warfare today has assumed different forms, which large conventional military establishments are struggling to deal with. Consider these snapshots from the last decade:

- *Juz Ghoray, Afghanistan, October 2011:* A US Marine on patrol finds an improvised explosive device buried near a ridge called Ugly Hill. While working to defuse it, he spots another, in the process moving and stepping on a third, which shatters his right leg—causing him to become one of the 240 US service members to lose a limb in 2011.[13] He was lucky: 250 coalition troops lost their lives to improvised explosive devices that same year.

- *Mumbai, India, November 26–29, 2008:* After hijacking an Indian fishing trawler, ten Pakistani gunmen arrive via sea and proceed to stage terror attacks across the city, killing 168 people and wounding more than 300 before they are themselves killed or apprehended.

- *Monterrey, Mexico, August 25, 2011:* Gunmen from Los Zetas, Mexico's most violent drug cartel, attack a casino, shooting patrons and then setting it afire. More than 50 people die in the carnage.

- *Northeast of Socotra Island, Yemen, February 7, 2012:* Somali pirates attack and take over a Liberian-flagged, Greek-owned bulk carrier, and sail it back to the Somali coast—one of thirty-seven attacks, and the eleventh vessel to be taken hostage with its crew, since the beginning of the year.[14]

- *Washington, DC, May 2010:* The US Chamber of Commerce discovers that Chinese hackers have had access to its computer network throughout the previous year, during which they pilfered member information and some of its employees' e-mail logs and even controlled its building thermostats.[15] This is just one of hundreds of such attacks on US government, military, and corporate targets launched by hackers from China and elsewhere, many of them with government connections.

As these examples illustrate, the challenge for traditional military powers such as the United States is not just a new set of enemies but the transformation of warfare itself, driven in no small part by the darker side of the *More, Mobility,* and *Mentality* revolutions. The IEDs that have become the weapon of choice in Afghanistan, Iraq, Syria, and myriad other sites of conflict rely not on plutonium or complex alloys but, rather, on household or agricultural ingredients and consumer goods manipulated and assembled into bombs designed by those who have benefited from the spread of education—both fruits of the More revolution. Like the pirates who use fiberglass skiffs, cheap AK-47s, and rocket-propelled grenades to hijack huge multimillion-dollar ships, the terrorists who attacked Mumbai drew on the ready availability of weapons and communication technologies—

by-products of the More and Mobility revolutions that include the GPS that helped them navigate through Indian waters as well as the satellite phones, cellphones, and BlackBerries they relied on throughout the attacks to coordinate with one another, monitor the police, and transmit messages of their heinous deeds to the outside world. Thanks to the ease of travel and communication, even a lone terrorist can mount the kind of high-impact strike on a faraway target that once required bomber jets or missiles—think of "shoe bomber" Richard Reid and "underwear bomber" Umar Abdulmutallab, both of whom almost succeeded in bringing down aircraft. By raising aspirations and expectations that are often cruelly unmet or easily distorted, the Mentality revolution has helped to recruit a pool of disaffected zealots, criminals, and would-be revolutionaries. And perhaps just as importantly, the lesson that a lone attacker or a small band of committed fighters can inflict severe damage on a major power has entered into the minds of millions of people and won't be unlearned.

These new capabilities do not demand the hierarchy and coordination that are the pride of the world's great militaries. As barriers to involvement in conflict have fallen, the advantages that once constituted the might of big armies and secured their ability to deter attack have lost some of their relevance. After the initial display of "shock and awe," the wars in Afghanistan and Iraq have not been the kinds of conflicts waged with massive artillery barrages, tank assaults, and supersonic dogfights, much less with the cold logic and calculated escalations of nuclear doctrine. Meanwhile, NATO forces have also had to learn how to fight in a different media environment—one in which their adversaries have been able to spread their message with greater ease through social media, and in which reporters, bloggers, and activists catalogue every allied casualty and ugly episode of collateral damage for presentation to a plugged-in and restless public.

The transformation of conflict has spurred intense rethinking in defense ministries and war colleges, and driven attempts to adapt organization and doctrine. Both the 2010 Quadrennial Defense Review, the principal guiding document of US military approach and budgeting, and the Defense Strategic Guidance released in January 2012 stress the growing importance of small and asymmetric conflicts with an eclectic range of antagonists;[16] the latter document puts "Counterterrorism and Irregular Warfare" at the top of the list of primary missions of the US Armed Forces.

American military planners are also worried that advanced precision weapons that can shoot down planes, sink ships, or target a single moving car on a highway are becoming increasingly available not just to rivals such as China and adversaries such as North Korea but also to nonstate actors. Thomas Mahnken, a former deputy assistant secretary of defense for policy planning and a professor at the Naval War College, has warned that "adversaries are acquiring precision-guided munitions, as well as the vital supporting capabilities needed to wage precision warfare with a minimum investment."[17] Drone technology, the pilotless vehicles that have revolutionized surveillance and the conduct of US operations against insurgents and terrorists, is being widely adopted and disseminated, raising the possibility of inexpensive mayhem for anyone willing to make a relatively small investment of a few thousand dollars.

THE BIG RISE OF SMALL FORCES

"A prince wishes to make war, and believing that God is on the side of big battalions, he doubles the number of his troops," wrote Voltaire in the eighteenth century. But just as constant throughout history are examples of small armed forces that have successfully harassed, halted, and sometimes even defeated these large military machines.

The battle of Thermopylae in 480 B.C. is an earlier case in point. Taking advantage of high ground and rugged terrain, a vastly outmanned Greek force held the Persian army at bay for three days, inflicting disproportionate losses on its enemies before eventually perishing in a heroic last stand. The Greeks lost the battle of Thermopylae, but they did weaken the Persian force and ultimately repel the invasion. From David in the Bible to the Vietcong in the Vietnam War, history is replete with smaller and less-equipped antagonists holding their ground and thwarting, if not militarily defeating, larger opponents.

Among the modern pioneers in this method of warfare are Che Guevara and Ho Chi Minh as well as Mao Zedong, whose guerrilla tactics in the Chinese civil war helped deliver China into communist rule. Differentiating guerrilla war from conventional war, Mao found the two to have opposite requirements with respect to size and coordination. "In guerrilla warfare," Mao wrote, "small units acting independently play the principal role and there must be no excessive interference with their activities." In traditional war, by contrast, "command is centralized. . . . All units and all supporting arms in all districts must coordinate to the highest degree." In guerrilla war, that sort of command and control was "not only undesirable but impossible."[18]

In current military language, guerrilla wars are "irregular" and "asymmetric." They are irregular because they are launched by an antagonist that, while armed, is not a traditional military force. And they are asymmetric because the opponents are mismatched in brute military power, as measured by personnel and materiel. Today, irregular and asymmetric conflicts have become the norm. In Afghanistan, for example, more than 430,000 Afghan and coalition troops have been unable to subdue a Taliban force barely one-twelfth as big. In Iraq, at the peak of the surge in October 2007, more than 180,000 coalition forces and nearly 100,000 Iraqi security forces were pitted against as many as 20,000 insurgents.

Russia had a similar experience in Chechnya: in 1999–2000, in what is called the Second Chechen War, more than 80,000 well-armed Russian troops were stalled for five months by an estimated 22,000 insurgents fighting for independence. Eventually the Russian army prevailed and restored Russian federal control over the territory, but not before launching a brutal campaign that resulted in tens of thousands of civilian casualties and the deaths of more than 5,000 Russian soldiers.[19]

Across Africa and Southeast Asia, one can find dozens of new and long-running insurgencies—from the Lord's Resistance Army in Uganda to the Moro Islamic Liberation Front in the Philippines. And military conflicts that are not tied to defending a particular territory, but instead are motivated by potentially borderless ideological, criminal, religious, or economic goals, are clearly on the rise. Of the military conflicts that erupted in the 1950s, only a minority were between states and nonstate armed groups. In contrast, during the 1990s conflicts with armed groups were in the majority. In 2011, then-Deputy Secretary of Defense William Lynn explained that conflict is evolving from "intense but short periods" to "longer and more drawn-out engagements."[20]

Smaller forces are proving successful with increasing regularity, at least in terms of advancing their political goals while surviving militarily. The Harvard scholar Ivan Arreguín-Toft analyzed 197 asymmetric wars that took place around the world in the period 1800–1998. They were asymmetric in the sense that a wide gap existed at the outset between the antagonists as measured in traditional terms—that is, by the size of their military and the size of their population. Arreguín-Toft found that the supposedly "weak" actor actually won the conflict in almost 30 percent of these cases. That fact was remarkable in itself, but even more striking was the trend over time. In the course of the last two centuries, there has been a steady increase in victories by the supposedly "weak" antagonist. The weak actor won only 11.8 percent of its conflicts between 1800 and 1849, as compared to 55 percent of its conflicts between 1950 and 1998. What this means is that a core axiom of war has been stood on its head. Once upon a time, superior firepower ultimately prevailed. Now that is no longer true.[21]

The reason is due in part to the fact that, in today's world, the resort to barbarism by the stronger party—for example, indiscriminate bombing and shelling of civilian populations in World War II, the use of torture by the French in Algeria, or the targeted assassinations of the Vietcong under the Phoenix program in South Vietnam—are no longer politically acceptable. As Arreguín-Toft argues, some forms of barbarism—the controversial Phoenix program, for example—can be militarily effective in relatively short order against the indirect attacks of a guerrilla warfare strategy. But in the absence of a true existential threat to a stronger state, especially a democracy where military policy can come under intense public scrutiny, no such strategy is politically viable. As retired General Wesley Clark, a Vietnam veteran and former Supreme Allied Commander Europe of NATO, told me: "Today, a division commander can directly control attack helicopters 30 to 40 miles ahead of the battle, and enjoy what we call 'full spectrum dominance' [control of air, land, sea, space, and cyberspace]. But there are things we were doing in Vietnam that we cannot do today. We have more technology but narrower legal options." The "successes" of an autocratic Russia's savage tactics in Chechnya or of Sri Lanka's brutal suppression of the Tamil Tigers are bloody examples of what it takes for superior firepower to win today over a tenacious, if militarily weaker, adversary.

The prominence of political factors in determining the outcome of asymmetric military conflicts helps explain the ongoing rise of the ultimate small actor—the terrorist. We have come a long way since terrorism's roots in the state during the revolutionary French regime's "Reign of Terror" from September 1793 to July 1794. Although the US State Department has designated around fifty groups as Foreign Terrorist Organizations, the number of active groups is easily double that, some with dozens of members, others with thousands. Moreover, the ability of a lone individual or small group to change the course of history with an act of violence was evident even before the Bosnian Serb nationalist Gavrilo Princip's assassination of Archduke Ferdinand in Sarajevo helped start World War I.

What sets apart modern terrorism—as epitomized by 9/11; other Al Qaeda actions in London, Madrid, and Bali; the Chechen attacks in Moscow; and Lashkar-e-Taiba's attack on Mumbai—is the elevation of terror-ism from a matter of domestic security (i.e., for each country to handle in its own way) to a global military concern. Terrorist attacks by Osama bin Laden and his organization prompted governments from more than fifty countries to spend well over a trillion dollars safeguarding their popula-tions from potential attack. A key French defense strategy paper of 1994 contained 20 references to terrorism; its 2008 update mentioned it 107 times, far more frequently than war itself—"to the point," wrote scholars Marc Hecker and Thomas Rid, "that this form of conflict seems to eclipse the threat of war."[22]

THE END OF THE ULTIMATE MONOPOLY: THE USE OF VIOLENCE

The more small and nonstate actors have grown in relevance and effective-ness in modern war, the more they have undermined one of the core prin-ciples that guided politics and allocated power for the last several centuries. "The state," wrote Max Weber, "is an association that claims the monopoly on the legitimate use of violence." In other words, part of the definition and raison d'être of the modern state was its ability to centralize military power. Mustering an army and police was the prerogative of the state, and preventing the use of violence by other parties on its territory was one of its responsibilities, an element of the social contract grounding its legitimacy. That new monopoly on violence meant the end of medieval marauding bands and soldiers for hire, and the end of Russian-doll hierarchies of feu-dal lords and vassals, each with his own army, patrolling the same terrain. Military control was profoundly tied to sovereignty.

Today that monopoly has been fractured on multiple levels. Govern-ments from Mexico and Venezuela to Pakistan and the Philippines have lost control of swathes of national territory used by armed groups as the base for military activities that often support cross-border ambitions or en-terprises. Even the basis of guerrilla war has shifted. In the past, guerrilla movements typically sought to overthrow an invader or colonizer, and to gain or restore sovereignty. Where they operated, according to guerrilla theorists, popular support was key to their legitimacy. "The guerrilla fighter needs full help from the people of the area. This is an indispensable condi-tion," wrote Che Guevara. Now guerrilla warfare is increasingly borderless: it no longer subsists on popular support—for the simple reason that it is no longer tied to physical territory. Fighting the Taliban in Afghanistan may require winning the hearts and minds of the Afghan population, but fighting Al Qaeda and the imitators it inspired as they attack New York, London, or Madrid may require more the craft of intelligence agents than that of economic development experts. Meanwhile, facing increasing budgetary pressures, states have sought ways to reduce the burden of huge standing armies and "outsourced" a growing chunk of what used to be their sovereign responsibility.

The convergence between the modern state and the modern military was not just a matter of ideology or political philosophy. It was also deeply practical. It reflected the costs and the technology of war. For centuries the means of violence scaled up, from the rise of firearms through heavy artillery, tanks, fighter jets, and computer mainframes—all of which increased the cost and the logistical requirements for a military effectiveness.

Military theorists speak of four generations of warfare since the founding of the modern state. Each corresponds to a phase in world history but also reflects contemporary technological advances and tactical innovations. Until the rise of the machine gun, for instance, armies concentrated firepower by massing huge battalions of soldiers in lines and columns oriented to fight for small patches of territory. Battles resulted in fields strewn with dead bodies from close combat. The gruesome pattern played out from the Napoleonic War to the American Civil War, culminating in the trenches of World War I. This kind of combat rewarded the largest and best-organized armies, emphasizing size (and thus disposable manpower) as well as coordination. In the first half of the twentieth century, it gave way to heavy artillery, tanks and aircraft, and a model of combat in which these weapons cleared the way and infantry followed to take over the terrain. This was more effective—and more expensive, too. The cost of these new armaments only made it more necessary for armies to scale up. Surveying the landscape of the early twentieth century, Max Weber observed that there was no inherent reason why private, capitalist enterprises could not carry out war; but a strong, centralized structure could not be avoided. The requirements of scale, skills, and technology made the military the epitome of the modern, centralized hierarchical organization. A decentralized military, Weber argued, was bound to fail.

That consensus began to crack in World War II, under the hammer blows of Germany's Blitzkrieg and its defeat of static defenses like France's Maginot Line. The use of flanking, surprise attacks, and airborne troops required faster and more nimble action, the kind that officers on the ground would have to initiate with no time to wait for instructions from high command. Too much centralization could be a handicap. Later in the twentieth century, new conflicts brought forth the third generation of warfare in earnest. Nimbleness and flexibility became increasingly valuable. Sophisticated equipment like surface-to-air missiles grew more portable, allowing local commanders to make more consequential decisions. Still, the polarization of the Cold War, the arms race it prompted, and the hovering threat of classic interstate conflict meant that the world's main armies continued to emphasize scale over other priorities—as military theorist John Arquilla put it, "a reliance on a few big units rather than a lot of little ones." In the case of the US military, Arquilla noted, its structure changed little from the Vietnam era to this day. The US military, he added, "has a chronic 'scaling problem,' i.e. the inability to pursue smaller tasks with smaller numbers. Added to this is the traditional, hierarchical military mindset, which holds that more is always better—the corollary belief being that one can only do worse with less."[23]

Many of today's fighters would beg to differ. A Taliban insurgent setting an IED, a Colombian FARC rebel, a Hamas commander, a jihadi blogger sitting at a computer are all doing "better with less." They are not traditional enlisted soldiers or officer graduates of service academies, but they are no less relevant to military affairs today. And it is not just the "bad guys"—the terrorists, insurgents, pirates, and criminals—who are growing more numerous and more effective. On the side of the national armies of Western democracies is a growing array of private military companies that carry out military and security jobs once reserved for armies and police.

This, too, is not completely new. In the medieval and Renaissance periods, war-making and policing often took place through hire. But today's private military services market, which has been estimated at $100 billion a year, was virtually nonexistent a generation ago. And it has grown beyond supplies and logistics—important functions for any military campaign, but well behind the front lines. Private military companies have taken on some of the most sensitive tasks, including prisoner interrogation. In 2011, at least 430 employees of American contractors were reported killed in Afghanistan—more than the number of military casualties. If L-3 Communications, one such defense contractor, were a country, it would have the third-highest loss of life in Iraq and Afghanistan, after the United States and Great Britain.[24] "Not within the last two centuries," wrote scholar Peter Singer, an expert on the topic, "has there been such reliance on private soldiers to accomplish tasks directly affecting the tactical and strategic success of engagement."[25] Often starting as small companies out of anonymous office parks in the outskirts of London or suburban Virginia, firms such as Blackwater (now renamed Academi), MPRI, Executive Outcomes, Custer Battles, Titan, and Aegis took on key roles in different military operations. Some were bought by larger firms, some went out of business, and some remained independent. Among other recent opportunities, private military firms have found a market for their services in protecting commercial vessels from Somali pirates. Mercenaries, with all the ancient associations of the word, have turned into a booming and diverse industry.

American military thinkers coined the concept of fourth-generation warfare (4W) to describe a conflict characterized by a blurring of the lines between war and politics, soldier and civilian.[26] This is a conflict where a *violent nonstate actor* (VNSA) fights a *state* and where engagement is military not just in the narrow sense of armed hostilities but also in the sense that it plays out in media and public opinion, each side seeking to undermine the other's grounding and legitimacy as much as to defeat it in the battlefield. Terrorism, cyberwarfare, and propaganda are commonly used in a fourth-generation war.[27] The idea of fourth-generation war was initially formalized as early as 1989, when the Cold War was coming to an end. In that respect, the growing success of the fourth-generation adversaries of the United States, far less wealthy and well-equipped than America's armed forces, is all the more remarkable.

A Tsunami of Weapons

For decades the tools of war kept growing more complex, costly, and, as a result, harder to obtain. But though the United States and other countries still have their share of gold-plated wonders, the military aircraft best suited to warfare today is not a fighter jet but something far less expensive and far more flexible: the unmanned aerial vehicle, or drone.

A wide range of drones now serve as decoys, conduct reconnaissance missions, or launch missile strikes for a growing number of nations. Their cost ranges from as low as a few thousand dollars for a simple noncombat, short-range drone to about $15 million for a Reaper hunter-killer drone. Drones are not a new concept. But technological advances in recent decades have made them much more powerful, and their low cost and ability to fly unmanned make them more attractive for combat missions.[28] And they are finding nonmilitary uses—for example, by real estate agents filming houses from above, ecologists monitoring the rainforest, and ranchers following their herds of cattle as they roam the prairies. More than three dozen countries now operate drone fleets, and dozens of private companies are now offering to fly them on behalf of other countries that lack the support infrastructure to do so.[29] More disturbingly, ordinary hobbyists and private users abound: in the United States in 2012, a group called DIY Drones already had twenty thousand members. In 2004, Hezbollah flew a drone into Israeli air space; the Israeli military downed it, but the psychological effect of the violation, and the message it sent about Hezbollah's capacities, endures.[30] What happens when any disaffected, delusional, or deranged individual has the capacity to wreak havoc from the sky? As Stanford University's Francis Fukuyama, who has been building his own drone to take better nature photos, has observed: "As the technology becomes cheaper and more commercially available, moreover, drones may become harder to trace; without knowing their provenance, deterrence breaks down. A world in which people can be routinely and anonymously targeted by unseen enemies is not pleasant to contemplate."[31]

Drones are hyper-sophisticated compared with the most devastating weapon in military conflicts of the past few years—the improvised explosive device. IEDs come in multiple types with many combinations of munitions and detonating systems; they do not follow a particular standard and often can be assembled with readily available ingredients: agricultural supplies, or chemicals from a factory, drugstore, or hospital. They may lie at the opposite end of sophistication and technical requirements from the equipment in big-army arsenals, but IEDs are especially well-suited to today's decentralized wars. They require no complicated supply chain or time-consuming deployment. Instructions for manufacturing the devices are fairly simple and circulate over the Internet. The proliferation of loose munitions from places like Iraq, the former Soviet Union, and Libya further reduces the cost and complexity of manufacture. They are small and easy to camouflage and do not require the fighter to expose himself; their raw impact, killing or maiming the enemy, is stark and scary. In fact, the sheer contrast between the homemade quality of these weapons and the technological superiority of the forces that they undermine can feed a David-versus-Goliath narrative, scoring a public relations win for insurgents.

The amount of money that Goliath has thrown at the problem while the casualties mount only adds to that effect. The United States has spent more than $20 billion since 2003 to combat IEDs. A variety of groups and agencies within the US defense establishment have been tasked with this challenge, leading to such classic bureaucratic problems as working at cross-purposes, rivalries, poor coordination and, of course, waste. Even the acronym of the lead agency involved, the Joint IED Defeat Organization (JIEDDO), suggests its unwieldy character.[32] Innovations like special armored vehicles, mine-clearing robots, and special protective garments have saved the lives of countless soldiers and civilians. But trying to stem the IED tide remains difficult. In 2011, for example, the number of improvised explosive devices that were cleared or detonated in Afghanistan alone rose to 16,554 from 15,225, an increase of 9 percent. The number of Afghans killed or wounded by IEDs jumped 10 percent in 2011, compared with 2010; the IEDs alone accounted for 60 percent of all civilian casualties.[33]

Even more insidious and adapted to stealth warfare than IEDs is the ultimate weapon of today's guerrilla and terrorist campaigns: the motivated individual prepared to give up his or her life in order to execute the mission. By one tally, suicide bombers were responsible for twenty-two of the thirty most lethal terrorist attacks around the world between 1990 and 2006. Martyrdom is an ancient motivation, and suicide warriors always appear in times of war. But since the 1980s, suicide attacks have increased dramatically, and their frequency and deliberate strategic use have no recent precedent. The combination of premodern motives and postmodern possibilities has proven devastating. Again, the three revolutions amplify the impact of suicide bombers. They take advantage of today's unparalleled ease of travel, while the culture of martyrdom validates the perpetrator, brings in new recruits, and sharpens the effect of fear not only in the target population but also, thanks to the amplification of the media, far beyond. Moreover, the culture of martyrdom is ruthlessly effective, as it is almost impossible to completely defend against a suicide bomber whose only purpose is to approach the target, and has no interest in getting away.

Dispersed and stealth warfare uses resolutely modern tools as well, of course. The Internet has become just as essential as IEDs or suicide attacks in the new decentralized landscape of war. At the frontier of cyberwar are hacker attacks on civilian and military infrastructure, as well as distributed denial of service (DDOS) and other disruptions of websites and platforms relied upon by the target government or population. But even simpler to access is the constellation of online militant voices that amplify hostile messages, spread propaganda materials and threats, and attract new recruits to their cause. Whereas in the United States and Europe some of the strident public voices in the war on terror have been mocked for their lack of military experience, the suicide bomber who carried out a successful attack on a CIA base in Afghanistan in December 2009 was a former "jihadi pundit" who took up arms. The Internet is not just an amplifying tool for these causes; it can also be a device for radicalization.[34]

What all of these tools and techniques have in common is their sheer ease of access. As the head of Israeli military intelligence, General Amos Yadlin, pointed out in a late 2009 speech, Israel's enemies were still well behind Israel in military capability, yet they were catching up "by means of precision missiles, computerization, anti-aircraft weapons, GPS and pilotless aircraft." He added that off-the-shelf computer products available commercially now gave Israel's enemies significant abilities to encrypt their own communications and hack Israeli resources. "Cyberpower gives the little guys the kind of ability that used to be confined to superpowers," he said. "Like unmanned aircraft, it's a use of force that can strike without regard for distance or duration, and without endangering fighters' lives."[35]

General Yadlin's observation encapsulates the dilemma that now faces armies—and the governments who deploy them, and the citizens they are supposed to protect. The centrifugal force that has scattered power in politics, business, or religion has not stopped short of the military domain, as if it were untouchable. The decay of power has changed the terms and the possibilities of conflict, increasing the influence of small, nonstate and nontraditional players as the tools have generalized and the costs have tumbled. Media and communications disseminate the lessons of what works and help the effect feed on itself.

As these new, small military powers succeed, others waiting in the wings, or yet to be born, discover how to emulate them. This scenario does not mean that endless small-scale conflict is inevitable—but it does carry deep implications for anyone concerned with peace as a moral or practical priority.

It also has enormous implications for the way power is obtained, retained, and lost in our time.

THE DECAY OF POWER AND THE NEW RULES OF WAR

"Never again" is the universal motto of war's survivors. Yet a day does not go by without a reminder that violence, terror, and coercion remain potent forces shaping human lives and communities. The Cold War's "peace dividend" quickly fizzled in the face of the Gulf War, the first World Trade Center attack, the conflict in the Balkans, genocide in Rwanda, civil wars in West Africa, and more. Author Robert Kaplan warned of the "coming anarchy" as states propped up by the Cold War disintegrated and ethnic and religious tensions surged.[36] The shock of 9/11, the rise of Al Qaeda and its clones, and the prosecution of a "global war on terror" under one name or another since then have compounded the sense of a world besieged by new forms of low-level but high-impact violence. Although coming from different perspectives, analysts such as Kaplan and Amy Chua, author of *World on Fire*, have argued that the rapid pace of globalization and the weakening of states have made violent conflict more likely, and that attempts to create Western-style democracies where they do not currently exist are likely to backfire into violence.[37] Meanwhile terrorism, cyberwar, and narco-trafficking take place on amorphous, shifting, borderless fronts, liable to take their toll anywhere in the world on any given day.

Call it low-intensity conflict, small war, irregular war, or, as scholars Marc Hecker and Thomas Rid put it, "'War 2.0'—by any name, violent conflict today is drastically different from the forms that shaped the 19th and 20th centuries and that live on in History Channel documentaries . . . and in the defense spending patterns of most countries."[38] What is less clear is how to address this new landscape. Arguments for radical cutbacks and reform of the world's major militaries founder on vested interests, the impression that they convey weakness, and the bigger worry of eroding the strength of conventional deterrents. Traditional interstate threats have not gone away, be they unresolved border disputes from the Caucasus to South America, military buildups by countries like Iran and North Korea, or the sharp and mutual suspicion between the United States and China. Meanwhile, prescriptions for how to address the spread of violence by nonstate actors depend on competing opinions about its root causes, which analysts pin variously on economic inequality, cultural disruption, the spread of corporate-driven imperialism, fundamentalist Islam, instigation by state sponsors, and a host of other factors.

Looking at war today through the lens of the decay of power will not resolve such debates. But it can produce some needed clarity about what forms of conflict are here to stay, and what new realities any military strategy—whether that of a Western democracy, an aspiring superpower, a developing country, or a militant or insurgent group—must account for if it is to succeed.

Military Hyper-Competition Is Here

Easily available weapons; a blurring of the lines between soldier and civilian and military and consumer technology; and a rise in the number of conflicts whose stakes are less about territory than about money, commodities, and ideas set the stage for hyper-competition in the arena of war and security. Like major political parties or the behemoths of industry and banking, the great military institutions are encountering new competitors no longer held back by traditional barriers to entry. A major defense ministry like the Pentagon no longer has a lock on the tools and resources needed to prosecute a conflict. Skills that are valuable in conflict can now be gleaned not just in basic training, officer academies, and defense universities but in an insurgent camp in northwest Pakistan, a madrassa in Leicester, England, or a computer school in Guangzhou, China.

In this scattered landscape, the traditional military apparatus remains important and impressive. It possesses the advantages of public resources and the ability to make itself the top priority in government budgets; national sovereignty gives it the moral heft that attracts recruits and justifies investment and spending, and the political legitimacy to enter into alliances. It has tradition on its side. What it has lost is exclusivity. Two crucial monopolies—one philosophical, one practical—have vanished and exposed its vulnerabilities. First is the state's philosophical monopoly on the legitimate use of force. The second is a practical monopoly bestowed on the military by the geopolitical competition among sovereign states and the need for ever-more complex technology to win it. The rise of powerful nonstate actors and the breakneck diffusion of technology beyond the realms of specialists have destroyed that nuts-and-bolts advantage.

Today, national armies are attempting to adjust—with different speeds and results—to "full spectrum" warfare in which weapons are digital as much as physical, methods are psychological as much as coercive, and combatants are civilian and scattered as much as uniformed and coordinated. Hyper-competitive conflict does not necessarily mean more or worse conflict than before, whether measured in lives lost or economic benefits forsaken. Nor does it signal, by any means, the end of national armies. But it puts in a new perspective what a national army can be expected to achieve.

Military Might No Longer Equals National Security

The transition from conventional interstate war to decentralized small-scale conflict has largely ended the specialization advantage of a large military. Therefore, any national security strategy that relies on military might or superior firepower is suspect. Realizing this, the major armies have been trying to adjust. As noted above, a US military directive in late 2008 announced that irregular war was to be considered "as strategically important as traditional warfare"—a major statement of doctrine with implications for the whole scope of military planning, from personnel to equipment to training.[39] For the United States, a focus on irregular warfare means giving more importance to special operations, intelligence gathering, counterinsurgency, and what the military calls "low visibility operations," as well as more attention to operations in partnership with allies and local forces. According to plans announced in 2012, the US Special Operations Command, which has forces deployed in roughly seventy-five countries, will grow by about 6 percent from sixty-six thousand personnel in 2012 to seventy thousand in 2017.[40] With this growth comes the discovery that today's counterinsurgency, for instance, may be different from the kinds that were featured in special-operations manuals. As a recent National Defense University study pointed out, insurgencies today are less likely to follow an ideology and established leadership (à la the Vietcong) and more likely to be "coalitions of the angry" that can spring up almost spontaneously (à la the Palestinian intifada).[41]

Other militaries are going through their own parallel adaptations. China's People's Liberation Army has shrunk in size in the last two decades, trading surplus personnel for more modern technology. It has significantly increased its participation in United Nations peacekeeping missions, which was nugatory before 2000, and its navy is making more and more port calls. Moreover, kidnappings and killings of Chinese workers in places like Sudan have provoked new thinking about how China can enhance its ability to protect its increasingly numerous citizens and interests overseas. Military analysts scour the experiences of leading forces like those of the United States, China, India, Britain, France, and Israel in search of "best practices" to prepare for today's most likely military assignments: counterterrorism, counterinsurgency, humanitarian intervention, and peacekeeping.[42]

The possibility of war on the electronic frontier is a particular concern. A record of attacks in the last decade has set out the wide scope of the threat that nations face—for instance, attacks on systems to immobilize them or plant malicious agents, attacks on information networks to collect sensitive data or prevent communications, and attacks on key infrastructure such as power grids.[43] Cyber-warfare also includes "message war" actions such as distributing propaganda and redirecting websites. Various forms of cyber-attack have been reported against systems in the United States, Iran, Georgia, Estonia, Kyrgyzstan, Azerbaijan, and elsewhere. Privately owned services like Twitter and Google Mail have also been attacked—for instance, during the unrest in Iran in summer 2009. But cyber-war has yet to experience its analog to, say, 9/11—an event so massive in scale, damage, and visibility as to focus resources and galvanize public support. The evidence suggests that governments have been slow to adjust to cyberspace as a battlespace, and it is clear that hackers and cyber-attackers still enjoy a wide berth in terms of the opportunities they have to disrupt critical governmental functions. And time is of the essence: "Staying ahead of the game is important in light of the dizzying change of pace in the cyber world," argued Amos Yadlin, the Israeli military intelligence chief: "at most, a few months in response to a change, compared to the years that pilots had."[44]

The delay in making the adjustments needed to survive on the new, scattered landscape of war is not necessarily the fault of military minds, Arquilla, the military scholar, points out. "Awareness of these issues has been slowly but steadily growing over the past two decades," Arquilla wrote in 2010. "But senior commanders will tend to fall back on a fatalism driven by their belief that both Congressional and industrial leaders will thwart any effort at radical change."[45]

Moreover, it is not as if the arguments for traditional military buildup with advanced technology and superior firepower have vanished. The scholar Joe Nye, who coined the concept of "soft power," argued that military power "still structures expectations and shapes political calculations." Even when a conventional military is not deployed in active conflict, its deterrence role remains important. "Military force, along with norms and institutions, helps to provide a minimal degree of order," Nye wrote.[46] But if brute military force is no longer enough to ensure dominance, the question then becomes one of how resources are allocated among traditional vectors of power and their new, relatively untried alternatives. No one thinks terrorists can stop great powers from existing, but surely they can affect their behavior and deny them options that they used to take for granted.

Money Talks More Than Orders Do

Who, in fact, are the Zetas? On one level, they're just one of the many armed parties involved in Mexico's long-running drug war. This war is no metaphor: from December 2006 to early 2012, almost fifty thousand people died in drug-related violence.[47] The conflict has subtracted huge realms of both physical territory and economic activity from the authority of the

Mexican government. In this picture, the Zetas are especially powerful. They control key territory in northeast Mexico and watch over the bulk of drug shipments into the United States through the busy Laredo crossing. A militia of an estimated four thousand people, they are notorious for a reign of terror over the areas where they operate, and for their reach elsewhere in Mexico and across the US border. Among the many opponents Mexico faces in this battle, the Zetas may be the most daunting. But what sets them apart is their origins. The Zetas were recruited from Mexico's elite national military and police units to become the private army for the Gulf Cartel. Corruption and defection are common in Mexico, but the Zetas elevated it to a new scale. Now the Zetas are undergoing a further transformation. As the power struggle among rival cartels shakes out, the Zetas, once a militia of enforcers, have become a narco-trafficking organization of their own, battling for key markets and distribution routes and reportedly expanding into Europe through a tie-up with the Calabrian 'Ndrangheta.

The shift of the Zetas from government soldiers to private soldiers to traffickers illustrates the interchangeable nature of roles in conflict today. It has echoes in the rise of kidnapping as a business among Iraqi insurgents, themselves often veterans of Saddam Hussein's army; in the intermingling of the Taliban with the Afghan drug trade; in the rise of piracy. These examples illustrate how economic opportunity—from better pay to the windfalls of criminal enterprise—drives participants in conflict. Money has always been one motivation to take up arms (and sometimes to put them down); but in an environment of decentralized conflict where the most useful tools are ones that are easily obtained, economic incentives are especially strong and the merits of obeying a command-and-control structure are correspondingly weak. From crime to insurgency to private military firms, market opportunities abound for people with relevant training in weapons and logistics, which themselves involve more and more traditionally "civilian" technology.

In other words, *orders* carry less weight in conflict today than *material incentives*. In the traditional military, the level of pay is secondary; the primary motive for participation is loyalty, citizenship, a sense of mission or purpose—a phenomenon illustrated in striking fashion by military enrollments in the United States after 9/11. That sense of calling extends to some insurgencies—and to violent organizations as well, of course—that lure recruits with appeals to defend a land against occupiers or a faith against infidels. But the dispersal of military roles and the rise of nonmilitary ways to participate in conflict mean that the signals of the market—

prices, payments, opportunity costs—now shape patterns of violence to a degree not experienced in the modern West in at least a century.

The Decay of Military Power Affects Everyone

The centrifugal force that has scattered conflict, unpacked military capabilities, and transported these capabilities into a hybrid military/civilian realm has not limited its impact to large national armies. Even new players in conflict are at risk of falling prey to the same dispersal that has facilitated their own rise.

For examples, look no further than the jihadi movement. The 9/11 attack and the ones that followed in Madrid and London were the result of long months, even years, of planning and the effort of a network with a core leadership in the persons of Osama bin Laden and Ayman al-Zawahiri. More recent attacks traced to Al Qaeda have been smaller and—once thwarted—almost comical considering the personalities of the would-be "shoe" and "underwear" bombers. Why the difference? One reason may be the improved capability of counterterrorism agencies to disrupt large plots before they reach fruition. But another has to do with the effects on the jihadi world, and on Al Qaeda itself, of the decay of its power and capabilities. Studying the "cracks in the jihad," scholar Thomas Rid has examined the different niches that jihadis occupy. Local insurgencies fighting for terrain are typically not interested in global reach. Some jihadi insurgents have turned the corner into organized crime and trafficking, motivated by money over mission, not unlike the Zetas. Still more jihadis come from a Web-enabled diaspora in Europe, North America, and elsewhere. Some of these have found their way into full-fledged military operations; a case in point is Alabama-raised Omar Shafik Hammami, who went from popular high school student in middle America to major guerrilla leader in Somalia.[48]

The disparity of interests, senses of mission, and capabilities makes the jihadi world as fragile from within as it has looked menacing from without, argue Rid and his colleague Marc Hecker. The same internal fragility exists among the Taliban, whom military observers have separated into "big-T" ideologically-driven fighters and "small-t" members who are driven more by parochial concerns and monetary gain. A study of forty-five terrorist groups that ended their activities found that only a minority were actually defeated; twenty-six of the forty-five dissolved under the effect of internal strife. The franchise model that is attributed to Al Qaeda is misleading, Rid and Hecker further argue; it suggests a degree of command and coordination that overstates the reality. They suggest that "wikiterrorism"—loose and fragile transmission of ideology, methods, and allegiances—better describes the way jihadism propagates, making it at once more ubiquitous and less effective.[49]

DRONES, IEDS, A FULLY WEAPONIZED CYBERSPACE, PRECISION-GUIDED munitions, suicide bombers, pirates, wealthy and well-armed transnational criminal networks, and a host of other armed players have already altered the international security landscape. The future shape of this new landscape is ever changing and therefore impossible to map accurately. But there is one assumption that can safely be made: the power of large military establishments will be less than what it was in the past.

CHAPTER SEVEN

WHOSE WORLD WILL IT BE?

Vetoes, Resistance, and Leaks—or Why Geopolitics Is Turning Upside Down

ON MARCH 28, 2012, AN EVENT TOOK PLACE THAT WAS AS IMPORTANT as it was unnoticed. According to the calculations of Australia's Treasury, that day the collective size of the less developed economies surpassed those of the rich world. That day brought to a close what columnist Peter Hartcher described as "an aberration that lasted one and a half centuries . . . [as] China was the biggest economy in the world until 1840." He went on to quote Ken Courtis, a well-known observer of Asian economies: "The Chinese look at this and they say, 'We just had a couple of bad centuries. . . . In the blink of a generation, global power has shifted. Over time, this will not just be an economic and financial shift but a political, cultural and ideological one.'"[1]

Will it? The readers' comments to Hartcher's column offered a revealing synthesis of a debate that is consuming scholars and policymakers everywhere: Which countries will call the shots in the years ahead? Derek from Canberra wrote: "I don't think we've got much to worry about for several more decades. On paper China and India are power-houses, but most of their citizens don't even have access to sewerage or electricity." "Barfiller" added: "Let's not forget other 'emerging economy' considerations: border conflicts; water and resources rights; patents and other intellectual property; ethnic, religious and ideological differences; cultural diversity; historical arguments and wars; etc, etc. It won't be all sweetness and light for the newly developed nations." David from Vermont noted that it was necessary to take into account "the distribution of wealth within the populations of these countries. The difference between the 'wealth' of the average Chinese and their privileged comrades in the party is, in my opinion, an un-fillable gap (as per India)." "Caledonia," who wrote from Sydney, is more worried: "Well, if China's economy comes crashing down you will find yourself in an unemployment queue and feel lucky if you can get a job as toilet cleaner. If China sneezes Australia will catch a cold. If China gets a cold Australia ends up with pneumonia."[2] Implicit in these comments are fundamental assumptions about what makes a nation powerful, powerful enough to make it a *hegemon*—a nation with the capacity to impose its will on others. And as this chapter will show, not only have the factors that define a hegemon changed but the acquisition and use of power in the international system are also undergoing a profound transformation.

For centuries, the job of tending the rivalry between nations and scrabbling for territory, resources, and influence has been the noble calling of generals and ambassadors. During the nineteenth and twentieth centuries, the representatives of the so-called Great Powers wielded their respective country's military might and economic clout to win wars, harness alliances, secure trade routes and territory, and set the rules for the rest of the world. After World War II even more impressive creatures, the superpowers, came to perch on top of this group. And the dawn of the twenty-first century, with the Soviet Union consigned to the history books, found just one player paramount: the sole superpower, the hegemon, the United States. For the first time in history, many argued, the struggle for power among nations had produced one single, clear, and maybe even final winner.

Consider the evidence from WikiLeaks, which released a trove of more than 250,000 US diplomatic cables that, as the organization's leader Julian Assange luridly put it, "show the extent of U.S. spying on its allies and the UN; turning a blind eye to corruption and human rights abuse in 'client states'; backroom deals with supposedly neutral countries; lobbying for U.S. corporations; and the measures U.S. diplomats take to advance those who have access to them."[3]

The reaction of experienced analysts such as Jessica Mathews, the president of the Carnegie Endowment in Washington, is that this is not a surprise: "This is precisely what hegemony has always been. This is how dominant nations actually behave," she wryly noted.[4]

What many of these cables also show is a hegemon struggling to get things done, stymied by other countries' bureaucracies, politicians, nongovernmental organizations, and ordinary citizens. Dip into the cables for any one particular month and you would see:

- The United States wringing its hands as the European Parliament prepares to vote down separate measures on tracking terrorist financing and providing airline passenger name records
- The Russian Duma squeezing US credit card companies out of payment processing unless they join a national payment card system that significantly reduces their revenues
- A long-running battle to get the government of Turkmenistan to restore the landing rights of US military aircraft
- Frustration over the refusal of Kazakhstan's government to grant local tax exemptions for equipment and personnel to safeguard spent nuclear fuel—a crucial strategic effort

Even those countries theoretically in thrall to the United States are hardly obedient. Egypt, the recipient of billions of dollars in military and economic aid, imprisons high-profile staff members from US nongovernmental organizations. Pakistan offers sanctuary to Taliban and Al Qaeda terrorists, including Osama bin Laden. Israel defies US requests that it not build settlements on disputed territories. Afghanistan, a government that relies on assistance from the United States and its allies for a staggering portion of its budget, breaks with the United States on the conduct of the war on its soil. And Washington frets over the possibility that despite its strong warnings Israel may unilaterally bomb Iran's nuclear facilities. As former US National Security Adviser Zbigniew Brzezinski told me, the world has entered into a "post-hegemonic era" where "no nation has the capacity to impose its will on others in a substantial or permanent way."[5]

What happened to American hegemony is the subject of endless debate. The conventional wisdom has swung wildly in response to one unexpected event after another. At first, the sudden end of the Cold War and the ideological victory that it marked, combined with US economic growth and the communications and technology boom of the 1990s, seemed to prefigure a new unipolar world, one in which the sole superpower could thwart the hegemonic ambitions of all credible competitors. But then the 9/11 attacks, the unilateralism of the Bush administration, the return of high deficits, and the continued growth of China shifted the picture. As a result, the declinist view of American power picked up momentum. Reminders that empires throughout history have always come to an end were captured in book titles such as Cullen Murphy's *Are We Rome?*, published in 2007.[6]

The improbable election of Barack Obama gave pause to this argument as well. Suddenly, America's moral credit in the world was renewed, and with it the "soft power" of attraction that just a few years earlier had seemed to be fast dwindling. Yet the residual benefits of Obama's global appeal have, in turn, been sapped by the United States' ongoing financial crisis, deep and enduring fiscal imbalances, and energy-draining entanglements in Iraq and Afghanistan. In his 2012 State of the Union address, Obama would defensively say that "[a]nyone who tells you that America is in decline . . . doesn't know what they are talking about." The debate over America's global status goes on, driven as much by the latest headlines or economic statistics as by erudite theories of international relations or historical comparisons with the world order in centuries past.

Yet just as American power seems wobbly, so does that of some of its competitors. Across the Atlantic, the European Union—an ambitious project that many believed would form a counterpower to the United States—is mired in a devastating economic crisis, hampered by unwieldy governance, and slowed down by an aging population and a massive inflow of immigrants that the continent does not know how to absorb. Russia, the old rival and heir to Soviet resources and military capabilities, is another aging society, an authoritarian petro-state struggling to contain simmering popular discontent. Two decades of postcommunist crony capitalism, heavy-handed state intervention, and outright criminality have transformed the enormous nation into a hobbled and complicated beast that still owns a nuclear arsenal, yet is only a shadow of the superpower that preceded it.

As noted, those searching for evidence of a new ascending great power have an easy answer: there is vitality in the east. Indeed, according to the Global Language Monitor, which follows the world's top media sources, "the rise of China" has been the most-read news story of the twenty-first century.[7] China's economy surged ahead through the global recession. Its military capabilities and diplomatic weight continue to expand. Since the mid-1990s, the Asian economies have grown at twice the speed of those of the United States or Europe. Looking ahead, experts differ only on the speed at which the Western economies will be left in the dust. One forecast estimates that as early as 2020, Asia's economy will be larger than those of the United States and Europe combined. Another forecast finds China alone far outweighing the United States by 2050; adjusted for purchasing power, China's economy at mid-century will be almost double America's, India will follow close behind, and the European Union will come in at third place.[8] In Washington, such forecasts are laced with anxiety and alarm. In Beijing, they are flush with triumphalism. And as we saw above, Australians are as engaged in this debate as everyone else—and just as divided.

In China's wake come other credible contestants. In India, fast growth, its generally uncontested acceptance into the nuclear weapons club, and its technology and outsourcing boom have nurtured aspirations of big-power status. Brazil, a large country with an activist foreign policy and now, after displacing the UK, the world's sixth-biggest economy,[9] has raised its global profile as well, rounding out the so-called BRICS (Brazil, Russia, India, China, South Africa) group of emerging powers. Each has its own claim to regional sway and its role as an anchor, moderator, mobi-lizer, and sometimes bully of smaller nations around it. Moreover, each has resisted and encroached on the hegemon's prerogatives, whether in their bilateral dealings with the United States or in the United Nations and a variety of other multilateral fora.

Does the behavior of these states represent a threat to the stability of the world order that the United States must parry and deter? Are they merely seeking to take maximal advantage of the benefits that flow from Pax Americana and have little interest in overturning it? Does their emer-gence signal a deepening of the unipolar system around the United States, the early emergence of a major hostile opponent such as China, or a shift to a new multipolar order in which the United States is just one among a growing set of partners, rivals, and peers? And what if all or some of the BRICS are just enjoying a transient prestige and will soon become em-broiled in the problems that come from being poor countries full of polit-ical, economic, social, or ecological imbalances? Indeed, after their rapid growth, the economies of the BRICS and other superstars among the emerging markets are starting to slow down, a reality that can feed the simmering political discontent always present in fast-changing societies. Each of these views has its partisans who offer prescriptions about what their respective country must do to promote its own interest and, possibly, help preserve the global peace.

In subsequent pages we will look at why the question of hegemony consumes military and foreign policy thinkers, and why power shifts among the world's major nations have implications for everyone, far be-yond the superficial focus on who has the largest GDP, military, or haul of gold medals at the Olympics. But this chapter is about an underlying story—one all too often missed by those who debate and keep track of national fortunes. No nation, whether one on top, one striving to get there, or one of those seemingly stuck at the bottom, is immune to the effects of the More, Mobility, and Mentality revolutions and the decay of power that accompanies them. The staggering growth of output and population, the unprecedented mobility of goods and ideas and people, and the accompanying surge in popular aspirations are eroding the barriers to the projection of power—a reality that holds true for all countries regardless of size, income level, political system, or military force.

As those barriers fall, they are erasing the distinction between elite nations capable of playing power politics and the ex-colonies, client states, and far-flung marginal entities that the great powers could once lord over or ignore. Whereas sophisticated and expensive intelligence systems once gave a few countries an information edge, now off-the-shelf data and online resources help the little ones compete. Whereas billions of dollars in aid budgets once established goodwill and loyal regimes in a big power's sphere of influence, now the sources of foreign aid have multiplied, from smaller countries that punch above their weight to foundations whose endowments dwarf other countries' GDPs. Whereas Hollywood and the Comintern once exerted a strong cultural pull, now Confucius societies, Bollywood films, and Colombian telenovelas win over hearts and minds.

The growing capacity of small countries to ward off the designs of large ones is part of an overall shift that has empowered a much broader range of actors in international affairs. The likes of Al Qaeda, the Gates Foundation, and Al Jazeera have their own agendas largely unmoored from any specific country. Terrorists, insurgents, nongovernmental organizations, immigrant associations, philanthropists, private companies, investors and financiers, media companies, and new global churches have not made armies and ambassadors obsolete. But they are limiting what armies and ambassadors can do and influencing the international agenda through new channels and vehicles. Look at Kony 2012, a video created by a Christian activist and film director named Jason Russell urging the capture of indicted war criminal Joseph Kony. Within weeks of its release through YouTube (not through an established broadcasting company), it had garnered tens of millions of viewers, as well as donations, celebrity endorsements, and calls for action—not to mention howls of outrage from some Ugandans dismayed by the film's portrayal of their country. Of course arms sales, national aid programs, and the threat of invasion or trade sanctions still do more to shape international relations. Not every small country has managed to exploit the new ways to project power; but many have.

As America, China, Russia, and the other big-power rivals position themselves for military and commercial competition, they must also reckon with the influence of this new kind of activism on their domestic politics, economics, and culture. And as noted in the last chapter, the decay of power has significantly altered the terms of global conflict. Its transformative impact on how nations relate to one another in the everyday conduct of diplomacy—the web of ties that shape our lives and stitch together the prevailing world order—is no less profound. To appreciate its impact, we should look at the reasons why hegemony and the Great Game mattered so much in the first place.

THE STAKES OF HEGEMONY

Whenever global politics goes through major flux, the specters of conflict and anarchy raise their fearsome heads. Indeed, when the hierarchy of big powers changes, what is at stake is not just prestige but the stability and even survival of the international system itself.

When states seek to advance their national interests, those interests are bound to collide with those of other countries. The collision could be over territory, natural resources, access to water or clean air, shipping lanes, rules governing the movement of people, sheltering hostile groups, or many other subjects of contention. And that clash of interests tends to lead to border wars, proxy wars, territorial disputes, rebellions, nefarious secret-service operations, humanitarian interventions, violations by rogue states, and power grabs of all kinds. History offers stark lessons about what happens when regional powers are not able to prevent or contain such conflicts. For centuries, from the Thirty Years' War to the Napoleonic Wars to World Wars I and II, the scope and scale of war have advanced in a bleak and bloody progression.

Since 1945, many devastating regional conflicts have caused much devastation without expanding into all-out world war. Why this unprecedented extended global peace? A key part of the answer is hegemony. For six decades, countries have had no questions about where they stood in the hierarchy of nations and thus what boundaries they could not cross. In the bipolar system of the Cold War, most of the rest of the world fell more or less firmly into the American or Soviet sphere of influence, and the remaining countries knew better than to challenge this overall frame. And once the Cold War ended, one country, the United States, towered over all the others in military and economic might as well as cultural sway.

Hegemonic stability theory, developed in the 1970s by MIT professor Charles Kindleberger, underlies, more or less explicitly, much of today's debate. Its central insight is that a dominant power that has both the unique ability and the interest to ensure world order is the best antidote to costly and dangerous international chaos. If there is no hegemon, the theory holds, the only way to bring peace and stability is through a system of rules—norms, laws, and institutions that every country agrees to abide by in exchange for the benefits of peace and stability. Needless to say, this is a complicated alternative, no matter how worthy, and hegemony tends to deliver the goods more effectively.[10]

Writing about the world between the wars, Kindleberger argued that the economic and political turmoil of the time—the collapse of the gold standard, the Great Depression, instability in Europe, and the rise of the fascist threat—showed a failure of hegemony. Great Britain's willingness and ability to deploy the forces and spend the money to maintain supremacy were in decline. The only credible contender to step into that role, the United States, was locked in an isolationist stance. The absence of a stabilizing hegemon—one with both the ability and the political will to use its power to preserve order—contributed to the spread of the depression and ultimately to World War II.

Historians using a wide range of measures to estimate national power, from population and economic output to military spending and industrial capacity, have identified moments when the pure hegemony of one country—basically, the gap between it and everyone else—has been the clearest. Britain in the 1860s and the United States right after World War II, from 1945 to 1955, are two cases that "reflect the greatest concentrations of power in the system leader," according to the scholar William Wohlforth, who has analyzed these data extensively. But both of them pale in comparison with America after the Cold War. "The United States is the first leading state in modern international history with decisive preponderance in all the underlying components of power: economic, military, technical and geopolitical," Wohlforth wrote in 1999. He argued—in a view echoed by many other analysts—that the emergence of the United States as an overwhelmingly dominant power with no credible competitor across all the different arenas of international rivalry established a unipolar world. This was an entirely new configuration in world history, and one that had the ingredients not just to deliver global peace and stability but also endure over time.[11]

THE NEW INGREDIENTS

The very success of the United States in providing the world with hegemonic stability helped bring to the fore two new dimensions of power in the world system. One was "soft power"—the idea that a state's power might be expressed and reinforced through the appeal of its culture and ideas. The other was the extraordinary proliferation of organizations, treaties, international laws, and conventions to which more and more countries signed up in the second half of the twentieth century. This growing institutional framework created a system of global cooperation with far more participants, covering far more subjects, than had ever been anticipated.

Soft power had its rougher antecedents in imperialism, whether of the Roman, British, or French variety—the *mission civilisatrice* that sought to indoctrinate colonial subjects into the glories of western civilization, through the seduction of lucre and pomp, or the creation of educational, social, and cultural frameworks. The kinder, gentler, and more egalitarian modern version was posited by political scientist Joseph Nye—later a senior official in the Clinton administration—in a 1990 book titled *Bound to Lead: The Changing Nature of American Power*. The concept took hold, and Nye expanded it in a 2004 book called *Soft Power*. Its subtitle gives away the plot: *The Means to Success in World Politics*.[12]

Soft power as Nye envisions it is a kind of power that is hard to measure but easy to detect: the power of reputation and esteem, the goodwill radiated by well-regarded institutions, a desirable economy to work in or trade with, an attractive culture. This form of power might be less quantifiable than the number of fighter jets, infantry divisions, or billions of barrels of oil reserves, but its value is no less clear. In the 1990s, it was clear that Silicon Valley and Hollywood were adding to America's soft power by driving global technological innovation and spreading entertainment products laced with American culture. Soft power was not unique to the United States, but in the mid-1990s American dominance in this newly crucial arena of power seemed as thorough as it did in the traditional areas.

The world also enjoyed the highest degree of international cooperation in history. Starting with the founding of the United Nations in 1945, governments have steadily invested more and more in new tools of cooperation. From 1970 through 1997 alone, the number of international treaties more than tripled.[13] The US State Department publishes a listing of treaties currently in force for the United States that is almost five hundred pages long, listing thousands of treaties covering everything from polar bears and road traffic to nuclear fuel.[14] Today's widely agreed-upon norms of behavior for states and apparatus of treaties and organizations could scarcely have been imagined a century ago. They govern everything from treatment of prisoners of war to the management of fishery stocks and how much you pay for an international telephone call. Trade, finance, communications, migration, outer space, nuclear proliferation, endangered species, epidemics, terrorism, crime—all are underpinned by agreements or organizations that limit the options of nations and create a space to compromise and work out differences.

Scholars call this a regime—a set of rules and forums addressing a particular issue of common concern. And when a new global challenge takes shape—a recent example might be climate change or financial contagion—there is a healthy instinct to gather and attempt to construct a regime to deal with it together, rather than let every country fend for itself. It is a far cry from the predatory and narrowly self-interested politics among nations once held as a given by Machiavelli and Hobbes. Today, in a once unimaginable world of almost two hundred separate sovereign states, there is a greater moral consensus about the proper behavior of nations than humanity has ever known before.

The combination of hegemony and rules has been good for global stability. The two approaches have functioned together rather than in competition. The United Nations system itself, with its permanent seats and veto powers on the Security Council, was set up to entrench the authority of the winners of World War II, particularly the United States. The United States assumed many classic burdens of hegemony: posting troops in Europe and Asia and acting as global policeman, underwriting the Marshall Plan, contributing the lion's share of the UN's budget and that of other international organizations. Its rival, the Soviet Union, used ideology, oil, and weapons to prop up a bloc of satellite states in Eastern Europe and throughout the developing world. Undergirded by the threat of mutually assured nuclear destruction, the standoff between the two left little room for local conflicts to spread. Once the Soviet Union collapsed, the United States was left with all the attributes and burdens of a hegemon. It possessed vast military supremacy; the world's largest economy and investment and trading ties around the world; a strong and stable political system; a safe and well-defended national territory; and a robust network of diplomats, troops, and spies in every important corner of the world. Meanwhile, the impressive web of global agreements and forums kept disputes from becoming violent and channeled rivalries toward discussion and agreement. The theorists of hegemonic stability seemed vindicated: the hard power of guns and money, the soft power of culture and ideas, and the binding ties of institutions suggested that a long and virtuous Pax Americana lay ahead.

IF NOT HEGEMONY, THEN WHAT?

A decade later, the picture is more complicated. The body blow of 9/11 shattered America's illusion of immunity to domestic attack. Intractable conflicts in Iraq and Afghanistan showed the limits of its military supremacy. The financial crisis and great recession exposed weaknesses in its economy. Administrations of both of its major parties struggled with polarized domestic politics. Yet, at the same time, no clear rival has emerged. China and India have posted phenomenal growth but are far behind and have severe internal weaknesses. No major alliances or treaties have been signed by powers seeking to exploit America's vulnerabilities. The classic elements of the balance of power—whereby countries scheme to offset one another's alliances and limit one another's zones of influence—remain muted. A few countries are clearly vying for leadership in global talks on everything from trade rules to climate change, but this is a far cry from massing weapons on the border. Since the end of the Warsaw Pact, no military alliance has arisen to oppose American-led NATO. Yet the exercise of hegemony by America, divided politically at home, is uncertain at best. So what is happening? For the last several years this sense of unease has fueled a great deal of speculation and worry.[15]

One response has been to point to signs of American decline as the country's economic ability and political will to pay the costs of hegemony decrease. This is a recurring topic. A famous 1987 book by Yale historian Paul Kennedy, *The Rise and Fall of the Great Powers,* described five hundred years of shifts in the world power system and ended with cautions about the fragility of American dominance based on the experience of past empires, which came undone when they could no longer marshal the resources to support their overstretched military operations. The collapse of the Soviet Union seemed to refute Kennedy's prediction, but in the post-9/11 world it seemed relevant once again. And even boosters of American hegemony worried that the biggest risk to the world order was not the rise of some devious competitor but, rather, America's failure to live up to its role. In his 2004 book *Colossus*, prolific British historian Niall Ferguson argued the United States needed to do more to assume its responsibility of leadership as a "liberal empire." All the postwar rules and regimes were not enough to handle threats from rogue states, terrorism, or disease—all given new force by technology, Ferguson argued. "What is required is an agency capable of intervening . . . to contain epidemics, depose tyrants, end local wars and eradicate terrorist organizations." In other words, a capable and active hegemon.[16]

Views about the future of international rivalry span the gamut. Conservative scholar Robert Kagan anticipated that "the twenty-first century will look like the nineteenth," he wrote, with powers like China, Russia, India, and a unifying Europe jostling for supremacy.[17] Another view holds that even if the rival powers are not overtly challenging American hegemony, they are using techniques known as "soft balancing"—such as informal agreements, voting blocs in international forums, or turning down American diplomatic and military requests—to limit and undermine it.[18] Other thinkers argue that fears like Ferguson's are overstated, because American hegemony is not that damaged. Even in a world with new rivals and multiple poles of influence—a "post-American world," as Fareed Zakaria has put it—the United States enjoys unique advantages that reinforce, not diminish, its power.[19]

Still others fear that changes in the global economy and the way we live have been so radical that neither hegemony nor global rules are even possible anymore. They fear that a form of anarchy—the primeval state of the world system—is once again taking hold. As early as 1994, Robert Kaplan saw anarchy emerging from failed states and ethnic rivalries, the rise of unchecked terrorist and criminal networks, and the vulnerability of an interconnected world to the spread of disease and other catastrophes. An even more dire view is that of political scientist Randall Schweller, who compares changes under way in the world system to the onset, in physics, of the state of entropy, when a system becomes so disorganized that it changes nature in a way that is impossible to reverse. Information overload and the scattering of identities and interests will make international politics essentially random, Schweller argues. "Entropy will reduce and diffuse usable power in the system," he writes. "No one will know where authority resides because it will not reside anywhere; and without authority, there can be no governance of any kind."[20]

Clearly, the world system is in a state of flux. The above debates are important, yet they ring hollow when the main views on where the world is headed are so wildly different and subject to shifting conventional wisdoms. The decay of power helps to clarify the picture.

WHO'S AFRAID OF THE BIG BAD WOLF?
TRADITIONAL POWER AT BAY

Fundamentally, the tools that big powers use to get their way in the international system have not changed much. Weapons, money, and diplomatic ingenuity have usually carried the day. A robust army equipped with state-of-the-art equipment and staffed by a large and competent fighting force; a large economy, advanced technology, and a strong natural resource base; a loyal and well-trained cadre of diplomats, lawyers, and spies; and an attractive ideology or system of values have always been major assets to international influence. In every era of history, such attributes have conferred advantage on the most populous, economically advanced, politically stable and resource-rich nations. It is not the raw assets themselves that are shrinking. What is waning is the effectiveness, usability and impact of the traditional modes of power that they underpin: whether military, economic, or soft power.

From Overwhelming Force to the Age of Ad Hoc Allies

As we saw in the last chapter, one country—the United States—spends more on its arsenal, troops, and logistics than do all others combined. It is not a fruitless expense. Pax Americana—in which American military supremacy acts as the ultimate guarantor of stability—has been real. Indeed, the United States now formally guarantees the security of more than 50 countries.[21] The disparity in military spending between the United States and other countries endures, as does the phenomenal breadth of the US military presence in 130 countries, from large contingents in long-term bases to small units in training, peacekeeping, special operations, and counterinsurgency activities.

The United States also leads NATO, the most important military alliance in the world and, with the fall of the rival Warsaw Pact, the only one of its scale. This is as strong an indicator of hegemony as there could be. Alliances were always the core instrument of great-power politics, backing up diplomacy with the credible threat of military action, delineating spheres of influence and no-go areas, and deterring attack by guaranteeing mutual defense. They were, in other words, the building blocks of world order. And for many decades the pattern of alliances in the world remained steady. NATO and the Warsaw Pact enforced a rigid order on either side of the Iron Curtain. In the developing world, newly independent countries quickly got courted, co-opted, or coerced into alliances with the West or the communist bloc.

Today, more than a decade after the dissolution of the Warsaw Pact by its members in July 1991, NATO stands triumphant. In fact, three former Soviet republics and a further seven former members of the Soviet bloc have joined the alliance. NATO and Russia remain rivals: Russia resists having more of its neighbors join the alliance and opposes the deployment of NATO missile defense in central Europe. But they have also proclaimed themselves partners, not enemies, and since 2002 have had a dedicated council to smooth out their relations and solve any disputes. Beyond Russia, NATO has no other obvious potential enemy—a novel situation for a major alliance, and one that has forced it to seek out new ways to remain relevant. The chief case in point is its mission in Afghanistan, in which all twenty-eight member-states plus another twenty-one countries have supplied troops.

But its apparent supremacy conceals mounting weaknesses that reflect both the absence of an existential threat and the dilution of power among its participants. The Afghanistan mission has been heavily dominated by the United States, with many countries making modest or symbolic contributions. Several countries have withdrawn. Domestic opposition to the continued presence of Dutch troops in the mission contributed to the fall of the Netherlands government in February 2010, presaging withdrawal. Participants such as France and Germany have demurred at American requests for additional troops. Moreover, each contingent in Afghanistan has operated under different rules imposed by its own national military command departments or even its country's legislature. A provision hammered out in parliament in Prague or The Hague might limit what actions a NATO soldier might take in the field fighting the Taliban, training Afghan soldiers, or combating the opium trade. Such restrictions have prompted some American soldiers to rechristen the so-called International Security Assistance Force (ISAF) as "I Saw Americans Fight."[22]

While NATO strains under these contradictions, coordination among its members is rivaled by parallel structures. A long-standing defense organization, the Western European Union, overlaps with NATO. The European

Union has its own official defense policy apparatus, including the European Defense Agency and other bodies; it carries out its own overseas missions including peacekeeping, military assistance, and contributions to multinational forces. Of course, each EU member-country has retained its own military. Between NATO, national governments, and the many layers of EU bureaucracy, the Atlantic alliance is increasingly a hodgepodge of jurisdictions and forums with overlapping memberships, but with no decision-making hierarchy or clear lines of command.

The rise of the "coalition of the willing" as a new kind of multinational military enterprise testifies to the diminished force of alliances. The most notorious manifestation of this decline was the ad hoc group of countries who agreed to participate in or otherwise support the US invasion of Iraq in 2003. But it aptly describes the Afghanistan operation as well as security, peacekeeping, and humanitarian efforts from earthquake relief to patrolling the sea lanes off Somalia—where countries have pooled military forces despite no formal alliance having been triggered, and with no overarching authority forcing them to take part. Because the "willing" sign up on an ad hoc basis, their support is contingent on political developments in their respective countries, their continued willingness to pay the financial costs, and the side deals they can negotiate in exchange for taking part—in the case of several nations participating in the Iraq operation, for example, streamlined visa procedures for their citizens to enter the United States.

As for the actual new alliances that have sprung up in the world under Pax Americana, some are simply forums for military cooperation among members of a regional organization, similar to the EU. The African Union, for instance, has its own peacekeeping force to intervene in regional conflicts. A South American Defense Council is building military ties in Latin America. But these fall short of traditional alliances that are built on tight cooperation, sharing plans and technology, and the promise of mutual defense. One might have expected the rise of new alliances around a large rival power, such as China or Russia, in an effort to recreate a rival in place of the Warsaw Pact. Instead, the most active efforts—albeit largely unsuccessful— were those by Venezuelan president Hugo Chavez to form a military alliance with Cuba, Bolivia, and other sympathetic nations as a regional counterpower to the United States. The more representative "alliances" today are in fact between states and nonstate actors that they support—for instance, Iran's support of Hezbollah and Hamas, and Venezuela's reported role as intermediary between the Colombian FARC and organizations like the Basque militant group ETA.[23]

One military arena in which some of the traditional hierarchies remain intact is arms sales—at least of the traditional kind. The same dominant suppliers—the United States, Russia, China, France, Germany, Italy—still account for the overwhelming majority of arms deals, in a top tier that has held intact for decades. But official sales backed by government financing are only one part of the actual global arms business. As the UN secretary-general's April 2011 report puts it, "In recent decades, the arms trade has seen a shift from mostly direct contact between Government officials or agents to the ubiquitous use of private intermediaries, who operate in a particularly globalized environment, often from multiple locations."[24] This part of the arms trade, unregulated and often stateless, is out of control, and points to the diminished grasp of national defense ministries in the environment of armed conflict—yet another symptom of the decay of power.

The Decline of Economic Diplomacy

Alongside military alliances, great powers have traditionally used economic inducements as a way to get other countries to support their interests. The most direct method is bilateral aid—that is, directly from one government to another—in the form of loans, grants, or preferential trade or resource deals. Economic diplomacy can be punitive as well, in the form of trade barriers against a targeted country, boycotts, embargoes, or sanctions against their economic institutions.

Here again the methods persist, but their effectiveness as a means of power projection has diminished. For starters, thanks to the integration of the world economy, the dependence of any one country on supplies, customers, or financing from any one other country has loosened enormously. Falling trade barriers and more open capital markets were long-held goals of the United States and other rich nations in international trade talks. Their victory—along with the widespread promotion of the "Washington consensus" as a condition for lending by the World Bank, International Monetary Fund, and other institutions—has had the paradoxical effect of weakening the hold that the United States or former colonial powers like Britain and France once had over countries in their sphere of influence.

The imposition of sanctions against Iran in an effort to bring its nuclear program into compliance with international regimes is the exception that proves the rule. The United Nations, the United States, the European Union, and several other countries have imposed a widening array of restrictions on commerce with Iran, including an embargo on Iranian oil, curtailment of transactions with its central bank, and restrictions on travel and tourism. But the United States has had to grant exemptions to several of its allies who depend on Iranian oil and has faced the difficult dilemma of whether to impose penalties on friendly countries such as South Korea and India, and on rivals with significant retaliatory capacity such as China, for their unwillingness to curtail purchases.

The targeted use of state power through the allocation of aid to favored countries has become enormously diffuse as well. At the end of World War II, only five or six national aid agencies existed. Today there are more than sixty. In the 1950s, an overwhelming 88 percent of aid disbursed came from three countries: the United States (58 percent), France (22 percent), and Britain (8 percent). The bilateral aid field saw its first major expansion in the 1960s when Japan, Canada, and several European countries set up overseas aid agencies. The Netherlands and the Scandinavian countries soon became major players, contributing a greater share relative to their national income than did the United States, Britain, or France. In the 1970s, the oil windfall allowed Arab countries to set up development assistance funds that they used to support projects in Muslim countries and throughout Africa. The landscape expanded again in the 1990s, with Eastern European countries becoming donors; large emerging nations like India and Brazil have also become major aid issuers in their own right.[25] By 2009, the United States, France, and the UK accounted for only 40 percent of total official development assistance.[26]

And that is just the bilateral part of the picture, which accounts for 70 percent of aid flows. There are at least 263 multilateral aid agencies,[27] from the World Health Organization to regional groupings like the Nordic Development Fund or specialty agencies like the World Fish Center or the International Council for Control of Iodine Deficiency Disorders. On top of all this is the vast expansion of private aid through nongovernmental organizations that follow their own agenda. In 2007, total official development assistance (bilateral and multilateral) was about $101 billion, and private aid was about $60 billion.[28] The global private aid industry is estimated to employ more staff than the government and multilateral organizations with which it competes more and more effectively.

The proliferation of sources means that the typical recipient country is dealing with a great many partners, rather than a few that monopolize the scene and can exercise disproportionate influence on its government. In the 1960s, there were on average twelve donors channeling foreign government funds into each recipient country; in 2001–2005, the number had almost tripled to thirty-three.[29] The dispersion of economic power is even more pronounced when it comes to foreign investment. The days when the United Fruit Company acted as a transmission belt for US interests in the "banana republics" are well over. Multinational companies are no longer national champions for their home country, extending its interests and sometimes serving as more or less complicit agents in its foreign policy. Between the expansion of global markets, outsourcing and manufacturing facilities, the wave of mergers and acquisitions, and investment by individual tycoons, multinationals are as unmoored from the foreign policy of "home" countries as they have ever been. What specific national interest, for instance, would you attribute to the world's largest steel company, Arcelor Mittal, given that it is based in Europe, its shares are listed in the stock exchanges of six countries, and yet it is owned primarily by an Indian billionaire?

In fact, if any countries have seen their interests expand through foreign investment in recent years, it is emerging economies whose companies have become active international investors, especially in agriculture, natural resources, construction, and telecommunications. Brazil's Petrobras or China's CNOOC in oil, Malaysia's Sime Darby in rubber, Mexico's CEMEX in cement and Bimbo in food, South Africa's MTN or India's Bharti Airtel in mobile phone service are just a few of the many companies involved in the so-called South-South foreign direct investment (FDI) supported by increasingly strong investment promotion agencies, export-import banks, or political risk insurance. An estimated twenty-thousand multinational companies have their headquarters in emerging markets. Investments originating in developing countries are still a minority of global foreign investment, but they have skyrocketed from only $12 billion in 1991 to $384 billion in 2011. Of this, a growing proportion has gone to investments in other developing countries. In 2011, emerging-market investors accounted for more than 40 percent of global merger and acquisition activity. The ensuing distribution of executives, personnel, and brand-name visibility gives the lie to the antiquated idea of foreign investment as a political tool of rich nations.[30]

Economic diplomacy still has the best chances of translating to political clout in places where the needs are greatest and competition from other partners and the private sector is lowest. In recent years that has meant Africa, where China and the West are facing off in the closest thing we now have to an old-fashioned scramble for influence, against a background of promising oil reserves and political instability. Chinese influence in Africa has grown in the last decade, as the country has built roads, hospitals, and other infrastructure, lavishly outbidding Western firms for oil concessions and turning projects around rapidly—with few or none of the onerous policy or management conditions imposed by Western funding agencies. One of China's most recent high-profile gifts was a $200 million headquarters for the African Union in Addis Ababa. This generosity combined with professions of support for the sovereignty of recipient countries and a blind eye to rebellions and political unrest have earned China credit among African political elites and created strong competition for French and US companies and agencies. But as fast as Chinese influence in Africa grows, it too is vulnerable to decay as other countries—notably India, South Africa, and the Arab countries—expand their investments on the continent.

Soft Power for All

If the military and economic clout of the great powers has become diluted, their soft power dominance has been equally affected, though this is difficult to measure. The Pew Global Attitudes project, which has polled in an increasing number of countries since 2002, confirms that the global image of the United States declined in most parts of the world during the George W. Bush administration, particularly after the invasion of Iraq, and appeared to have improved—sometimes returning or exceeding 2002 levels, sometimes not—after Barack Obama's election. In Germany, for instance, 60 percent of those polled in 2002 had a favorable view of the United States, compared to only 30 percent in 2007, and 64 percent in 2009. In Turkey, favorable views of the United States dropped from 30 percent in 2002 to 9 percent in 2007, and rose back to 14 percent in 2009. Measured this way, America's soft power is far from uniform: in 2009 American favorability was 78 percent in Nigeria, 69 percent in Britain, 47 percent in China, 38 percent in Argentina, and 25 percent in Jordan. Moreover, by 2012, the "Obama dividend" was declining in many countries.

The same question posed of China offers similarly ambiguous results, with the biggest improvements in China's image reported in Nigeria (from 59 percent favorable in 2006 to 85 percent in 2009) compared with a drop in Turkey (from 40 percent in 2005 to 16 percent in 2009) and tepid results, in the 40–50 percent range, in many of the countries polled. Tellingly, in 2011, Pew reported that a majority or plurality of respondents in fifteen out of twenty-two nations said that China either will replace, or has replaced, the United States as the world's leading superpower. Opinions of the EU have been mixed—its overall image declined in thirteen of twenty countries from 2010 to 2011—while views of Russia tend to be negative and opinions of Iran even more so, with a few salient exceptions (for instance, in 2009, 57 percent of Lebanese had a favorable opinion of Russia, and 74 percent of Pakistanis thought highly of Iran).[31]

All this suggests that soft power is, at the very least, a volatile concept, highly vulnerable to short-term twists in world affairs, in an environment where news travels more rapidly than ever. That has not stopped numerous countries from embracing the concept and looking into ways to increase their soft power. The scholar Joshua Kurlantzick traces China's shift to a soft power strategy to 1997, when the country couched its refusal to devaluate its currency as "standing up for Asia." Since then, China has become the major provider of aid to many Southeast Asian countries, expanded aid and projects in Africa, accelerated distribution of its national television programs, and opened Confucius Institutes for language teaching and cultural programs around the world. In February 2012, China Central Television launched an effort to produce programming for the United States, opening a studio in Washington, DC, with more than sixty international staff.[32] China is also becoming a destination for global artists and architects; and a sense of its growing importance is prompting parents around the world to consider enrolling their children in Mandarin classes. For China, soft power is an explicit strategy.[33]

In India, by contrast, soft power is less a policy priority and more a concern among analysts who hope that the country has already amassed a soft power advantage by virtue of being a democracy and having attracted generations of Western tourists, seekers, and now investors. "India has an extraordinary ability to tell stories that are more persuasive and attractive than those of its rivals," argues Shashi Tharoor, the author and former UN high official turned Indian government minister and politician.[34] The head of India's overseas culture programs cited the popularity of yoga as a component of soft power.[35] Vague as all this can sound, one area in which India's soft power is generally accepted is Bollywood, the world's largest film exporting industry; it has won fans across Asia, Africa, the Middle East, and Eastern Europe for decades and is now breaking into the Western commercial mainstream.

If media penetration and popularity are among the more reliable indicators of soft power, as evidenced by both Hollywood and Bollywood, they also reveal a landscape where telenovelas from Mexico and Colombia, low-budget films from Nigeria, and reality shows from South Africa are broadening the range of influences. In Russia and Eastern Europe, just as the end of the Cold War threw huge arsenals of surplus weapons onto the world market, the end of state television monopolies created a vast vacuum for cheap telenovelas from Latin America to fill, giving birth to addictions—and also markets. In Southeast Asia, a whole generation of fans knows South Korea not for its confrontation with the North nor for its time under dictatorship in the 1970s, but for its video games, pop music stars, and the *Winter Sonata* TV series. The Korean government capitalizes on this by sponsoring concerts and offering language and cooking classes at its cultural centers in the region. Once an opportunity to extend soft power comes into view, capitalizing on it is easy—and often very cheap.[36] The latest Korean cultural beachhead is the United States, where the rapper Psy created a sensation with his "Gangnam Style" dances and songs. (Gangnam is a posh neighborhood in Seoul.) "K Pop," another Korean superstar, also won over legions of fans: the *New York Times* reported that R&B singer Jay Park's songs and albums have hit No. 1 on the R&B/Soul charts on iTunes in the United States, Canada, and Denmark since 2010. Together with the global spread of consumer names such as Samsung, Hyundai, Kia, and LG, these cultural inroads are helping to strengthen South Korea's global brand: in the Anholt GfK Roper Nation Brands Index, which surveys twenty thousand people in twenty countries to put together a ranking of the top fifty country brands, South Korea has risen from thirty-third in 2008 to twenty-seventh in 2011.[37]

THE NEW RULES OF GEOPOLITICS

One of the best examples of smaller countries that have used coalitions of the willing, economic diplomacy (i.e., a lot of money), and soft power to advance their interests must surely be Qatar. It led the way in toppling Libya's Moammar Qaddafi by supplying rebels with money, training, and more than twenty thousand tons of weapons, and called early for the arming of rebels in Syria.[38] It has attempted mediation in Yemen, Ethiopia, Indonesia, and Palestine and—importantly—in Lebanon. Through an $85 billion investment fund, Qatar has bought into businesses from Volkswagen to the Paris St. Germain Football Club. And it is not only behind what is perhaps the most influential new news organization, the network Al Jazeera, but has been building up its reputation as a cultural center with top-rated museums of Islamic and Middle Eastern art as well as high-profile purchases of pieces by the likes of Warhol, Rothko, Cezanne, Koons, and Lichtenstein.[39]

But you don't have to be sitting on top of a small fortune in hydrocarbon resources to play with the big boys. A small group of countries that are not necessarily neighbors or bound by a common history can achieve results more quickly by simply choosing to work together than by going through cumbersome international organizations. And a more geographically ambitious foreign policy, one focused only on immediate neighbors, is within reach of a larger number of countries now; countries that lag in grasping this opportunity stand to lose their competitive edge.

None of these principles denies the value of a large military or a commanding resource base. But all of them flow logically from the decay of power, and they form the basis for a new kind of international politics.

JUST SAY NO

When they set up the United Nations' system, the winners of World War II made sure to design it in ways that would protect their interests. The United States, Soviet Union, China, France, and Britain, for example, gave themselves permanent seats on the Security Council, the body that was to handle the most serious international crises. They also ensured that they would retain the power to veto any resolution. This arrangement was an innovation in international affairs and, in this case, it worked as its designers had hoped it would. The ability of the five permanent members (all of them nuclear powers) to block any action that threatened their interests gave them another useful tool to wield in the complex rivalry that resulted from the division of the world between the Western and Soviet spheres of influence. Of 269 uses of the veto between 1946 and 2012, more than 225 came before 1990.[40] The Soviet Union was the most active veto wielder in the 1950s and 1960s, and the United States thereafter, mainly to stop resolutions condemning Israeli policy vis-à-vis Lebanon or the Palestinians. In the past decade, the Security Council veto has rarely been used; neither France nor Britain has employed it at all in over fifteen years. Since 2006, however, China and Russia have used their veto power to defend rogue nations such as Zimbabwe, Myanmar, and Syria from censure and sanctions.

But if the UN veto by traditional great powers is mostly dormant, other veto powers are flourishing. One arena in which the veto has proved extremely effective for individual nations is the European Union. In 1963, when the community had only six members and was dominated by the French-German alliance, Charles de Gaulle vetoed Britain's application to join. He renewed his opposition in 1967—even though all five of France's partners supported the British application. Only after de Gaulle died in 1969 did France soften its stance, resulting in the admission of Britain, Denmark, and Ireland in 1973. The French veto was an example of a major power—one of the two dominant players in the European Economic Community of the time—using the veto to stop others from usurping its national interest, not unlike the Security Council instrument.

As a result of the steady expansion of the EU and the principle of unanimity for key decisions, considerable power was given to one new nation after another, to the extent that some analysts have wondered why the existing members were so eager to admit new ones at all. Each wave of new members has gotten benefits, often financial, by threatening to hold up new initiatives. Fear of a British referendum on EEC participation in 1975 got France and Germany to agree to new financial terms of membership that were far more favorable to the UK. Later Greece, which joined in 1981, and Spain and Portugal, which joined in 1986, were able to get financial benefits from their fellow members in exchange for not blocking new treaties aimed to advance integration, such the Maastricht Treaty and the development of the common currency.

The EU now uses a system of "qualified majority voting" with a complicated formula that apportions votes to each country by population and requires 255 out of 345 votes for a measure to pass in the Council of Europe. This still creates safeguards for smaller states, preventing a small number of large countries from ramming any initiatives through. But key issues such as new common policies and further expansion of the union still require absolute unanimity, and each year finds small countries using this veto power to hold up various measures. For instance, Poland vetoed a key EU-Russia trade partnership in 2007, until Russia lifted a ban on imports of Polish meat. Lithuania vetoed the same deal until its EU partners agreed to endorse its position on a variety of disputes with Russia, including the issue of compensation for Lithuanians who were deported to Siberian labor camps. The Netherlands has blocked EU accession talks for Serbia over failure to hand over accused war criminals to the International Criminal Court in The Hague. In these ways, small countries have used their veto power to gain concessions—sometimes on major issues, but sometimes on ones that might seem parochial—from larger EU states or from other nations seeking to deal with the EU as a whole.

By digging in their heels, small countries can hold up any number of international initiatives—and they are not hesitating to do so. The failure of the Copenhagen climate summit in December 2009 was blamed on many factors—the reluctance of the United States and China to make a deal, the intransigence of large industrial or developing countries—but in the end, what stopped the adoption of even a weak accord was the objection by a previously unimagined coalition: Venezuela, Bolivia, Sudan, and the tiny Pacific island nation of Tuvalu. The Sudanese representative likened rich-country proposals to the Holocaust, while the Venezuelan representative cut her hand on purpose to ask if it would take blood to be heard.[41] Their acts were dismissed as farcical, but their nations' objections added to the mood of confusion and dissent of what already was a fractious meeting. In the end, the summit did not adopt the accord but, rather, "took note" of it—making a mockery of the efforts of the United States, EU, China, Brazil, India, and other big-country negotiators and sending a discouraging signal about global commitment to a common approach to climate change.

The EU succeeded in forging an agreement at the UN's Durban climate talks in December 2011—only to find its own climate-change policy thrown over three months later by a veto from Poland, which is heavily dependent on coal.[42]

Why do vetoes work so well for small nations today? One major and paradoxical reason is the proliferation of organizations intended for international cooperation on numerous issues. The more of these, the more opportunities for a country to potentially take a stand on a parochial, ideological, or even whimsical issue, often for short-term domestic political reasons rather than because of any defense of principle. But small-country vetoes also work because large countries no longer have the same range of carrots and sticks to force compliance. The decay of military and economic power makes small countries less vulnerable to strong sanctions from traditional patrons and trading partners. And the proliferation of news and communication channels allows small countries new ways to make their case directly to the global public, fomenting sympathy and support, rather than see it limited to closed-door negotiations.

FROM AMBASSADORS TO GONGOS: THE NEW EMISSARIES

"American ambassadors—an obsolete species?" The question was posed as early as 1984 by Elmer Plischke, a distinguished practitioner of that now-fading field, diplomatic history. Plischke pointed out the changes that were eroding the primacy of ambassadors as representatives of their nation, including easier travel and communications technology, the rise of ways for governments to communicate directly with publics in other countries, and the diluting effect of the proliferation of nation-states, including so many very small ones, each with its own diplomatic corps deployed.[43] All of these transformations, of course, have only accelerated in the ensuing three decades.

The idea of diplomacy as a field in decline is not new. In 1962 the scholar Josef Korbel, a Czech emigré and Madeleine Albright's father, wrote about the "decline of diplomacy" as old values and procedures developed over centuries in the diplomatic profession began to crumble. Among these were discretion, manners, patience, thorough knowledge of the relevant topics, and the shunning of premature publicity. "The modern diplomatic world has trespassed much too frequently against these basic rules of diplomacy," Korbel wrote, "and one is compelled regretfully to add that the sin cannot be attributed exclusively to its Communist sector." In addition to the decay of these traditional values, Korbel pointed out the bypassing of diplomats by politicians at summit meetings and state visits, when for many years heads of state and even foreign ministers rarely traveled abroad. And he pointed out that democratic regimes create spaces for other countries to present their case directly, even when they do not reciprocate; thus, he noted, Soviet leaders had access to the American press while Americans enjoyed no such direct access to the Soviet population.[44]

These days, those direct-access channels have exploded into a cornucopia of political, ethnic, and religious advocacy groups; pleas by well-to-do immigrant communities on behalf of their home nation, or emigrants on behalf of their host; friendly news coverage and public relations inserts in newspapers; sponsored events by cultural or tourism organizations; the activities of paid lawyers and lobbyists; and a wellspring of blogs, forums, advertising, and propaganda in cyberspace. For some nations, the leading edge of overseas advocacy is not the embassy staff, with its protocol and security restrictions, but the Gongo. What is a Gongo? It is a government-organized nongovernmental organization: an impostor that purports to be part of civil society but is in fact instigated, funded, or directed by a government or people acting on its behalf.[45]

One Gongo, for instance, occupies a pleasant, innocuous office building in Chiyoda-ku, Tokyo, close to the Imperial Palace. Chongryon, the General Association of Korean Residents in Japan, has about 150,000 members and serves an ethnic community several times larger. It runs about sixty schools, including a university; it also owns businesses, including banks and gaming interests in Japan's popular pachinko parlors. But it delivers passports as well. That's because Chongryon serves as the de facto embassy in Tokyo for North Korea, which has no diplomatic relations with Japan. In its schools, it faithfully advances the ideology of Kim Jong-Un's regime. Over the years North Korea has become isolated and impoverished, but Chongryon has carried on. It lost direct North Korean government funding, and Japan withdrew some of its tax privileges. When it fell into debt, a former Japanese intelligence officer tried to swindle it out of its headquarters. Chongryon encourages Japan's Koreans to maintain their national identity and shun Japanese institutions, but it was happy to see the Japanese courts rule to restore its ownership of the building.[46]

Not all Gongos are pernicious: America's National Endowment for Democracy, a private nonprofit created in 1983 to support democratic institutions around the world, is funded by the US government. That makes it a Gongo. And its work as such has drawn the ire of antagonists including Egypt (which imprisoned and sought to try several of its staff), the Russian government, and a Chinese newspaper that called US-backed democracy promotion "self-serving, coercive and immoral."[47] Other Gongos work in the cultural sphere; among these are the British Council, Alliance Française, Goethe-Institut, and Instituto Cervantes, which promote the arts and teach the language of their respective countries overseas. Numerous religious groups operating in foreign countries have the backing of Saudi Arabia, Iran, and other countries that seek to advance not just the Islamic faith but a particular geopolitical agenda. Gongo ventures can be extremely creative: one, for instance, is the annual program by the Chavez government in Venezuela to subsidize cheap heating oil for thousands of families in the northeast United States, through gifts from the Venezuelan state oil company to a Boston energy company run by former congressman and political scion Joe Kennedy.

As these examples show, Gongos are a mixed bag—and they are not going away anytime soon. Why? Because lower political, economic, and information barriers make them vastly preferable to the rule-hobbled work of a deputy chief of mission, political officer, or science attaché. Deploying a Gongo on a subject of immediate concern can be much cheaper than ramping up personnel and resources in the diplomatic corps—or, for that matter, paying an expensive lobbyist or public relations firm. And cyberspace generates its own Gongos, in the form of bloggers, videographers, and other online voices that advance a country's point of view and may be amenable to friendly encouragement and underwriting.

ALLIANCES OF THE FEW

The multiplication of working partnerships, some more formal than others, among countries involved in one issue or another reflects the shifting lines of power in geopolitics today. The Cairns Group, founded in 1986 to reform agricultural trade, gathers nineteen food-exporting countries, including Canada, Paraguay, South Africa, Argentina, and the Philippines, that push for cutting both tariffs and subsidies. And the BRICS group, which, as noted, is an acronym for five large emerging markets—Brazil, Russia, India, China, and now South Africa—held its first summit meeting in Russia in 2009, though the acronym was coined by a banker for Goldman Sachs eight years earlier and had spread in financial circles before the politicians latched on. Russia also belongs to the G-8 of industrial nations; Mexico and South Africa joined Brazil, India, and China as the "plus 5" in the expanded G8+5. There are two different G-20s, one consisting of finance ministers and central bank governors of nineteen large nations, plus the EU; the other a grouping of developing countries that are now more than twenty in number. The memberships of the two overlap. New trade blocs and regional cooperation agencies are simmering in all parts of the world. And the Bolivarian Alliance for the Americas (ALBA), an alliance begun by Venezuela and Cuba in 2005, has seven members including Ecuador, Nicaragua, and the Caribbean nations of St. Vincent and the Grenadines, Dominica, and Antigua and Barbuda. It resembles a trade pact but has larger political aspirations, and among the benefits it shares among nations are eye care (provided by Cuba and subsidized by Venezuelan oil).[48]

The key common feature is that none of these groups is trying to be a universal alliance. By allowing admission only to members with a common outlook or concerns, they more resemble the "coalitions of the willing" in America's Iraq and Afghanistan wars than they do the United Nations or the international climate-change negotiations. In March 2012, for example, the members of BRICS discussed the creation of a common development bank to mobilize savings between the countries and promote the opening of further trade links, particularly between the other members and Russia and China.[49]

Such groupings also have a higher chance of accomplishing whatever it is they set out to do. Truly global agreements have grown exceedingly rare—especially ones that actually work. The last global trade deal was in 1994, with the agreement to create the World Trade Organization; the United States has yet to ratify the Kyoto Protocol, and many signatories have missed their targets; and the United Nations Millennium Declaration, signed by 192 countries in 2000, set out numerous global social goals to be achieved by their target date of 2015. The Copenhagen fiasco, with its vast expenditure of diplomatic effort for barely a symbolic outcome, is far more characteristic of multilateral initiatives that aim for universal adherence.

The alternative is what I have called minilateralism. At its most fine-tuned, minilateralism consists of gathering the smallest number of countries necessary to make a major change to the way the world addresses a particular issue—for instance, the ten largest polluters, the twenty largest consumers of endangered fish stocks, the dozen major countries involved in aid to Africa as donors or recipients, and so on. Minilateralism can serve small countries too, when it takes the shape of alliances of the few that have a greater chance of succeeding, but also of not being shut down by dominant powers whose leverage is diminished. In turn, minilateralism is vulnerable to the decay of power. Because many of these associations are ad hoc and lack the moral pressure of global membership, they are also more vulnerable to dissolution or defection when a member-government falls, its population dissents, or its policy preferences change.[50]

Anyone in Charge Here?

The leveling of hierarchy means that a small number of dominant nations (let alone a single hegemon) no longer hold sway over the direction of international cooperation and how the world will handle present and future crises. It also means the bypassing of the traditional diplomatic establishment—foreign ministries, embassies and their staff, national aid agencies, and other bilateral services—that has controlled the terms of engagement across borders. Diplomats were once the gatekeepers and guardians of certain norms of interaction. Now they have been disintermediated, and the advantages of traditional statecraft blunted, in a landscape of small-country initiatives, promotion by nonstate actors, and channels of direct access to overseas public opinion.

The edifice of cooperation and deterrence built in the last seven decades has been strong enough to see through decolonization, ward off invasions and conquests, and limit secessions. The dissolution of unwieldy unions that had been held together by ideology and force—the Soviet Union, Yugoslavia—stand as the exceptions that confirm the rule. So sovereign states remain, and they still possess the trappings of sovereignty, which are not insignificant: armies, border controls, currencies, economic policy, taxation. The rivalry among states—along with its expression through the Great Game of negotiations, alliances, agreements, propaganda, and confrontation—is here to stay.

The tail will not always wag the dog, either. The power of the United States or China is vastly superior to that of a small European, Latin American, or Asian state both on paper and almost always in practice. It is the effectiveness of that power that is lagging, not its potential. The American president will have his or her phone call taken at any hour anywhere in the world. He can barge into a meeting of fellow leaders and redirect the conversation. The clout of the Chinese premier by that measure is growing. These are the dynamics that unfold at international conferences and summit meetings, and they have an impact on the outcome. Keeping tabs on them is more than a matter of jingoism or attachment to bygone ways: it does make a difference.

But the decay of power means that obsessing about which great power is on the rise and which one is declining, as if geopolitics in the end reduced to a zero-sum game among a global elite, is a red herring. Yes, each issue on which they face off is significant on its own merits. The alignment of military forces between the United States, Russia, and China is certainly worthy of concern. So is the nature of China's response to American entreaties that it manage its currency differently. So are differences between the United States and the European Union on trade policy, agricultural subsidies, and the prosecution of war criminals. So are the stances of India and China on carbon emissions. But none of this signifies the fall of one hegemon and the rise of another in its place. Future superpowers will neither look nor act like those of the past. Their room for maneuver has tightened, and the capability of small powers to obstruct, redirect, or simply ignore them will continue to grow.

So, does this mean that the alternative view is correct? Is the world spiraling toward an updated, twenty-first-century version of Hobbes's war of all against all, made more complicated by the cross-cutting and blurred lines between nation-states, nonstate actors, unmoored financial flows, charities, NGOs and Gongos, and free agents of all kinds? The default answer is yes—unless, and until, we adjust to the decay of power and accept that the ways we cooperate across borders, both inside and outside the framework of governments, must change.

There is no reason we cannot do so. The collapse of the world system has been repeatedly predicted at times of technological change and cultural and demographic flux. Thomas Malthus predicted that the world could not carry an expanding population. Yet it did. Witnessing the industrial revolution and the expansion of global markets and trade in the nineteenth century, the Marxists anticipated a collapse of capitalism under the weight of its internal contradictions. It did not. World War II and the Holocaust deeply shook our faith in the moral character of humanity, yet the norms and institutions the world established in response have endured to this day. Nuclear annihilation, the cardinal fear of the 1950s and 1960s, failed to occur.

Today's panoply of international threats and crises—from global warming and resource depletion to nuclear proliferation, trafficking, fundamentalism, and more—come as the hierarchy of nations is in flux and the very exercise of state power is no longer what it used to be. The juxtaposition can be jarring. Each new massacre, bombing, or environmental disaster jolts us anew, and the laborious, ambiguous results of conferences and summit meetings seem to offer little consolation or hope. It may seem that no one is in charge. That feeling, and the trends that provoke it, will continue. But looking for a current or new hegemon or a committee of elite nations to reassert control is a fool's errand. The solutions to the new challenges of international cooperation—ultimately, of sharing the planet—will emerge in a landscape where power is easier to obtain and harder to use or even to keep.

CHAPTER EIGHT

BUSINESS AS UNUSUAL

Corporate Dominance Under Siege

FOR DECADES, THE "SEVEN SISTERS"—GIANT, VERTICALLY INTEGRATED companies like Exxon and Shell—dominated the oil industry, the "Big Five" ruled accounting, and the "Big Three" controlled car-making, as did three networks in television and, later, two computer companies in information technology. The same pattern prevailed in many other sectors: a few companies dominated their respective markets, and they were so large, rich, global, powerful, and entrenched that dislodging them was unthinkable.

Not anymore. Across every sector of the global economy, these static structures are gone, and competition for the top slot is fiercer than ever. Shell or IBM or Sony may still be at or near the top, but they have seen their market power decline and their dominance abate as new competitors have gobbled up large chunks of their traditional markets. Moreover, corporations that used to be household names have disappeared—no more "Kodak moments," to name just one storied brand that in 2012 ended up on the ash heap of history.

The list of companies at the top now routinely includes new names, including many hailing from places not known for spawning world-class businesses—Estonia (Skype), India (Mittal Steel), Brazil (Embraer), and Galicia in Spain (Zara) among them. And whether newcomers or not, those at the top are no longer assured as lengthy a stay among the leaders as in the past.

We are not talking about the displacement of one behemoth by another. More often than not, the space once controlled by old leaders has been filled by a different set of players that rely on new rules, sources of power, and competitive strategies. The very nature of the power that the old companies and their masters once enjoyed has changed.

How so? The oil industry is an extreme, and therefore illuminating, example. The "Seven Sisters," the companies that dominated the field from the 1940s to the 1970s, were not simply replaced by others like them; indeed, the oil industry is now more fragmented and less vertically integrated. The creation of new futures markets and the trading of more oil on a spot basis have dramatically changed the way oil is bought and sold. The industry is full of new "independents": smaller companies that compete with, and in some cases even outrun, giants like ExxonMobil, Chevron, and BP. New players in the oil industry also include state-owned companies that have become more competitive and far more assertive in controlling their nations' energy sources. Giant hedge funds that exert unprecedented influence over ownership, accountability, and finances are now part of the oil industry landscape and may behave as active shareholders of the large companies or as providers of capital to smaller firms. In the past, only the "Seven Sisters" had access to the vast financial resources needed to participate in the oil market. Today, thanks to the combination of new players (hedge funds, private equity firms), new financial instruments (derivatives), and other institutional arrangements (new stock exchanges), it is possible for smaller companies to acquire the capital needed to compete in projects that once were the sole preserve of the oil giants. Finally, all these industry participants must contend with unprecedented scrutiny and intervention by governments, shareholder activists, environmental groups, institutional investors, labor unions, and the media—among others.

As Paolo Scaroni, the CEO of the Italian oil giant ENI, told me: "When I look back at how the leaders of the main oil companies of the 1960s, 1970s or 1980s used to make decisions and run their businesses, I am amazed at the freedom and autonomy they enjoyed. From where I sit, it's obvious that nowadays any oil company CEO has far less power than those who came before us."[1]

Something similar is happening to banking. Several established big banks disappeared or were taken over as a result of the global financial turmoil that erupted in 2008, and this led in turn to further concentration. By 2012, five banks (JPMorgan Chase & Co., Bank of America Corp., Citigroup Inc., Wells Fargo & Co., and Goldman Sachs Group Inc.) held assets equal to half the size of the US economy. Much the same is true in the UK, where for the past two decades the "Big Five"—Barclays Plc, HSBC

Holdings Plc, Lloyds Banking Group Plc, Royal Bank of Scotland Group Plc, and Santander U.K. Plc (which was Abbey National Plc until Spain's Banco Santander bought it in 2004)—dominated the sector.[2] But in the last few years, public concerns fueled by the financial crisis and scandals like the rigging of interest rates by Barclays and the complicity in illicit money transfers (HSBC, and Standard Chartered) have created a backlash, which in turn sparked a wave of new regulations that limits the autonomy these banks traditionally enjoyed. Moreover, new players such as British entrepreneur Richard Branson, whose Virgin Money bought up the ailing Northern Rock Plc and aims to become a consumer powerhouse, are indicative of new competitive pressures the traditional megaplayers in banking are facing. As one analyst told *Bloomberg Markets* in 2012, "There is more structural change going on in the U.K. market than at any time in recent history."[3]

But the big challengers to the dominant big banks are the hedge funds and other new financial players that have access to resources as deep as those of the large banks yet can move faster and with far more flexibility. In early 2011, as the global economy was still sputtering, this is what the *Financial Times* reported about the health of hedge funds:

> The top 10 hedge funds made $28 billion for clients in the second half of last year, $2 billion more than the net profits of Goldman Sachs, J. P. Morgan, Citigroup, Morgan Stanley, Barclays and HSBC combined, according to new data. Even the biggest of the hedge funds have only a few hundred employees, while the six banks employ 1 million between them. According to the data, the top 10 funds have earned a total of $182 billion for investors since they were founded, with George Soros making $35 billion for clients—after all fees—since he set up his Quantum Fund in 1973. But John Paulson's Paulson & Co is closing in on Mr Soros's fund as the hedge fund to have made the most money for investors, after scoring net gains of $5.8 billion in the second half of 2010.[4]

Like their oil peers, the top bankers also lament their diminished freedom of action. Jamie Dimon, JPMorgan Chase's CEO, presides over a larger bank than did his predecessor, William Harrison, but as his constant complaints about government regulation and the pressures of activists suggest, he also is more limited in what he can do. His argument that the public and regulators are better off trusting the banks' self-regulation and competition became harder to defend when in 2012 he revealed that his

bank suffered an estimated $6 billion in losses hidden by some of his col-
leagues and unnoticed by trusted members of his top management team.[5]
The newspaper industry offers another telling example. The standard
narrative of its misfortunes is that Craigslist and Google took away a critical source of revenues (classified advertisements) from the industry's traditional leaders. But what happened to newspapers is far more dramatic and
cataclysmic than a mere shift in market share in classified ads from one set
of companies to another. The power that the owners and executives of
Craigslist now have is very different from the power once wielded by the
Graham family, the owners of the *Washington Post*, or the Ochs-Sulzberger
family that controls the *New York Times*. These controlling shareholders—
like the Murdochs, Berlusconis, or the many media-owning families around
the world—still have clout, but they have to use it, and fight to retain it, differently from their predecessors.

Does this mean that ExxonMobil will be displaced by an independent
oil company, JPMorgan Chase by a hedge fund, or the *New York Times* by
The Huffington Post? Of course not. These are large companies with immense resources and hard-to-replicate competitive advantages that ensure
their dominance in the industry. On the other hand, the same could have
been said in the 1990s about once-dominant and now bankrupt Kodak or
in 2007 about the world's largest insurance company AIG, which one year
later had to be saved from extinction by an unprecedented $85 billion gov-
ernment bailout?[6] Who would have said in early 2012 that one of the
world's most powerful bankers, Barclay's Bob Diamond, would lose his job
in a matter of days after it was discovered that his bank was involved in ma-
nipulating interest rates? Large companies that go out of business and
once-larger-than-life business leaders who end up in the street, or even in
jail, are nothing new. What *is* new is that, as shown in the pages ahead, the
probability that a company will fall from its standing at the top of its league
has increased, as has the probability that a company or business leader will
suffer a damaging "reputational accident."

Moreover, the broader and more consequential effect of the decay of
power in the business world is not that large companies are now more
prone to disappear but, rather, that they face a more dense and limiting
web of constraints on their ability to act.

The business sectors that have undergone a structural revolution are as
numerous as they are varied: from travel to steelmaking and from book-
selling to the manufacturing of passenger jets. In fact, the challenge is to

find an industry where this has not happened and where the power of the top players is not more constrained and, indeed, decaying.

In the Land of Bosses, Authority, and Hierarchy

Who's in charge here? In the business world, this question calls for a clear answer. In the military, hierarchy comes naturally. And the same is true in corporations; they are not democratic institutions. In an environment where decisions about resources, prices, procurement, and personnel are made every minute and show up in the bottom line, there needs to be a place where ultimate accountability, credit, and blame rest. The title *chief executive officer* suggests orders, discipline, and leadership. It comes with the traditional symbols and perquisites of corporate authority: the corner office, the corporate plane, memberships in fancy clubs. And of course, the salaries. From the end of World War II to the mid-1970s, the median real value of executive pay was remarkably flat.[7] But from 1980 to 1996, the real value of CEO compensation in the S&P 500 grew by more than 5 percent per year; overall, CEO pay levels after 1998 were roughly double what they were at the start of the decade. To varying degrees, executive salaries in the rest of the world have followed that trend.

Nice work if you can get it. Yet just beneath the surface of high-flying privilege lurks another reality. Power in the corporate sector is diminishing—and harder to hold onto when you get it.

This is not anecdotal: the statistical evidence clearly shows that the hold of CEOs on their jobs has become tenuous. In the United States, still home to the largest population of big companies, CEO turnover was higher in the 1990s than in the two previous decades. And since then the trend has sharpened. The CEO of a Fortune 500 company in 1992 had a 36 percent chance of holding that office five years hence. But a CEO in office in 1998 had only a 25 percent chance of keeping it five years later. According to management consultant John Challenger, the tenure of the average CEO has halved from about ten years in the 1990s to about five and a half in recent years—a trend that has been confirmed by several studies. Another study found that nearly 80 percent of CEOs of S&P 500 companies have been ousted before retirement.[8] Rates of both internal turnover (the kind forced by boards) and external turnover (due to mergers and collapses) rose from the 1990s to the early 2000s. In 2009, another study found that 15 percent of American CEO positions turned over each year.[9] The data vary depending on the sample of firms, but the core trend is apparent: things have grown more and more slippery where "the buck stops."

And this trend is global, not just American. The consulting firm Booz & Company tracks CEO changes in the 2,500 biggest companies listed in global stock markets. In 2011 alone, 14.4 percent of the world's top CEOs left their jobs and the turnover rate was higher among the 250 largest companies, as it has been since 2005. This trend has also been occurring over the past twelve years. On average, more than 14 percent of chief executives of the top 250 companies by market capitalization have turned over, compared with 12 percent of companies ranked 251 to 2,500. This figure included terminations due to planned retirements, illness, and the like, but the study found that forced successions—CEOs being shown the door—were on the rise in both America and Europe. The rest of the world, where business is growing the fastest, was catching up to the West in this area, too. In Japan, traditional business culture makes it nearly taboo to push out a top executive, yet forced successions quadrupled there in 2008 and have continued to be higher than their historical trend. Booz & Company also found that CEOs around the world are much less likely than before to be chairman of the board—another measure of the growing limits to corporate executive power.[10]

As it is for bosses, so it is for their firms. Sojourns at the top of corporate league tables have noticeably shortened. This, too, is not an ephemeral trendlet of the last few years, though the economic crisis certainly made it more pronounced; rather, what we're seeing is a deep transformational phenomenon.

Again, the statistical evidence is conclusive: whereas in 1980 a firm in the top fifth of its industry ran only a 10 percent risk of falling out of that tier five years later, by 1998 that risk was up to 25 percent.[11] Among the top 100 companies in the Fortune 500 listing in 2010, 66 were survivors from the 2000 list. Thirty-six hadn't existed in 2000. On the basis of a detailed statistical analysis, Diego Comin of Harvard and Thomas Philippon at New York University found that in the last thirty years "the expected length of leadership by any particular firm has declined dramatically." This, too, is a global trend. And it coincides with the growing geographic scope of competition. The Forbes 2012 ranking of the world's 2,500 biggest companies found 524 based in the United States—more than 200 fewer than five years prior and 14 fewer than the year before. More and more of the world's largest companies have headquarters in China, India, Korea, Mexico, Brazil, Thailand, the Philippines, and the Gulf states. Mainland China is closing the gap between itself and the United States and Japan, the two countries with the largest number of top global companies, and is now the third-largest country in terms of membership, with 15 more companies than it had in 2011. New entrants like Ecopetrol of Colombia and China Pacific Insurance of China are coming in, while the likes of Lehman Brothers and Kodak (both dead), Wachovia (absorbed by Wells Fargo), Merrill Lynch (now owned by Bank of America), and Anheuser-Busch (taken over by a Belgian-based conglomerate with roots in a once-obscure Brazilian provincial brewing company) have fallen from consideration.[12]

WHAT IS GLOBALIZATION DOING TO BUSINESS CONCENTRATION?

The disappearance of well-known companies and once-cherished brands does not mean that in many business sectors concentration isn't as high as ever and in some cases even higher than before. A pet-food recall in 2007 in the United States, for example, revealed that only one contract manufacturer actually made more than 150 products with various names. Two companies control 80 percent of the US beer market, two companies account for 70 percent of American toothpaste, and so on. In an example cited by author Barry Lynn, an Italian company, Luxottica, controls not only several big optical retail chains in the United States but also many of the brand-name lines of eyewear that they sell.[13] Leonardo del Vecchio, Luxottica's major shareholder, is one of the world's wealthiest people, ranking 74 in Forbes's list of the world's billionaires.

Globally, industry concentration levels vary a great deal by sector. The diamond industry remains tightly driven by the dominant player, De Beers, which asserts prices and governs the flow of rough diamonds to the enterprises that cut and finish them. De Beers's 60 percent of the rough-diamond market gives it an overwhelming lever on prices. In the computer chip business, one manufacturer, Intel, controls 80 percent of the market for CPU processors. Other industries in which concentration is high enough to rouse the attention of American or European antitrust agencies are crop seeds (where Monsanto and DuPont dominate), payment networks (where Visa and MasterCard reign), and of course Internet searches (where Google accounts for 63 percent of search activity in the United States—and 90 percent of search growth).

But other industries have become less concentrated despite years of apparently aggressive merger activity. In fact, as business professor and author Pankaj Ghemawat argues in *World 3.0*, "In most situations, globalization appears to promote more competition, not more concentration."[14] A salient example is automobiles. Industry data show that the top five motor vehicle manufacturers worldwide accounted for 54 percent of production in 1998, and only 48 percent—a small but significant decrease—in 2008. Expanding the analysis to the top ten manufacturers still showed a decrease in concentration. The trend is long-standing. In the 1960s the top ten manufacturers accounted for 85 percent of the world's car production; that share is now down to about 70 percent. In part, the increased fragmentation of the market reflects the emergence or global spread of new players from countries like Korea, India, China, and elsewhere.[15] In 2011, for example, Hyundai was not only the world's fifth-biggest automaker but also its most profitable.[16] In looking at concentration among the top five companies across eleven industries from the 1980s to the 2000s, Ghemawat found that the average five-firm concentration ratio had fallen from 38 percent to 35 percent; that decline is even more pronounced if we reel the numbers backward to the 1950s.[17]

THE POWER AND PERIL OF BRANDS

Many long-cherished corporate names have performed sudden vanishing acts. Once-prestigious names in retail, banks, airlines, even technology— remember Compaq?—are receding into faint memories. On the other hand, some of the world's most ubiquitous brands barely existed a few years ago, such as Twitter, founded in 2006. As consumers, we have largely grown accustomed to such trends. Indeed, consumers have been the inadvertent agents of some of this turnover, which has been partly driven by an increase in the rate and impact of brand disasters—incidents that shake the reputation of a company and its products to the core, causing share prices to plummet and consumers to flee. A study conducted in 2010 found that whereas two decades ago companies faced an average 20 percent chance of encountering a "corporate disaster" for their reputation in a five-year period, that chance is now 82 percent.[18] Is this because oil spills, failing brakes, and impolitic statements are four times more common today than twenty years ago? No, but their diffusion and reach are faster and far greater, and their louder echo often portends grave consequences.

In this context it should come as no surprise that the most visceral indicator of economic power—individual wealth—is subject to quick changes as well. (Since 2012, *Bloomberg News* has provided a daily ranking of the world's top twenty billionaires, updated daily at 5:30 P.M. New York time.) The number of billionaires in the world has soared in recent years; it reached a record 1,226 in 2012.[19] A growing proportion are Russians, Asians, Middle Easterners, and Latin Americans. Interestingly, the billionaire who gained the most wealth between 2007 and 2008, Indian industrialist Anil Ambani, was also the one who lost the most the next year (though he still ranked 118 in 2012).[20] According to a 2012 study by wealth intelligence firm Wealth-X, between mid-2011 and mid-2012 Chinese billionaires lost almost a third of their combined wealth.[21]

No one is shedding any tears for the plight of the mega-rich. But the turbulence in the world's wealth rankings rounds out a picture of insecurity at the top of the business world—whether of bosses, corporations, or brands—that is heightened relative to any time in recent memory, in a business arena that is more global and diverse than at any time in the past.

The turmoil at the top makes an odd contrast with the widely prevailing idea that we live now in an era of unprecedented corporate power. The boom of the 1990s doubtless brought fresh glamour and prestige to corporate careers, and the rise of the high-tech economy created a new generation of business heroes out of the chiefs of Apple, Oracle, Cisco, Google, and the like, as well as superstar players in the world of securities and banking. In Europe, regulatory reforms, privatization, and the creation of a single market gave birth to new corporate icons. Swashbuckling billionaires emerged in Russia, and former Third World nations once derided as recesses of state control and poverty produced burgeoning business empires, brands, and tycoons. Critics from the Left raised alarm at the new dominance of capital. Boosters praised it. But no one disagreed that it existed.

The global recession and financial crisis have done little to clarify our picture of corporate power. On the one hand, the need for governments to rein in unbridled corporate behavior again became apparent. But so did the notion that certain businesses—banks, insurers, automakers—were "too big to fail"; they could not be allowed to go out of business without immense adverse regional, national, or even global consequences. Some, like General Motors and Chrysler, were saved by government intervention. Others, like Lehman Brothers, were allowed to go under. Banks deemed too shaky to survive were sold to larger ones, creating ever-larger behemoths and bolstering claims of critics who saw power concentrating in a tight-knit, untouchable financial elite. Unquestionably, corporate giants exist today on a scale barely imaginable a few decades ago. Some industries have consolidated a great deal. And clearly antitrust and other key regulations, whether in North America, Europe, or elsewhere, have fallen behind some of the tools and techniques that businesses—especially in finance—employ on a daily basis.

So which is our reality? Unbridled corporate power that foists costs and liabilities on governments and taxpayers while preserving high pay and profits for executives—or insecure business leaders constantly at risk of being squeezed by new entrants and technologies, thwarted by reputational disasters, scrutinized by market analysts, and ultimately removed by rebellious shareholders and impatient boards? In other words, what is happening to the power held by large corporations and their top executives?

Market Power:
The Antidote to Business Insecurity

To understand the fundamental forces that are transforming corporate power in the twenty-first century, we need to explore a concept that was introduced in Chapter 2: market power.

Pure economic theory assumes cutthroat competition, which means that upheaval is the normal state of affairs in capitalism inasmuch as competition kills some companies and rewards others. The ideal state known as "perfect competition" leaves no space for monopolies, cartels, or a small number of dominant companies to prevail, let alone endure for years.

Reality is obviously different: some companies persist while others go under; legendary investors and executives rule for decades while others vanish as fast as they appeared; some brands seem to be ephemeral artifacts of passing fashion while others are able to outlast any number of technological transformations, market expansions and contractions, and management changes. Some large companies make it impossible for others to compete in their market, and small groups of companies in the same sector collude to extract the most profits for the longest possible period of time. Also, the very nature of some sectors where low barriers to entry are the norm facilitates the entry of new competitors (restaurants, garments); in others the barriers are so high that it is very hard for new companies to challenge the incumbents (steel mills, mobile telephony).

In other words, capitalist business contains a wide variety of patterns and expectations that manifest themselves in the symbolic language of our investor and consumer society. They produce enduring competitive oppositions (Boeing versus Airbus, Coke versus Pepsi, Hertz versus Avis); they turn brand names into vernacular common nouns (Xerox, Hoover, Kleenex); they invest some (Rolex, IBM) with prestige and others (Timex, Dell) with practicality. When they obliterate, they do so ruthlessly. Be it Pan Am, Woolworths, Kodak, or Wang—the end of a corporation, whether dissolved or absorbed into another, is a vanishing act.

What stokes this constant motion of symbols, products, people, and names is in large part the day-to-day action of sellers and buyers in the market—as well as risk-taking, accidents, mistakes, happenstance. But it is also power. And this is where market power comes in: it is the power that dwells in being able to charge prices for products and services that are above marginal cost, and hence generate and sustain extra profits, without ceding market share. The more market power a company possesses, the more autonomously it can set its own prices without worrying about rivals. The more market power is present in a given sector or marketplace, the more entrenched its industry structures and the more static its league tables.

In real life, products are not interchangeable, and even when they are, they are differentiated by brands and promoted by advertising. In real life, companies do not have access to the same information. They do not enjoy the same laws and rules for running their operations or solving disputes, the same tacit or overt backing from governments, or the same access to precious resources. Intellectual property restrictions carry rather different weight in Switzerland than they do in China. A US firm with a large "government affairs" division dedicated to lobbying politicians in Washington, a Russian company founded by an oligarch with personal friendships in the Kremlin, and an Indian company finding its way through the tangle of decades-old licensing and bureaucratic requirements face drastically different regulatory environments from one another, let alone from a start-up seeking to enter an industry for the first time. Companies also differ with respect to the internal resources they have to train personnel and develop new products. All of these differences in business scope, resources, and operating environment affect the cost of doing business, decisions to expand, and the choice of whether to take on an activity in-house or to farm it out to a supplier or contractor. In short, they produce the structure of industries.

A whole field of economics—industrial organization—arose almost a century ago to make sense of industry structure and explain what made it change, or not change. As discussed in Chapter 3, the field drew on the insight of Ronald Coase, the British economist who in 1937 first propounded the notion that transaction costs helped to explain why firms and industries took particular shapes.[22]

Individually or together, the companies that dominate a particular industry or marketplace spend a great deal of their energy working to keep things that way. For a company, the aim is to present a unique and attractive selling proposition—one that is hard for any other to imitate, or replicate. It can protect that position by means of exclusion and by means of collusion. Exclusion might involve driving out competitors by undercutting them on price, pulling ahead of them on quality or product innovation, or deluging the market with advertising. Collusion could take the form of setting up obstacles that make it difficult or impossible for a new competitor to enter—in particular, when the companies that dominate a space tacitly (or overtly) coordinate pricing and sales strategies or technology standards, or use public relations campaigns and industry associations to argue for regulations that give them shelter. Whatever enabled incumbents to exclude and collude also limits the horizon for new competitors, and therefore creates barriers to entry that could be insurmountable.

This explains why economists who seek to identify market power at work often move past the numbers to investigate the more qualitative question of how daunting the barriers to entry are in a given field. There are quantitative measures of market power as well, but they are hard to use.

More useful are the measures that economists use to determine market power in a given industry rather than at the level of an individual firm. A variety of such measures are available. A simple one is the top-firms concentration index, which adds up the total market share of the leading firms (the top four, five, or ten in sales or assets, for example) in a given industry or economy.[23]

But market power goes beyond concentration alone. In some highly regulated economies or industries, relatively small companies might benefit from market power simply by being inside the fence of government protection or political favor. Think, for example, of a taxi company that has the exclusive rights to service passengers arriving to a specific airport. Likewise, the simple presence of industrial concentration does not necessarily mean that the firms act as an oligopoly, using overt or tacit collusion to keep prices high; the competition between them might be intense and vicious. Other factors that contribute to market power, such as the ability to lobby for favorable treatment and laws, do not stem directly from industry concentration. A trade association that represents a scattered industry (e.g., accountants or dentists) might achieve lobbying results as successful as those of one acting on behalf of a concentrated industry (e.g., cement or basic telephony).

To understand the workings of market power, therefore, a single quantitative measurement is not enough. Rather, the extent of market power and, with it, the stability of an industry's structure and the advantage of shelter that its dominant firms enjoy are best gauged by looking at the presence and effectiveness of barriers to entry. And when we do this, a salient trend quickly becomes clear: *across the board, the traditional barriers to entry that shaped industry structure for the better part of the twentieth century have grown porous or fallen altogether.*

Axioms of corporate organization have been overturned. As a result, market power is no longer what it used to be. The antidote to business insecurity and instability is losing its effectiveness. And the advantage long considered to be built into corporate scale, scope, and hierarchy has been blunted, or even transformed into a handicap.

BARRIERS ARE DOWN, COMPETITION IS UP

The classic barriers to entry in business are well known. *Size,* for example, prevents smaller companies from taking on larger ones. And *economies of scale* make it cheaper to mass-produce items, justifying such innovations as the large-scale modern factory and the assembly line. When a few, large manufacturers are able to capture a large portion of the market, they can spread their total fixed costs (administration, for example) over a large number of units, thus lowering the average cost of each individual unit.

A related set of barriers originates in *economies of scope.* Experience in related but not identical businesses can give a company an advantage that its rivals lack. For instance, a company that has large contracts to supply airplanes to the air force will have enormous advantages when competing in the market for passenger airplanes. While economies of scale are a function of volumes, economies of scope emerge when a company is able to use its unique knowledge and core competencies in different markets. *Access to scarce resources,* such as mineral deposits, fertile soil, or abundant fisheries, becomes a barrier when potential competitors can't access similar resources. *Capital* is of course another obstacle. Launching a new airline or a telephone or steel company requires huge capital expenditures that few newcomers can afford. *Technology* is another common barrier to competition: a formula, manufacturing process, or any form of exclusive intellectual capital not available to would-be competitors also dampens competition. The same is true for a *brand name:* competing with Coke and Pepsi is hard not just because of their size but also because their products enjoy enormous brand appeal.

And then there are the *rules:* the laws, regulations, ownership codes, tax policies, and all the other requirements to operate in a given location and industry. All these (and many variations—there is no single standard list of every barrier to entry in business) typically entrench the position of dominant firms in any given industry and hold new entrants at bay.

Which brings us to the core question about the transformation of power in the business world: What might cause barriers to entry to suddenly fall and thus make long-entrenched companies more vulnerable to power-loss? One obvious answer is the Internet. Examples of how it has helped to dislodge established monopolies are as legion as the possibilities of the medium itself. In fact, few sectors have been untouched by the revolution in information and communication technologies.

Yet, as is also the case in other arenas discussed here (politics, war, etc.), beyond the information revolution there are forces at work that have altered the way power is acquired, used, and lost in the business world.

In the last three decades, for example, government actions have drastically altered long-fixed business structures. Margaret Thatcher and Ronald Reagan launched a wave of policy changes that spurred competition and changed the way of doing business in a variety of sectors from telephones and air travel to coal mining and banking. Starting in the late 1980s, developing countries from Thailand to Poland to Chile implemented their own revolutionary economic reforms: privatization, deregulation, trade opening, elimination of barriers to foreign investment, freer currency trading, financial liberalization, and a host of other competition-boosting changes. The development of the European Union with its opening of internal borders, new regulatory apparatus, and the introduction of the euro has had a huge impact on the competitive landscape, as has the expansion of global and regional trade agreements.

These policy initiatives have had at least as much impact in changing the global business environment as the advent of the Internet. Indeed, some analysts attribute as much as one-quarter of postwar trade growth in the advanced economies to policy reform, primarily in the form of tariff cuts.[24] The integration into the global economy of China, India, and other large markets that had been kept relatively closed by protectionist and autarchic economic policies brought billions of new consumers and producers into world markets. These epochal policy shifts were amplified by other revolutions in technology; together they led to a world in which the old barriers to entry could no longer protect incumbents from the assaults of new challengers.

Disruptive technologies began to appear in almost every industry. Small-scale solar, wind, and biomass energy plants are bringing electricity to vast populations that have never had it, lifting lives, promoting the development of small-scale industry, and challenging the dominance of traditional utilities. Miniaturization and portability have changed manufacturing in marvelous ways—and, in the process, have lowered barriers to entry that once seemed immutable. In some industries it is no longer necessary to build very large facilities to gain an interesting market share. While mini breweries will not displace the likes of Heineken and mini steel mills will not overtake a giant like ArcelorMittal, smaller firms such as these are now able to capture sufficient market share in their geographical areas to introduce more competition in markets where choices have been limited. And as noted above, financing for good business ideas has become more available thanks to fundamental changes in the financial industry. In most countries, access to capital is no longer the insurmountable barrier to the creation or expansion of a new company as it once was.

The ramifications are nearly endless, ranging from staffing requirements to insurance costs to the ability to move operations from site to site quickly. Containerization has streamlined shipping and allowed efficient, reliable intermodal transportation of goods of all kinds. In 2010, the volume of container traffic was more than ten times that in 1980.[25]

Almost all of the technologies that we either see in museums (the steam engine) or take for granted (the radio) represented a disruption in their time. But today's technological revolution is unequalled in scope, touching almost every human activity in the world at dizzying speed.

Looking further, we find that almost every major change in the way we live today, relative to even just a generation ago, spells the erosion of barriers to entry. Indeed, the *More, Mobility,* and *Mentality* revolutions and their degrading effects on the power of incumbents are clearly visible in the business world. The examples are many: The integration of the world's capital markets by wire transfers and electronic banking have changed the way capital is allocated and moved worldwide. Whole new cultures of investment—from venture capital and angel investors to micro-lending— have taken hold and connect money with users near and far. Migration has transported business knowledge and practical experience in ways that regulatory change and investment incentives cannot rival. It has also created world-spanning financing networks across diasporas as well as niche markets for entrepreneurs attuned to community needs.

The combination of these forces is what sets apart today's convulsions of capitalism from those that preceded them. There is more of everything, it moves wider and faster, and people's expectations have dramatically changed. A global market; the largely unfettered movement of vast sums of money, goods, brands, technology, and talent across borders and uses; the rise in value of knowledge and branding relative to natural resources and physical equipment; the emergence of credit in places where it was once scarce or nonexistent—all of these are among the now-familiar forces that have reshaped national economies. In so doing, they have not just changed the playing field on which businesses compete. They have also thrown open competition to new players, ushering in credible and savvy rivals that barriers of regulation, resources, knowledge, capital, or reputation had long kept out. As those barriers have grown porous, the conditions have emerged for fragmentation and displacement of traditional players in the long term, even though short-term trends in some industries and countries seem to point toward concentration.

Of course, this general trend admits exceptions. But a quick look at some of the most daunting past deterrents to competitive entry reveals the thoroughness of the underlying transformation.

Physical Assets

In 2007, News Corporation, controlled by Rupert Murdoch, achieved a long-held goal when it bought a hallowed property, the *Wall Street Journal*, for $5.6 billion. A few weeks earlier, Google had purchased the Internet ad–serving firm DoubleClick (founded in 1996) for $3.1 billion and Microsoft had bought the even less-known ad-serving firm aQuantive (founded in 1997) for $6.3 billion. While the venerable *Journal* with its seasoned journalists, bureaus, presses, portfolio of buildings, and fleet of trucks (all assets owned by the Dow Jones company) sold for a hefty sum, a pair of online advertising firms with just the briefest of histories and virtually no physical assets whatsoever sold for a combined total almost twice as high. An artifact of an overheated, bubble market for Internet properties? Indeed, Microsoft announced a $6.2 billion write-down of its aQuantive purchase in 2012[26]—but that's only part of a continuing story that found another, more recent expression in the 2012 purchase by Facebook (itself an Internet creation of recent vintage and of staggering valuation) of Instagram, a company with a dozen employees and no revenue, for $1 billion. For that money, Facebook could have bought the *New York Times,* Peet's Coffee, Office Depot, or Cooper Tire & Rubber, to name just a few companies with a similar valuation.

The share of physical assets in the value of firms has plummeted across all industries. The material resources they control—factories and offices and all those other physical assets—bear a decreasing relationship to the price that these companies fetch when they offer shares on the market or get acquired. Today, scholars estimate, anywhere from 40 to 90 percent of a company's market value comes from its "intangibles," a category that includes everything from patents and copyrights to the way the company is run and the brand premium and "goodwill" it commands among its customers. Not all of these intangibles can be easily measured—which has not stopped economists from trying.[27]

Of course, some industries are still predicated on very expensive operations, such as drilling for oil or building airliners. And some companies still have an immense advantage due to their access to desired assets: for instance, the Russian mining mammoth Norilsk controls 30 percent of the world's known nickel reserves and 45 percent of its platinum in Siberia. But even within these industries, the increasing importance of intangible assets holds true. Lorenzo Zambrano, the CEO of CEMEX, a Mexican cement company that has broken into the industry's top ranks and become a global player, told me that "knowledge management" was the crucial factor behind his company's ability to compete internationally with larger, more established rivals. Knowledge management, the "information systems, business models, and other 'intangibles' which have to do more with knowledge than with cement," explain the company's success, says Zambrano.[28] CEMEX is another example of a new, innovative player from a country (Mexico) not known as a cradle of globally competitive companies that has upended the traditional power structure of an old, highly concentrated industry.

Scale and Scope

The logic of economies of scale has long been an axiom of the modern corporation: the larger the production capacity, the less it costs per unit to manufacture, and the harder for smaller competitors to match the cost and price structure of bigger incumbents.

This logic has extended to relying on the economies of scope gained in a given business to diversify into another where the skills and core competencies are used as a competitive advantage vis-à-vis existing or potential rivals in the new business. An example is PepsiCo, which owns the Gatorade brand, and by applying its marketing and distribution skills to the sports drink, has made Gatorade one of its top sources of revenue.

Managerially, the logic of scale and scope has extended to keeping any number of administrative and support functions in-house; entrusting them to others would threaten efficiency, accuracy, or trade secrecy.

Today there are still large-scale industries where sunk costs and other factors lead to the emergence of large companies with a propensity for tight central control. (Consider nuclear power, for instance, with its advanced technology, its safety and security issues, and the expenses involved in getting everything right the first time.) But these are exceptions. Many of today's business success stories come not just from industries where economies of scale are less salient but from companies that defied the axiom altogether.

As a result, the principles of economies of scale, scope, and corporate organization are being violated in any number of ways, to the benefit of the business heretics. One example is the small-batch production of mass-market goods. The Spanish apparel company Zara, which began as a cottage industry making bathrobes and only stepped outside of Spain in 1988, exceeded the sales of the American giant The Gap in 2007—and by 2012, in the midst of a global economic slowdown, its sales of almost 18 billion were almost 25 percent higher than The Gap's, having previously left in the dust its European competitor H&M.[29] Operating in a broad-based, consumer segment of the fashion business, Zara (the flagship brand of Inditex, the holding company created by Zara's founder) is famous for producing apparel in small batches rather than farming out big production orders as its competitors do. It also tailors its retail strategy closely to its many overseas markets (more than 5,500 stores in close to eighty countries).[30] Zara needs just two weeks to design and manufacture a new product and get it to stores; the industry average is six months. Moreover Zara launches around ten thousand new designs each year.[31] In Zara's business at least, it turns out that the advantage of speed—being sensitive to changes in customer taste and addressing them immediately—far outweighs the benefits associated with huge shipments of mass-produced goods.[32] Zara is just one more example of a large and growing number of companies whose success is based more on speed than on scale—often in industries where large scale used to be the critical success factor.

Another violation of the axioms of scale and scope lies in the ability to set up a remote operation to perform services that once would not have been contracted out at all, let alone across long distances. Consider the activities encompassed under the rubric of "outsourcing." At first, this simply meant contracting with outside vendors for materials or sending goods away for assembly or some other phase in the manufacturing chain. Then outsourcing spread to services—initially, the lower-skilled services like basic accounting or call centers for fielding basic customer issues. But now, the scope of outsourcing extends to telemedicine—doctors who issue diagnoses or laboratory experts who process tests or accountants in India who file tax returns for US companies.

A constellation of small firms whose geographic location is an increasingly less relevant factor turns out to be capable of delivering specialty and knowledge-intensive services at lower cost but equal quality to the in-house shops painstakingly cultivated by the old industry giants. And no country has a lock on the provision of such services. After opening a research center in India in 1998, IBM in 2010 opened one in São Paulo, Brazil, which has the most Java programmers in the world and the second-most mainframe programmers. In 2011, companies in Latin America and eastern Europe opened fifty-four new outsourcing facilities, versus forty-nine in India.[33]

The fact that the reasons for outsourcing are familiar does not make them any less powerful. Take the widespread availability of instantaneous, efficient communications. E-mail, instant messaging, and voice-over-Internet (VoIP) telephony do not just make our lives more convenient; they also dilute the traditional business advantage that used to reside in office buildings where colleagues saw each other in person, or in meetings arranged through in-house travel agents, inter-office mail, Centrex internal phone networks, Intranets and local area networks, and so on. Each of these once required its own hefty investment, amounting to many deterrents for start-ups or new entrants and discouraging contracting-out of essential functions. That business advantage of incumbents is for all intents and purposes gone.

One term that has vanished from the economics lexicon is *natural monopolies*. This used to designate businesses with economies of scale so intense that it made no sense to have more than one provider. Electric power, fixed-line telephones, and water supply were prime examples. The only question was whether their monopolies should be state-owned or, instead, private and regulated. But now these industries are increasingly contestable, as economists put it: technology allows them to be organized in ways that let multiple providers compete for customers. The result is a dramatic expansion of choice. In Africa, Bharti Airtel, the region's leading mobile-phone service, has partnered with a pay-as-you-go solar micro-utility called SharedSolar to offer airtime and electricity to Bharti's 50 million subscribers on the continent.[34] A consumer in Melbourne, Australia, can select among fifteen power suppliers. Heresy a generation ago; now standard practice.

As scale and scope have lost their competitive edge, other advantages have come to the fore. Speed used to be a benefit of scale. Now speed trumps scale, and equal access by smaller and new competitors to the tools that enable fast customer identification, product and service development, and fulfillment and delivery is helping to turn scale from an advantage to, if anything, a burden.

Branding

One classic way of gaining a comforting market position is by deploying and defending a brand. Branding—with a name, a logo, and all the advertising and associated campaigns that a well-known and alluring name permits—helps to protect a product from becoming an undifferentiated commodity, whereby it matters little or not at all who manufactured or delivered it, and to endow it with the possibility of becoming an emotion and an experience. Famously, an early revolution in branding came in 1947 when the United Fruit Company devised the name *Chiquita* to label its bananas.[35] Previously, a banana was nothing more than a banana, no matter who grew it or where. All that differentiated two bananas was size, ripeness, and taste—factors seemingly independent of the producer. But the invention of a friendly name and logo allowed the creation of advertising stories around them. The success of the brand was so great that in 1990 it became the company's new name.

As this example illustrates, the whole point of branding is to deter competition. The more effective the brand, the more it contributes to the company's market power. And today, the ways to differentiate a product are more abundant than ever. They range from traditional tools such as logos, packaging, TV advertising, and sponsorships to new tools such as purchasing corporate naming rights, ensuring visible product placement, advertising across media platforms, and seeding viral marketing campaigns. The ways to tell a story about a product have proliferated, and they no longer require massive advertising budgets entrusted to the top New York or London agencies. As another illustration of how new and unexpected challengers succeed at eroding the dominance of long-established players, consider the example of a business that did not exist a few years ago—advertising through social media like Facebook, Twitter, and YouTube—and is poised to capture a large and rapidly growing share of the advertising dollars that for years went only to traditional media like TV, radio, newspapers, and magazines. Effective niche marketing—that is, marketing to soccer fans, Russian-speakers, videogame enthusiasts, wheat farmers, vegetarians, and so on—is available at prices that need not scare off new entrants. And a clever site can draw Web surfers to the name and products of a company they had previously never heard of half a world away.

A field has sprung up in economics to measure the component of a company's market value that can be attributed to its brand. In 2011 a study by Interbrand, a leading consulting firm in this area, found that the McDonald's brand—the name, product monikers, restaurant design, and golden arches—accounted for more than 70 percent of the company's valuation. Coca-Cola's brand was worth 51 percent of its value; Disney, IBM, and Intel derived from their brands 68 percent, 39 percent, and 22 percent of their value, respectively.[36]

The 2011 ranking of companies by the monetary value of their brands turned up a mix of old-economy stalwarts and newer technology-led players: Coca-Cola led the pack, followed by IBM, Microsoft, Google, GE, McDonald's, Intel, Nokia, Disney, and Hewlett Packard rounding out the top ten.[37]

Accordingly, it makes sense for companies to invest a huge amount of money in building up their brand. And smart ones are constantly evolving. IBM, for example, has recast itself from a maker of PCs, disk drives, and other computer equipment into a tech visionary that uses brainy consultants and analytics software to solve thorny global problems—an effort captured in its 2012 "Smarter Planets" ad campaign. But even brand advantage has grown slippery. Some of the most dynamic brands whose contribution to the total value of their firms has grown the fastest in recent years are upstarts like Skype (now owned by Microsoft). Just as brands have surpassed physical assets as a component of company value, the brand advantage itself is becoming harder to hold on to as new players establish their name.

Access to Capital

Few obstacles to enterprise are as crippling as the lack of access to capital. Rare are the entrepreneurs who have on hand the money they need to fund an idea or pilot a product. Typically, those with this luxury are large companies with money to invest in research and product development or enough spare cash to spend on a "loss leader." The more limited and restrictive the channels for raising funds, the more closed the market is to new competitors. And around the world, access to capital has been limited indeed, requiring onerous applications to stingy banks for credit that comes with high interest rates. The United States was historically the greatest exception to this pattern, contributing to its leadership role as a hub of innovation for the world.

Today, the United States remains one of the easiest places in the world to obtain credit—but only the tenth easiest. According to the World Bank, the five countries where credit is easiest to get are Malaysia, South Africa, the United Kingdom, Australia, and Bulgaria. This surprising sampler of countries is evidence of large changes not only in the location of capital sources but also in their nature, as whole new sources of credit have opened up and traditionally restricted ones have become more broadly available.

One major trend of the last two decades is the spread of "VCs" and "angels"—types of investors once largely based in the United States—to major new markets in Europe, Russia, Asia, and Latin America. As previously noted in the context of the Mobility revolution, one of the forces behind the international dissemination of venture capital and the private equity models has been the movement of bankers, investors, and engineers who cut their teeth in the United States, then returned home to replicate its investment methods. In Taiwan, the first venture funds set up on the American model were born in 1986–1987, led by managers who had returned from engineering studies and careers in the United States. More recently, venture capital firms have proliferated in India and even China, where they face comparatively more restrictions; returnees and financiers with feet in both worlds—say, in Bangalore and Silicon Valley—

have been central to this growth. Berkeley scholar AnnaLee Saxenian, an expert on this topic, considers "emerging technology areas" like Shanghai and Bangalore to be no longer copies but, rather, extensions of Silicon Valley. She says that the apt analogy for the movement of talent and entrepreneurial ideas and funding is no longer "brain drain" but, as mentioned in Chapter 4, "brain circulation."[38]

Innovation

"I don't know how you could possibly have a high innovation environment at a big pharma. It's hard for me to imagine how you could nurture an environment of innovation and risk taking, and produce champions." That statement came from John Maraganore, the CEO of a small, Cambridge, Mass., pharmaceutical company in 2007.[39] From his point of view, it was merely an expression of the obvious. Compared with decades of corporate standard practice, however, it was nothing less than radical.

Radical, but true. The multibillion-dollar pharmaceutical companies such as Pfizer and Merck may market some of the most innovative and transforming new drugs, but chances are they did not develop them. Rather, small specialized companies—some formed out of biology research departments at universities, some in hothouse innovation regions like Hyderabad, India, also known as "Genome Valley"—synthesize these new drugs. They then sell the drugs—or, in some cases, the company itself—to the large corporate giant.[40] Actually manufacturing the drugs may be the task of another outsourcing company. One example is FerroKin Biosciences, which has seven employees who work from home, and a collection of about sixty vendors and contractors who provide all the pieces of the drug development process. Started in 2007, it attracted $27 million on venture capital, moved its drug from development into Phase II clinical trials,[41] and was purchased in 2012 by Shire Plc, a UK-based specialty biopharmaceutical company.

Companies like Shire, and Big Pharma majors like Merck, retain a distinct advantage over such homegrown efforts in advertising and distribution. It would not be realistic just yet for a small pharmaceutical manufacturer in Hyderabad or Shenzhen to outfit its own army of sales representatives to bring samples (and pens and bags and lunches) to doctors and hospital staff in Florida, Perth, or Dorset.

The change in the locus of major product innovation is nothing short of revolutionary. For years, large companies in every field from pharmaceuticals to automobiles, chemicals, and computers conducted their own research and development in closely guarded and well-funded units that were essential to company pride and prestige. From the 1980s on, however, companies like Cisco and Genzyme gained prominence despite not having these in-house R&D capabilities. What business scholar Henry Chesbrough calls an "era of open innovation" has taken hold.[42] In some industries, Chesbrough points out, open innovation was the norm all along: Hollywood, for instance. Now, chemicals and telephone and aircraft manufacturers have come closer to the Hollywood model, overturning the wisdom of the old titans in these fields. And new power players in their industries like Acer and HTC have gone from offshore innovation shops whose names never appeared on their products to full-fledged competitors with their own brand names.[43]

It makes sense: "We know this kind of product category a lot better than our customers do," the CEO of Taiwan-based smartphone maker HTC told *Businessweek*.[44] A host of other still-obscure companies is primed to follow suit. In pharmaceuticals, outsourcing drug manufacture is a long-standing process, but drug discovery was long closely held. On the other hand, the outsourced drug discovery market has grown faster than overall drug R&D since 2001; it expanded from $2 billion in 2003 to $5.4 billion in 2007 and is estimated to be currently growing at 16 percent per year.[45]

None of this bodes well for large companies. As the business scholar Clayton Christensen argued in a famous book, *The Innovator's Dilemma*, even the very best large companies operate by a set of procedures that make them good at harnessing "sustaining technologies" (the new technologies that help make existing products better) but terrible at identifying and capitalizing on disruptive technologies (the new technologies that usually emerge at the margins of an existing market but eventually stand to remake it). Among classic disruptive technologies, Christensen lists the likes of mobile telephony, micro-turbines, angioplasty, PlayStation, distance learning, Internet Protocols, online retailing, and home patient care. New developments such as these, at first uneconomic relative to standard processes, ended up flummoxing the very same business giants that were always considered impeccable leaders in their field, leading to the eventual demise or decline of onetime paragons such as DEC or Sears Roebuck.[46]

Size and the operating procedures that come with it contributed mightily to these stories, Christensen explains. For instance, the need of large corporations to analyze market opportunities according to established metrics prevented them from grasping the contours of nascent markets emerging around new technologies. Lower short-term profits from these new markets go against the culture of maximizing quarterly share prices. And the dilemma replicates itself with each wave of innovation: as the first companies to exploit disruptive technologies gain and grow, "it becomes progressively more difficult for them to enter the even newer smaller markets destined to become the large ones of the future."[47]

Christensen offers principles for business leaders to confront the innovator's dilemma. But with research and development capital flowing more freely to more locations and less and less up-front investment required in physical plants, scarce inputs, communications, and marketing, the dilemma is poised to relentlessly grow, not decrease, in intensity.

Government Restrictions

Historically, government-imposed restrictions limited the competitive landscape in service of a higher goal: protecting fledgling local firms from cheaper imports, or advancing a particular social agenda by controlling the nature and location of investments.

But that trend crested about thirty years ago, brought down by poor results and a wholesale shift in global policy thinking. Now governments around the world have shed state-owned enterprises, unbundled monopolies, liberalized their trade and investment regimes, and improved the business environment for entrepreneurs in a process that has become well known. One telling indicator: In 1990, the average trade tariff was 23.9 percent worldwide (ranging from 38.6 percent in low-income economies to 9.3 percent in OECD countries). By 2007, it had fallen to 8.8 percent worldwide, ranging from a low 12 percent in low-income countries to a minuscule 2.9 percent among OECD members. Even the economic crash of 2008 failed to reverse the trend.[48] As advanced economies were crashing, it became fashionable to predict that the natural reaction of these governments was to protect jobs and companies behind higher barriers to imports. That did not happen. The same was true about the possibility that countries would impose limits to the entry of foreign investors. That, too, didn't happen.

The truly global movement toward relatively free, open economies with broad capital markets and limited state ownership is one of the well-told tales of the last generation. With it often comes the caution that at some point the pendulum might swing back—if not fully, then to a considerable extent. And indeed, it might appear at first glance that with the global recession of 2008–2009 came a swing back toward more government regulation and control in key industries.

But measures such as bank bailouts in the United States, temporary nationalizations in the UK, and efforts to update regulations in the financial sector to handle the trade of exotic derivatives should not be mistaken for a reversal of the much larger global trend. In fact, according to the World Bank, the pace of pro-business reform worldwide hit a record high in 2008–2009, in the midst of the global slowdown. In that year, the bank counted a record 287 reforms, enacted in 131 countries, that made business easier. In total since 2004, three-quarters of the world's economies have made it easier to start a business. Almost two-thirds have made credit easier to obtain. More than half have made registering property, paying taxes, and trading across borders easier. Add the significant number of countries that have made it easier to go through bankruptcy, enforce contracts, obtain construction permits, and the like, and the overall picture is one of dramatically lightened government obstacles to business activity—thereby exposing once-sheltered companies to competition. All kinds of barriers to the entry of new competitors are falling, and contrary to the common wisdom those imposed by governments are among those declining the most. And staying down.[49]

NEW ENTRANTS AND NEW OPPORTUNITIES

This is not the place to proclaim the death of all old industries, companies, and names. Plenty of evidence indicates the contrary. Many centenarian firms are doing just fine. Some massive and established corporations such as Coca-Cola, Nestlé, ExxonMobil, and Toyota will be here for a good while longer; others perhaps less so. But whereas getting caught up in predicting the prospects of a particular major corporation is a useful exercise for stockholders, it is a distraction from the big story taking place all around us—namely, the advent of a whole parade of new competitors. Following are a few.

The New Southern Multinationals

Meet Alejandro Ramirez, a young entrepreneur from Morelia, Mexico, who is one of the leading players in the Cineplex business—in India.

India is famously the country with the world's largest film industry, at least when measured by the number of commercial movies made each year. Where India lags significantly, however, is in modern multiplex cinemas that offer the country's exploding middle class domestic and foreign films on high-quality screens. There are only about a thousand modern film screens in this country of over 1.2 billion people. Ramirez's company, Cinepolis, will fill this gap by adding five hundred more screens in the next few years. Cinepolis, which began as a one-screen movie house in the 1940s in a provincial Michoacán state, has grown to become the largest multiplex company in Mexico and across Central America.[50]

Not only is Cinepolis the most aggressive new player in Indian movie houses; it is the first foreign investor to enter that sector in India. "How did it occur to you to diversify to the Indian market?" I asked Ramirez. "It wasn't my idea," he replied. "Two students at Stanford's business school had to prepare a business plan for one of their courses and came up with this opportunity and brought it to me. We worked together, refined it, got the capital, and were on our way. Almost immediately we discovered that the potential was even larger than we had anticipated."[51]

Cinepolis is just one of a growing number of players from countries like Mexico, India, Brazil, South Africa, and Turkey in other developing economies—that is, in sectors that previously were undeveloped, limited to domestic investment, or controlled by larger, Western-based multinationals. South-South cooperation was a dream of the Third Worldist movement of the 1970s, whereby economies of the developing world would help empower one another through direct trade, investment, and aid that bypassed the "North." It was a state-led, socialist dream, and the kind of investment now flourishing is quite different from what it imagined. Nevertheless, South-South investment is today one of the shaping trends of global business.[52] United Nations data show that outward foreign direct investment (OFDI) from developing and transition economies began to outpace OFDI from rich countries in 2003.

Twenty of the fifty-four bilateral investment treaties signed in 2010 were between developing countries, and they increased further in importance, both as recipients of FDI and as outward investors. Foreign direct investment outflows from developing countries reached an unprecedented 29 percent of total direct investment flows in 2010, and this strong growth continued in 2011 and 2012 despite global economic woes.[53]

The number of developing-country firms in the league tables of the world's largest companies is continually growing. And researchers from the World Bank and OECD have argued that official statistics underestimate the scale of OFDI from developing countries, in part because it is a new and often unanticipated reporting category, and in part because of the volume of unreported capital flight.[54]

Among the beneficiaries of this trend are a host of companies, in sectors ranging from construction and telecommunications to textiles and oil, that are largely unknown in Europe or North America but increasingly recognized brands in the rest of the world. In mobile phones, for instance, India's Bharti Airtel and Reliance, South Africa's MTN, Egypt's Orascom, and United Arab Emirates' Etisalat all rank within the world's top fifteen. Others are less known yet significant in their respective industries: for instance, Sri Lankan textile manufacturers have spread operations elsewhere in South Asia and the Indian Ocean, and Turkish multisector conglomerates have become major players in Russia, the Balkans, and the Middle East. (Indeed, Turkish companies have been big beneficiaries of the international effort to rebuild and develop Afghanistan's infrastructure, including construction of the US Embassy in Kabul.) Increasingly, firms such as these have been taking the jump away from their regional comfort zone, where there are language or cultural commonalities, to invest (like Cinepolis) when they detect opportunity far from their home base. Antoine van Agtmael, who coined the term *emerging markets,* told me that he feels confident that by 2030 firms based in emerging markets will outnumber those in today's advanced economies.[55]

The South Comes North

A related phenomenon is the rise of acquisitions of major North American and European firms by companies based in developing and transition economies, creating a new breed of global multinational that has either its headquarters or its corporate roots in what was until recently a closed-off, state-heavy economic system. India, Mexico, Brazil, South Africa, and China are among the major provenances of these companies. A good example is the aforementioned Mexican cement giant CEMEX, which operates in nearly forty countries. CEMEX's internationalization catapulted it to nearly top place in the world building-materials market (in a dogfight with French-based Lafarge) and raised the American share of its business to 41 percent, compared to only 24 percent in Mexico. Although CEMEX had to retrench as the global economy sputtered, it is still a major global player in many developed countries in a field that once was the exclusive province of rich-country companies.[56] Examples also include the parent firms of the two largest players in the American beer industry. Anheuser-Busch is controlled by Belgian-based InBev (itself formed when Brazil's Ambev brewer sought to expand overseas) and largely led by Brazilian management. Meanwhile, the custodian of the rival beer brand to Budweiser is SABMiller, formed when South African Breweries bought Miller Brewing Company in 2002, on the heels of successful acquisitions in markets like the Czech Republic, Romania, El Salvador, Honduras, and Zambia. Brazil's Vale (formerly known by the clunky name Companhia Vale do Rio Doce) became the world's second-largest mining company in 2007 after acquiring a Canadian rival, Inco. And the world's largest steel company, ArcelorMittal, resulted from an acquisition spree by Indian billionaire Lakshmi Mittal. His Mittal Steel had cracked the Fortune Global 500 only in 2005.[57]

The unwieldy compound names of ArcelorMittal and Anheuser-Busch InBev show that these stories are as much about mergers and acquisitions as they are about the dynamism of new entrants from unlikely places. While these mergers will surely bring about concentration and new oligopolies with substantial market power, we should remember that they often involve companies that only a decade ago were a fraction of the size of the companies they were able to take over. The same could happen to them: a company based in an improbable location and flying completely under the radar may be the one taking over these new giant companies. That was the story of the last decade, and the forces propelling this trend are only becoming stronger.

Once-parochial companies in small, protected markets could not have leveraged up to take control of top firms in major global industries were it not for the drastic fall in entry barriers precipitated by the opening of financial markets, the spread of business education and culture, access to capital, transparent and more easily available corporate data, deregulation, trade and investment openings, growth, mobility, globalization, new technologies, and other forces discussed here. The internationalization of companies based in poor countries is a powerful example of the More, Mobility and Mentality revolutions at work.

The Scattering of Exchanges

Among the victims of hyper-competition in the global business landscape are the markets themselves—that is, the stock exchanges where most shares are traded and that media, politicians, and the public monitor for clues about the health of the overall economy. Hallowed markets such as the New York Stock Exchange and the London Stock Exchange have rapidly lost ground to alternative marketplaces. In the US market, the traditional powerhouses NYSE (founded in 1792) and NASDAQ (founded in 1971) now barely command half the volume of trades on the public exchanges; as of 2012, the electronic exchanges Direct Edge (founded in 1998) and BATS Exchange (founded in 2005) account for about 9 and 10 percent, respectively, while dozens of other exchanges share the rest. Mushrooming exchanges and constant trading by automatic computer algorithms have contributed to market volatility, accounting for drastic falls and instant recoveries in the share price of particular firms.

The NYSE is not the only major bourse to be losing ground to new rivals; the same is true of the London Stock Exchange, Deutsche Börse, and other old-fashioned stock exchanges. As it is, Kansas-based upstart BATS (which stands for Better Alternative Trading System) runs more trading volume than any exchange other than NYSE or NASDAQ, surpassing Tokyo, London, Shanghai, Paris, and all the rest. One indicator of the struggle facing old exchanges is the loss of value of their own shares. Shares in NXSE Euronext (NYX ticker) plummeted from peaks of $108 in 2006 to about $22 in 2012. Revenues have fallen as well: in 2009, revenues from trading operations by the London bourse operator, London Stock Exchange Group Plc, fell by more than one-third.[58]

Rival exchanges are only one aspect of the new scattered financial markets. Another is the advent of "dark pools" exchanges, which began informally among institutions that seek to trade anonymously (without making orders, prices, or volumes known to the public) to avoid revealing their strategies. Dark pools go against the principle that markets should be transparent in order to achieve efficient outcomes; they are also fingered as a major cause of volatility and distortions in share prices, as well as a potentially unfair advantage for their participants. How to deal with dark pools is a matter of debate for regulators around the world, and views are split as to just how dangerous they are for the global financial system. What is clear is that they are proliferating.[59] The Securities and Exchange Commission estimated that the number of active dark pools in the US market shot up from ten in 2002 to more than thirty in 2012. In January of the latter year, according to *Bloomberg News,* dark pools handled almost 14 percent of US equity trading.[60] An earlier estimate by the SEC said that dark pools accounted for more than 7 percent of total trade volume on US exchanges—a relatively small fraction, perhaps, but enough to have large ripple effects.[61]

The Triumph of Private Equity and Hedge Funds

The financial crisis and global market setbacks of 2008–2009 were assumed by many to have brought to an end the dominance of private equity funds and hedge funds in the markets. Over the previous decade, these little-known and often small operations gained control of enormous companies by means of leveraged buyouts, aggressive trading, and shareholder activism. After recovering from the popping of the Internet bubble at the start of the decade, private equity firms led successive record buyouts for the rest of the decade, culminating in the $45 billion purchase of the energy company TXU in 2007 by Kohlberg Kravis Roberts (KKR) and Texas Pacific Group (TPG).

MEANWHILE, HEDGE FUNDS PROLIFERATED, GOING FROM THREE thousand funds to ten thousand funds between 1998 and 2008; by 2011, the hundred largest had $1.2 trillion in assets under management.[62] In 2012, hedge funds took part in half of US bond trading, 40 percent of equities trading, and 80 percent of trading in distressed debt. In 2011, *Bloomberg Markets'* twenty largest hedge funds, led by Bridgewater Associates with $77.6 billion, had almost $600 billion in assets.[63] The expansion of hedge funds was paralleled, albeit at a smaller scale, in Europe and Asia.

Lines began to blur as hedge funds took ownership stakes in more and more companies, acting like private equity firms while also displacing traditional banks. By 2007, the share of the primary leveraged finance market (i.e., trading in loans) handled by traditional banks slipped below 50 percent for the first time; it had been 90 percent as recently as 2000. In response, banks were purchasing shares in hedge funds themselves, thereby only accelerating the blurring of roles.

Hedge funds became the straw stirring the drink in terms of market activity and pressure on boards and management. In the United States, at a time when they held 5 percent of assets under management, they were also involved in 30 percent of trading activity. They exerted immense pressure on corporations without regard for brand and history, as when a fund (incongruously) called the Children's Investment Fund pushed so hard for the Dutch bank ABN AMRO to be sold or broken up that it had to accept being sold to British bank Barclays. Vast amounts of money came and went in the form of massive bets, in the spirit of the most famous bet of all—when George Soros bet $10 billion against the British pound in 1992, collecting a billion-dollar profit. In 2006, a thirty-year-old trader for a fund called Amaranth lost a cool $6 billion on a natural-gas bet gone wrong. Winners in the industry walked away with gargantuan pay: in 2006, the top twenty-five hedge fund managers together reportedly earned the equivalent of the GDP of Jordan. Yet chances are that most of these people were barely known even to their neighbors in the tony Connecticut suburbs of Greenwich and Westport where hedge fund managers are known to roost.

In 2008, hedge funds lost an estimated 18 percent of their value. Yet there were plenty of exceptions, including George Soros, along with the fund run by the then not-yet-notorious figure John Paulson, who made billions betting against troubled subprime mortgage instruments, and a cohort of other obscure people who made hundreds of millions of dollars in the midst of a market bust.[64] Perhaps not surprisingly, the market recovery amid the bailouts of 2009 proved profitable to hedge funds, although industry observers noted that a shake-out was under way. In fact, one argument in defense of the lightly regulated sector is that it produces winners and losers so definitively and efficiently that it acts as a kind of constant corrective helping to bring stability to the markets; according to Sebastian Mallaby, author of *More Money Than God* (a best seller on hedge funds), they "do not so much create risk as absorb it."[65]

But hedge funds have also fallen under the regulatory gun and now face more constraints. In 2011 it was reported that due to new financial regulations, George Soros decided to close his funds to investors and would thereafter concentrate exclusively on managing his own funds. Volatile markets can also inflict enormous losses on these risky vehicles. John Paulson's fund suffered a significant setback when its market bets didn't pan out. (It lost $9.6 billion in 2011, the biggest-ever loss by a hedge fund.)[66] At the same time, however, other hedge funds with names, approaches, locations, and technologies that are as surprising as they are innovative took their place as the biggest profit-making machines in the world. Hedge fund colossus Bridgewater, for example, made $13.8 billion for its investors that year.[67]

ONE LESSON THAT SEEMS CLEAR IS THAT SPECIFIC FUNDS MAY COME and go, and their manager's compensation may veer from merely large to the enormous and back, but the proliferation of these small, obscure shops with a huge capacity to affect markets and prices is bound to continue. In this new financial world, individual brainiacs armed with computer algorithms are frequently outwitting and outmaneuvering huge banks held back by cumbersome rules, complex internal practices, and slower-moving hierarchies.

Hedge funds are to traditional power in financial markets what Somali pirates are to the power held by the world's most advanced navies.

IN SUM, NEW ENTRANTS SUCH AS HEDGE FUNDS, NEW STOCK EXCHANGES, dark pools, and previously unknown start-ups that suddenly upend an entire industry are harbingers of things to come: more volatility, more fragmentation, more competition, and more micropowers able to constrain the possibilities of the megaplayers.

Indeed, neither the public clamor about the dislocations created by economic globalization nor the massive shocks produced by the financial crisis of 2008 and the ensuing Great Recession have derailed the process of international economic integration. It continues largely unabated, and the predictions of a protectionist surge prompted by the attempts of countries to fence in their economies to protect jobs have been proven wrong. International trade and investment flows continue to grow and to feed the forces that constrain the power of traditional business players.

WHAT DOES ALL THIS MEAN?

One of the paradoxes of our era is that, at the same time that corporations have become larger, more ubiquitous, and more politically influential, they have also become more exposed to risks that not only can hurt their sales, profits, and reputation but in, some cases, may even put them out of business. The list of companies that seemed untouchable by competitors or governments, and whose permanence was taken for granted but are no longer around, is long and continues to grow. The same is true for titans of banking and industry whose power and invulnerability proved to be far more fleeting than anyone—including them—had expected.

Even the large corporations that continue to thrive and are highly unlikely to be driven out of business by market forces face a more constrained set of options. For example, ExxonMobil, Sony, Carrefour, and JPMorgan-Chase still have immense power and autonomy, but their leaders are more constrained today than they were in earlier periods. They cannot exert their huge power with the same liberty enjoyed by their predecessors—and the consequences of misusing it are more immediate and dire than in the past.

As we saw in this chapter, corporate power isn't what it used to be.

CHAPTER NINE

HYPER-COMPETITION FOR
YOUR SOUL, HEART, AND BRAIN

WE NATURALLY LOOK FOR EVIDENCE OF SHIFTS IN POWER IN THOSE areas where its impact is most dramatic and brutal: on life and death, war and peace, the control of governments and the rise and decline of enterprises. And in each of these areas, we have seen that the decay of the power of the megaplayers is opening new paths for small and hitherto marginal actors, some of whom may gain access to capabilities that can limit the options of the once powerful.

But power dwells also in the church or religious group that collects the tithes and regiments the life choices of its adherents; in the union that gathers workers' dues and negotiates on their behalf for better wages and labor conditions; in the charity that brings private funds to bear on social works at home and fighting poverty abroad. Power also rests in the university whose research labs produce the most important scientific findings and innovations or whose graduates land the most prestigious jobs; in museums and galleries and music record labels; in symphony orchestras, book publishers, and movie production houses. And, of course, there is power in the media, the channels and filters we turn to for information, and whom we trust to be honest and useful, or to pull others toward our own point of view.

The stakes vary. Most, fortunately, fall short of life and death. Harvard versus Yale resembles Manchester United versus Chelsea more than it does, say, the US military versus the Chinese People's Liberation Army or Al Qaeda. As purely economic enterprises, the fates of the BBC, the *New York Times, El País,* or other prestige outlets affect far fewer workers and livelihoods than does, say, the profit and loss of Monsanto or WalMart, even if their influence on debate and policy matters acutely to media circles and helps to keep our democracies healthy. On the other hand, the distribution of power in the philanthropic world among foundations and donors has intense and immediate effects on billions of people near and far, determining which projects are funded (and how) and which emergencies are deemed most urgent. The importance of workers' ability to organize themselves to improve their economic fortunes needs no explanation. And the power of organized religion on other spheres of life and the intensity of rivalries between faiths is likewise obvious: the evidence—all too often bloody—scars history.

That is why our panorama of the great change taking place in the workings of power today needs to extend beyond business, politics, and war. The aim is not to be exhaustive. We will, however, examine what has happened to the power of long-dominant organizations in four areas that directly affect a large proportion of humanity: religion, labor, philanthropy, and media.

RELIGION: THE NINE BILLION NAMES OF GOD

"They are stealing our sheep." So one Jesuit described the tide of change sweeping Christianity in Latin America, long a Catholic bastion.[1] Who are "they"? The new evangelical, Pentecostalist, and charismatic Protestant churches that have sprouted across the region in the last thirty years— much as they have in the United States, Africa, and elsewhere—are giving the Catholic Church fits, and swiftly emptying its pews. A 2005 survey found that the proportion of Latin Americans who consider themselves Catholic dropped from 80 percent to 71 percent in the decade between 1995 and 2005. Worse still for the Church, only 40 percent said they actually practice their faith, a dramatic drop in a continent where the Catholic Church was dominant for centuries. In Brazil, for example, half a million Catholics leave the church each year. Whereas in 2000 the Catholic population represented 73.6 percent of Brazil's population, by 2010 that percentage had decreased to under two-thirds, or 64.6 percent. Only two-thirds of Colombians now call themselves Catholic, one-third of Guatemalans have left the Catholic Church since the 1980s—and the statistics go on.[2]

In La Paz, the capital of Bolivia, some former Catholics told reporters they felt "abandoned" by the Church. "It didn't really exist for me," one said. Now, they belong to the New Pact Power of God Church, a charismatic ministry where ten thousand people pray in multiple shifts every Sunday.

Scenes like this are common across Latin America. But the sheep have not been stolen. The sheep aren't sheep anymore: they are consumers, and they have found a more attractive product in the market for salvation.[3]

The roots of the modern evangelical movement trace back to an early-twentieth-century African-American ministry called Azusa, which was based on concepts drawn from the Bible story of the Pentecost. The movement that arose, Pentecostalism, gathers a broad range of larger denominations and independent local churches that share a few core concepts about individual deliverance (through being born again) and elements of worship such as speaking in tongues. But the autonomous churches that have garnered millions of adherents to become a social and political force in the United States, Brazil, Nigeria, and many other countries are not all Pentecostal; they include other kinds of evangelical and "charismatic" groups, each with a typically self-proclaimed prophet or apostle, but quickly forming their own chapters and hierarchies. Many preach the so-called prosperity gospel, which holds that God smiles on the accumulation of wealth in this life and will reward material donations to the church with prosperity and miracles. Indeed, in a recent Pew survey of religious attitudes in the United States, where 50 of the largest 260 churches are now prosperity based, 73 percent of all religious Latinos agreed with the statement "God will grant financial success to all believers who have enough faith."[4]

The rise of Pentecostal and charismatic Christian churches, and not just in Catholic or mainline Protestant–dominated countries, has been staggering. Estimates vary, partly because of the fluidity of terms and boundaries, but the impact is still clear. A Pew survey in 2006 estimated the proportion of "renewalists"—both Pentecostals and charismatics—to be 11 percent in South Korea, 23 percent in the United States, 26 percent in Nigeria, 30 percent in Chile, 34 percent in South Africa, 44 percent in the Philippines, 49 percent in Brazil, 56 percent in Kenya, and 60 percent in Guatemala.[5] Even in "non-Christian" India, renewalists make up 5 percent of the population; put another way, there are well over 50 million Pentecostals and charismatics in India, and some estimates claim that China has at least twice as many. Many renewalist churches are completely local, often not more than a storefront congregation of the kind familiar in black and immigrant neighborhoods of North American cities. Others have sprouted major organizations with hundreds of chapters and an international presence.

Though Pentecostalism first arose in the United States, historic American missions like the Assemblies of God are no longer the fastest to spread around the world. The big exporting countries in the redemption business today are Brazil and Nigeria. In Brazil, the Universal Church of the Kingdom of God, founded in Rio de Janeiro by pastor Edir Macedo in 1977, now has five thousand chapters. It spread to the United States in 1986 and has a presence in almost every country. Its latest plan, which received authorization from the Brazilian government, is to build a ten-thousand-person megachurch in São Paulo that will be the equivalent of eighteen stories high, modeled on Solomon's Temple. "We will spend tons of money, without a doubt," Macedo said.[6]

Another large Brazilian denomination, the Reborn in Christ Church, was founded in 1986 by a husband-and-wife team known as Apostle Estevam and Bishop Sonia; it owns newspapers, radio stations, and a TV channel. In 2005, it sponsored a new political party, the Brazilian Republican Party, which joined a coalition with President Lula da Silva's Workers Party in the 2006 elections. Yet another Brazilian church grew out of the epiphany of a surfer and former drug addict named Rinaldo Pereira. In the span of ten years, his Bola de Neve church formed more than one hundred chapters with up to several thousand members each. The church name means "snowball"—an apt title these days for a grassroots evangelical ministry.[7]

In Nigeria, meanwhile, the Redeemed Christian Church of God, founded in Lagos in 1952 but whose spread truly began in the early 1980s, operates in one hundred countries. Its pinnacle annual prayer meeting at a revival camp along the Lagos-Ibadan expressway gathers up to a million devotees. In the United States, it claims about three hundred parishes with fifteen thousand members and growing.

In the wake of these new leaders in the transnational market for souls, many other churches are spreading—divine fruits of the More, Mobility, and Mentality revolutions.[8] In fact, the roughly 2.2 billion Christians around the world are so dispersed that, as a recent Pew report put it, "no single continent or region can indisputably claim to be the center of global Christianity."[9] The share of the Christians in the population of sub-Saharan Africa, for example, has risen from 9 percent in 1910 to 63 percent a century later.[10] Talk about the Mobility revolution: in 2010, Christians made up almost half of the world's 214 million migrants, opening new possibilities for the expansion of the faith and spreading it further beyond the reach of any centralized denominational authority.[11]

As I have argued when discussing the ascent of the micropowers in previous chapters, the point is not that these new challengers will dislodge the megaplayers. The point is that they will deny them options that in the past the big players could take for granted. The new charismatic churches, for example, will not dislodge the Vatican or the Anglican Church. But they will narrow the range of possibilities and reduce the power of these large institutions.

The success of the new denominations inevitably comes to the detriment of mainline Protestant groups like the Anglicans and Lutherans, and most of all, the Catholic Church. Until a few decades ago, the Vatican's principal problems were the gradual secularization of Europe and the aging population of priests. These were serious issues, and the Church sought to modernize in response, notably through the decisions of the Vatican II council—for instance, by requiring Mass to be given in local languages rather than in Latin. But nothing prepared the Vatican for the competitive challenge of the Pentecostal and charismatic churches, not just at the far limits of its reach but in places like Latin America long considered the faith's backyard. Already in the 1970s and 1980s, the Church faced internal dissent with the emergence of liberation theology in Brazil and elsewhere in the continent. The threat of liberation theology has diminished, particularly with the spread of democracy in the region.[12] But the inroads of the new denominations and the greater intensity of renewalist religious practice (more people attending longer services and adapting more aspects of their life to the church's requirements) are chipping away at the influence of the once overwhelmingly dominant Catholicism. "If the church doesn't make changes to its centralized structures and authoritarian messages, it will suffer a genuine collapse in Latin America within roughly fifteen years," in the estimate of Elio Masferrer, the chairman of the Latin American Religious Studies Association.[13]

Scholars and analysts were slow to take in the scale of the trend, perhaps because they found it easy to dismiss Pentecostal worship as odd or exotic. Now, however, it is unavoidable, as evangelical groups have grown influential in politics (fielding candidates for office in countries like Brazil) and the media (launching radio and television networks in many countries). Neither the Catholic Church nor the mainline Protestant denominations have found a way either to halt the spread of these small and fast rivals or to stanch the defection of their own adherents, with all its implications for revenue and relevance.

Why? In part, that failure has to do with doctrine, and the ability of the evangelical churches to offer a message based on wealth and spectacular services—with their faith healings and deliverances—that contrast with

Catholicism's austere and repetitive rituals. But the core advantage, the one that makes the rest possible, is organizational. The changes in the composition and practice of Christianity are as drastic a case of the decay of power, away from large hierarchical and centralized structures and in favor of a constellation of small and nimble autonomous players, as the world has known.

The essence of the Pentecostal and evangelical advantage lies in the ability of these churches to spring up without regard to any preexisting hierarchy. There are no lessons to receive, instructions to await, or ordinations to earn from the Vatican or the Archbishop of Canterbury or any other central leadership. In the classic case, unless they have emerged from an already existing evangelical church, a pastor simply appoints himself or herself (while Catholicism still forbids women priests, there are any number of Charismatic women apostles, bishops, and prophetesses) and puts out his or her shingle. In this respect, the church resembles nothing so much as a small business launched in a competitive marketplace without funding from a central source; it must succeed on the basis of the members it draws, the services it provides them, and the tithes and collection revenue they can be persuaded to give.[14] As John L. Allen, a reporter covering the Vatican and author of *The Future Church,* has observed: "Barriers to market entry in Pentecostalism are notoriously low. Any Pentecostal who feels dissatisfied with the offerings of the local church is free to move on to another, even to start his or her own church in a basement or garage."[15]

The churches that succeed are the ones that adapt to local circumstances in the manner of a well-imagined niche business, in every respect from the doctrine of their teachings to the location and timing of worship, amenities and community services such as child care or job-finding assistance or support groups of all kinds, and business and media initiatives. Immigrants, indigenous groups like the Mayans in Guatemala, or other communities with needs that political leaders and mainstream churches have neglected are perfect targets for these new churches. In many Latin American countries, the historic ties of Catholic bishops with the political elite rendered them less sensitive to the conditions of the poor and especially of indigenous people.[16] The rigid hierarchy of the church and the need for doctrinal sanction from the Vatican prevented them from adjusting, and left room for the evangelical churches to outflank them. An explicit message about wealth and prosperity and an emphasis on individual actions and redemption fit settings where poverty and exclusion have been the norm. But the evangelical churches can also minister with more sensitivity to the communities where they operate, react in real time to economic and political events, and adopt the styles and sounds of local culture. As one evangelical pastor in Potosí, Bolivia, put it: "Our churches are more open, the songs use local rhythms, and I visit my people every day."[17]

Meanwhile, the barriers that previously held small upstart churches from having an impact beyond, say, their neighborhood or ethnic community have completely collapsed. The communications revolution and the rise of private media have ended the advantage of large organized churches in spreading the message, giving any self-declared pastor the ability to reach television viewers, radio listeners, or Web surfers and sending blessings beyond borders and collecting money in return. With more access to global media platforms has come the spread of the model first honed by American televangelists. Heightened migration and travel have increased the reach of the more flexible renewalist churches and given them a potential foothold demographic in many countries from which to grow. And the more adherents these faiths gain, the less weight there is to the moral opprobrium of exclusion or excommunication from the Catholic Church. The cost of heresy is down.[18]

Other major religions such as Islam and Hinduism seem less vulnerable to the rise of charismatic Christianity, probably for deep-seated cultural reasons. But to one degree or another, Islam, Hinduism, Judaism, Taoism, Shintoism, and others are also much less centralized and hierarchical than the Catholic or mainline Protestant churches. The Grand Rabbi of Israel, the Grand Mufti of Cairo, and the high priest of a major Hindu temple carry a certain moral weight and may enjoy decision-making authority in their country or region, but they have rival leaders within their own faith who can offer different rulings on any matter. Within Islam, for instance, political factors make certain tendencies (Sunni versus Shia, or Wahhabi versus more liberal interpretations) dominant in different Muslim countries, yet influential scholars offer competing visions of the faith to adherents around the world via often-sophisticated media operations. Egypt-born, Qatar-based Imam Yusef al-Qaradawi, for instance, reaches an estimated 60 million viewers through his television program on Al Jazeera.[19] Hinduism, meanwhile, has always been highly decentralized, with numerous sub-traditions, sects, and faith communities and no single governing authority. On a smaller scale, Indian religious exports from the Vedanta Society to the Hare Krishnas via Amma, Sai Baba, Osho, and the Maharishi share some of the organizational advantage of the Pentecostal groups, and have exploited it with similar success.

LABOR: NEW UNIONS AND NONUNIONS

Just as the Catholic Church confronts a growing challenge to its power from upstart denominations that have proved more nimble and flexible in meeting the needs of today's salvation seekers, so, too, have established unions struggled to maintain their clout in the face of efforts by new unions to fulfill the needs of workers shaped by the More, Mobility, and Mentality revolutions. "Are American unions history?" asked a headline in the opinion pages of the *Washington Post* in 2012. Harold Meyerson—a self-described democratic socialist and a pro-labor journalist—goes on to remind his readers that "in the U.S. private sector unionization has fallen below 7 percent from a post–World War II high of roughly 40 percent."[20] It is clear that the power of the US labor movement has been waning, and surely the drop in its membership is a driver of this decline. But declining membership is not the only reason. The power of traditional labor organizations has also decayed as a result of forces that, as discussed in these pages, affect all traditionally powerful actors. In fact, while the sway of the labor movement is broadly declining, megaplayers like the AFL-CIO have been more affected than some of the new, nontraditional rivals that have appeared in this field, such as the Service Employees International Union (SEIU). Here, too, we see that the barriers that used to protect the incumbents from the competition of their rivals have become easier to penetrate, circumvent, or overwhelm.

THE HISTORY OF UNIONS PARALLELS THE HISTORY OF MODERN enterprise. One could argue that trade unions in Europe have even deeper roots in the professional associations and guilds that stretched back into the Middle Ages. But the advent of factory-scale industry in the nineteenth century was almost immediately accompanied by the emergence of organizations meant to improve conditions and advance the rights of industrial workers. Although unions formed in Britain and France earlier in the century, most of the forerunners of the unions in the oldest industrial nations were founded in the second half of the nineteenth century. And although the structure of the union movement varies from country to country—for instance, between those where unions are mostly specific to certain companies and those where unions cover entire industrial sectors or multiple sectors—confederations intended to assemble all of these disparate parts and give them a strong, centralized, unified voice have been around since the late nineteenth century. The organization that became

Britain's Trades Union Congress (TUC) was founded in 1866. France legalized unions in 1884 and its largest federation, the CGT, was founded eleven years later. In the United States, an organization called the Knights of Labor was an embryonic national federation in the 1870s and 1880s; one of its offshoots, the American Federation of Labor, founded in 1886, would centralize the union movement for several decades.

Even among just these three countries, the histories diverge in the twentieth century: although the TUC has remained the umbrella group for virtually all labor unions in England to this day, France's CGT saw the rise of rival national federations (CFDT, FO) with less radical political orientations; in the United States, the Confederation of Industrial Organizations (CIO) took a more radical line until it merged with the AFL in 1955, forming the AFL-CIO, which would serve as the umbrella for union labor in America for half a century. For the last several decades in the industrialized world—where unions have the most penetration, recognition, and history—the typical set-up has consisted of one or several (two to four) national confederations, assembling several dozen major branches (either components of the national organization or independent but affiliated unions) usually organized by industry. Germany, for instance, has one major national confederation; Spain has two; Italy has three; Russia, where unions were once regimented components of the Soviet communist system, has four.

But as much as unions get credit for major breakthroughs in working life, at least in rich countries ("the folks who brought you the weekend," as the American sticker slogan says), the story of the great trade unions for several decades now has been one of decline. The numbers vary, and not every comparison is valid given the differences in structures from country to country. Still, both union density (the percentage of workers who are members of unions) and bargaining coverage (the percentage of workers covered by a collective bargaining agreement, whether they themselves are union members or not) have been declining in most OECD countries, in some cases steeply. In the United States, union density has plummeted from 36 percent after World War II to just 12 percent today. In the private sector, the drop has been even sharper, from about one-third half a century ago to less than 8 percent now. Union density in the OECD countries varies from 5.8 percent in Turkey to 68.3 percent in Sweden (according to 2008 data), but in almost every case the numbers have been at best stagnant, and more often declining, in a trend that has held in much of Europe for several decades.

The last period of strong growth of union membership across many
industrial countries was in the 1970s.[21] Even as of 1981, the AFL-CIO could
muster 250,000 workers to come to Washington to protest President Ronald
Reagan's firing of air traffic controllers in a Solidarity Day held that September. Fast-forward three decades, to a protest held at the National Mall in
2010, and the labor unions could pull together only a small fraction of that
number, with turnout lower than at Glenn Beck's Tea Party rally five weeks
earlier.[22] And in 2012 another important defeat confirmed the waning
power of the US labor movement as, despite a massive effort, unions failed
to win a recall election against Governor Scott Walker of Wisconsin.

The causes of this general decline include familiar factors: globalization and technological innovation have made it easier for employers to
move jobs to other countries or to eliminate them altogether, changing the
balance of power in favor of employers. Though the point of collective
bargaining might have been precisely to protect workers from this situation, the forces that gathered in favor of flexible and global labor markets,
often supported by governments ideologically committed to market-
oriented reforms, usually proved too strong. Moreover, unionization historically thrived in industries and occupations that rely on unskilled labor,
which is easier to organize. As automation replaced unskilled laborers in
various heavy industries, or those jobs went overseas where unskilled
labor was less costly, unions needed to move into new sectors such as services that needed fresh organizing. Few did. In many places, tales of corruption and complacency among unions were also part of the mix.

But changes in the attraction and effectiveness of unions have an organizational component as well. The structure of unions, from the specialization of individual unions or locals by company and industry sector up
to the centralized national federations, logically mirrored the structure of
dominant firms whose workers were to be unionized and represented.
Unions evolved to take on the large, hierarchical, modern corporations
that anchored capitalist business for most of the twentieth century before
globalization and flexibility pushed those firms to start downsizing, outsourcing, and moving to part-time and contract labor.

A major innovation area for unions in the last twenty years has been to
find ways to pressure companies whose operations span more and more
countries, as well as to protect worker pay scales at home by fighting for
more stringent labor standards in other countries. But occasional victories
in these areas only soften the edges of the general pattern. In the United
States, the one area where unions have gained ground in the last few de-

cades has been the public sector (teachers' unions, for example, or unions of municipal and county workers)—precisely the fields where the labor market has changed the least, and where employers still rely on centralization and hierarchy.

Where workers have won victories in recent years, the organizations they have used to deliver the win have been traditional unions that have radically rethought their structure and methods, new unions that have formed to bypass the old structures, and sometimes vehicles that are not unions at all.

Between 1996 and 2010, the Service Employees International Union (SEIU) more than doubled its ranks, to 2.1 million members. And it did that by riding the wave of the More, Mobility, and Mentality revolutions. Many of its members, for example, labored in health care, the growing field responsible for more people living longer, healthier lives. Many of its members were also recent immigrants, beneficiaries of the trends in global mobility that were reshaping markets and workplaces. And like their predecessors in factories and warehouses, all of them were driven by an aspiration to better themselves and achieve the gains that first lured them to the United States. Led by Andy Stern, recognized as an innovator not just in American labor but also in politics and social mobilization,[23] the union secured major victories with collective bargaining deals for some of the most vulnerable workers in the United States, such as janitors and child-care workers, many of whom work multiple part-time jobs and do not speak good English.[24] Historically, these groups had been neglected by a union movement focused on factories and traditional industries. To organize them required not just a bright idea on the part of Stern and his team but also new tools, including alliances outside the labor movement with community and immigrant groups, and a deeper involvement in elections than simply raising money and turning out the vote on election day for local Democratic Party candidates. Stern's negotiating tactics with business also broke from traditional methods. For instance, he pioneered an arrangement whereby collective bargaining for a particular workplace would kick in only after a majority of the market in question was unionized, thus sparing employers from the competitive disadvantage of being the first or only ones to sign a union contract.

The SEIU is still very much a union rather than some mutant new breed, and it has faced the burdens of size and unwieldiness in its own right. Among Stern's innovations was the combination of union locals into "mega-locals" of a million workers or more, in hopes of securing stronger bargaining power—but at the cost, his critics argued, of flexibility, internal democracy, and actual results. And its rival Change to Win, which was born in 2005 and thus far has not been able to scale up SEIU's successes, represents an endorsement of the federation model, not a repudiation. But the nitty-gritty involvement of SEIU with community and immigrant groups, churches and nontraditional allies suggests that in order to maintain their own relevance, the large industrial unions of the past need to embrace new methods and languages and share power with smaller, outside parties.

There is no country where more workers have more at stake than China, the world's largest industrial economy by population. China has fueled its intense economic growth by encouraging the development of a massive infrastructure of factories, many owned by foreign firms or their local subsidiaries, where thousands of workers, mostly young migrants from the countryside, work long hours and live in company dorms and eat and socialize with one another. These factory campuses can serve a population of up to several hundred thousand. The high demand for workers has meant that firms have gradually had to improve conditions, but worker organizing has been taboo. Like many authoritarian countries, China has a system of official labor unions that are part of the overall Communist Party architecture, less vehicles for worker demands and benefits than agencies that contribute to social control. Therefore, rather than attempt collective bargaining, individual workers have responded to poor conditions by job-hopping. And the young labor force typically works in the factories for a number of years only in order to prepare for marriage or send money home.

But Chinese plant workers have taken increasingly bold—and effective—collective actions to demand better treatment from their employers while bypassing the irrelevant official union structure. Strikes, which experts say have quietly gathered momentum in the factory towns of southern China, burst into world view in early 2010 with conflicts at Honda car parts and other factories. The workers demanded the right to form independent unions to hold real management-labor talks, while at the same time creating them de facto, surprising even Chinese labor advocates with the sophistication of their organization and election of shop stewards. The young workers also impressed observers by their adept use of technology to organize strikes and avoid, say, having to gather all of the leaders to meet in person where they might get arrested. They knew to avoid the main Chinese messaging service QQ.com because of its high population of government spies.

Honda, Toyota, the Taiwanese firm Foxconn (which manufactures iPhones), and other industrial employers agreed to wage and food and housing allowance increases, albeit not as large as the workers demanded. This success might not have happened without the labor shortage then developing in the overheated economy. Still, what happened in China demonstrates how much easier it has become for workers to self-unionize at the local, plant level when official unions are unresponsive or uninterested in serving them.[25]

Some emerging models in labor activism have come through organizations that are not unions at all—in fact, ones that have taken root in industries and areas where unions have found organizing to be too complicated and costly. One example comes from Los Angeles, where the Garment Worker Center—a small, compact team of activists drawn from progressive lawyers, immigrant rights groups, and representatives of ethnic communities—managed to score major victories against companies that relied on sweatshop labor. With a large number of small factories mostly staffed by undocumented workers with poor English, working up to twelve-hour days in conditions that often violated health and safety rules, the sector was urgently in need of intervention but extremely difficult for a traditional union to take on. But the Garment Worker Center led successful boycotts that spurred settlements with several of the clothing labels that used these workers' production. Small in size, and drawing on resources from multiple organizations in different specialties, worker centers are complementary to unions but operate on a nearly opposite model. They are also on the rise: from just 5 worker centers in the United States in 1992, to 160 in 2007.[26]

PHILANTHROPY: PUTTING THE BONO IN PRO BONO

The last two decades have seen a revolution in global giving. Even with the impact of the global recession, the available data suggest that more donors are giving more money to more people than ever before. To take just one rough number, from 2003 to 2010, the combined amount of official and private development aid from around the world rose from $136 billion to $509 billion.[27] Americans in 2010 contributed $291 billion to various causes,[28] and the number of US grant-making foundations continues to grow, from 21,877 in 1975 to 61,810 in 2001 and then 76,545 in 2009.[29] Together, private individuals and institutions are beginning to catch up with and in some cases displace official government efforts overseas. During the 1990s, for example, international giving by American individuals and institutions quadrupled. It doubled again from 1998 to 2007, reaching $39.6 billion, a sum more than 50 percent larger than the World Bank's total annual commitment. And charity is also getting a new face, whether the eighty-one American billionaires who as of 2012 had signed the Giving Pledge to give away most of their fortunes, the hundreds of thousands of cellphone users who texted millions of dollars in earthquake relief donations to Haiti, or the legions of "venture philanthropists" who gather in workshops, make field visits to inner-city schools or rural projects overseas to inspect firsthand the projects they fund, and exchange ideas and best practices in forums online.

Big foundations (Rockefeller, Carnegie, MacArthur, Ford), big relief agencies (the Red Cross, Oxfam, Doctors Without Borders), and big government agencies (USAID, Britain's DFID, multilaterals like the World Bank) still play a major role in channeling funds and technical support to the world's afflicted and poor. In fact, by many measures including total outlays, they still dominate the field. But the momentum is with new players: mega-foundations that have vaulted to preeminence such as the Bill and Melinda Gates Foundation, which became the world's largest in barely a decade; individual and small-scale foundations, which have mushroomed in the last fifteen years; and a constellation of private-aid platforms, marketplaces, aggregators, and advisers that are building new models from micro-loans for one Indian mother's sewing machine to public-private financing initiatives for new city buses.

Today's revolution in philanthropy shares two major traits of the previous one a century ago, when the titans of industry set up the Carnegie Corporation (1911), the Rockefeller Foundation (1913), and, a bit later, the Ford Foundation (1936)—massive and influential institutions that for decades were global models. Now as then, the transformation of philanthropy under way is following a period of spectacular wealth creation, this one stemming from information technology, communications, and life sciences instead of from railroads, steel, and petroleum. And once again the hub of innovation in philanthropy is the United States, the country where private giving is most tightly woven into the fabric of business culture.

A proponent of "scientific philanthropy," Andrew Carnegie believed in delivering charity according to the principles that worked in modern industry, the same principles that built the new corporate giants of the early twentieth century. He urged that the wealthy of his era "apply to their philanthropy the same entrepreneurial skills and zeal for efficiency that they employed in its accumulation." Logically enough, the result was the creation of huge institutions with a wide range of activities. The boards and program officers of the big foundations became key players: their funding patterns were bellwethers for other donors, and their choices of projects were models for would-be recipients.

Small individual donors, meanwhile, had few options for direct involvement in the projects their money supported. Channels for charity were not lacking: organizations such as the United Way, March of Dimes, Red Cross, the Salvation Army, and numerous religious groups collected donations in churches, shops, and workplaces and applied them toward the causes they deemed most needy and best fitting their philosophy. In other wealthy and emerging economies, a top tier of relief organizations developed over time. By the 1970s and 1980s, residents of wealthy countries could expect to get in the mail year-end and emergency appeals on behalf of disaster victims (MSF, Oxfam), endangered species (WWF), political prisoners (Amnesty International), and so on. All were worthy, but only a few gave small donors the chance to make a lasting commitment to a specific project or recipient, let alone communicate with recipients or send insights and share experiences along with their money. For that, you had to be rich.

Today's new breed of philanthropists offers a different vision, one informed by their backgrounds, their needs, and their own experiences in the marketplace. Start with their origins. The Bill and Melinda Gates Foundation, with its creation in Seattle in 1994, may be the 800-pound gorilla of modern philanthropy, but it is far from the only foundation born out of the wealth generated by the new economy. In California, for example, the number of foundations jumped by 71 percent from 1999 to 2009, and giving more than doubled from $2.8 billion to $6 billion.[30] Such growth helps to explain the shift in philanthropic gravity in the United States over the last decade: in 2003 the West surpassed the Midwest in overall giving for the first time, and in 2006 it overtook the Northeast, the bastion of American philanthropy.[31] While many of these new individual givers—the number of family foundations shot up by 40 percent from 2000 to 2005—are tech moguls of one stripe or another, some are also celebrities practicing what one wag at *The Economist* dubbed "celanthropy" (celebrity plus philanthropy): Bono with his One Foundation, Matt Damon promoting access to clean water, and Brad Pitt developing greenhouses to rebuild New Orleans. Mega-star athletes, such as Tiger Woods or

Andre Agassi, have foundations that control tens or hundreds of millions of dollars in assets. But many more are the small personal foundations of middling, journeymen NFL, NBA, or European soccer professionals whose names are little known beyond ardent fan circles.

For many of these new givers, the attitudes and methods of traditional philanthropy are anathema. Rather than give to big institutions, for example, they want to create their own. For the donor, a potential benefit of an individual foundation is the ability to select who gets what funds, and on what terms, without delegating those functions to some other agency. It helps set up a "short route" for philanthropy, cutting out intermediaries whose presence risks absorbing administrative costs as well as diluting or diverting the donor's intent.

Instead of funding the opera, libraries, or museums, they are much more likely to tackle concrete problems, applying their own business experience and methods. While such "outcome-oriented" philanthropy has been around for more than a century and bore fruit in the campaigns that led to the Green Revolution, its evidence-based, goal-focused approach has been championed in the last two decades by veterans of the tech community, who have applied their entrepreneurial mindset and engineering skills to some of the world's most intransigent problems.

Indeed, for many of these new players, philanthropy is no different than a business investment. A deliberate echo of venture capital, "venture philanthropy" reflects the application to charitable giving of that type of investment—selective and hands-on, aimed for the medium- to the long-term, and combining debt and equity stakes. Like venture capitalists, venture philanthropists have particular tastes and favored investment profiles. An organization called Venture Philanthropy Partners, for instance, aids groups that serve children in the Washington, DC, area. It doesn't just give money but also provides technical support and day-to-day involvement in the life of the groups it funds, and stringently monitors their progress. A group called Acumen Fund supports entrepreneurs in developing countries who meet very particular criteria: their venture must be a product or service that directly serves the poor, and it must be scalable to reach a population of at least 1 million. One recipient, for instance, was a start-up to provide rural retail and information kiosks in India. Acumen delivers support partly in grants, but mostly in loans and equity investments, largely blurring the line between business and philanthropy. The amounts involved are still small: in 2007, Acumen's loan portfolio was $27 million. Still, when one considers it was founded with only $400,000 in 2001, and that it is just one of a flotilla of new venture philanthropies, the speed of its success underscores a broader trend.[32]

But the most radical transformation in philanthropy today is the rise of tools that allow small individual donors or lenders, operating at a scale of just hundreds or even tens of dollars, to make the kind of specific, directed, involved contribution to a particular recipient or project that was impossible outside one's immediate neighborhood or circle of acquaintances.

This transformation has taken place mostly on the Internet. Kiva, founded in 2005, bundles small contributions as micro-loans to recipients around the world who are identified by name and can send updates to their individual funders. GlobalGiving, set up by two former World Bank employees in 2002, follows a related model in which donors support specific projects that they select. Using the global Web-based payments network PayPal, ventures like these are able to carve a short route between donors and recipients while keeping their own costs low and their organizations lean. Of course, the route can get only so short: Kiva and GlobalGiving rely on local micro-finance institutions and NGO sponsors to winnow their potential applicants and channel funds on the ground. The availability, competence, and institutional support for those remaining intermediaries are essential to the method's success. Still, the model allows anyone with an Internet connection and a few spare dollars to support, say, the conversion of taxis in Bolivia to natural gas, student loans in Paraguay, or a garment business in Cambodia (to cite some recent examples from Kiva).

Short-route philanthropy has yet to reach the volumes of money that large foundations or, for that matter, government agencies churn out, but it has become a new paradigm for giving. Individual fundraising for projects of all sorts is possible through services like Kickstarter, which enables would-be recipients to promote their project for a period and receive funds only if they raise the target amount of commitments during that time. A measure of the appeal of this approach is its adoption—and use as a marketing tool—by corporate philanthropy, as firms like American Express, Target, JPMorgan Chase, and Pepsico hold contests where Internet voters decide which among competing projects the company will support.

In the new philanthropic realm, where old-line foundations represent just one end of the spectrum, with short-route individual gifts via Internet at the other, the space between is now populated by funds, services, and advisers that are making the philanthropy business more complex, plural, and decentralized. The Wealth & Giving Forum, Social Ventures Partners International, Philanthropy Workshop West, The Big Give, and many more groups do everything from helping small foundations become more efficient and teaching newly wealthy individuals how to be hands-on philanthropists to advising on the design and monitoring of projects and creating forums for donors to compare experiences and practices.

This new, small-scale private giving is not poised to replace large foundations. Big-ticket funding by the Bill and Melinda Gates Foundation has given major impetus to worldwide research and treatment of diseases like malaria. A gift of $100 million from the Doris Duke Foundation in 2007 added 20 percent to the funding available for research on climate change for a five-year period. A gift in the same amount by Joan Kroc, heiress to the McDonald's fortune, turbo-charged America's National Public Radio. Medium and small-scale venture philanthropy, to say nothing of small-donor gifts via Kiva and similar platforms, address a different segment of the recipient community. By the same token, these new tools are not likely to displace official aid by government agencies. In fact, the scholars Raj Desai and Homi Kharas have found that Kiva and GlobalGiving donors base their choices on criteria that are different from those used by official aid administrators. Kiva donors, for instance, do not worry much about the overall political or economic situation of the country in which a recipient is located, so long as they like that person's project. This means that the new small-scale giving complements, rather than replaces, the old approach.[33]

But the new philanthropy has demolished the idea that only large foundations and public agencies have the expertise to design charitable projects and the efficiency to run them. The legal and bureaucratic obstacles that hamper official aid are well known; continuing waste, delays, and corruption have rekindled the long-standing critique of aid articulated by the economist P. T. Bauer at the London School of Economics and now given new voice by the Zambian economist Dambisa Moyo.[34] Major private aid organizations such as the American Red Cross in the wake of the Southeast Asia tsunami in 2004 and Hurricane Katrina in the United States in 2005 have been dogged by scandal and public suspicion. This is not to say that the newer, smaller charities are immune to waste and corruption. In the wake of the January 2010 earthquake in Haiti, small donors flocked to make $5 donations by text message to Yéle Haiti, the relief organization of singer Wyclef Jean, only to learn several weeks later that the group was suspected of major mismanagement.

But the premise of venture philanthropy and the new short-route vehicles and platforms is that the collective expertise of donors and recipients—the parties at either end of the ultimate transaction—can be assembled in a way that improves on what the old architecture of foundations and aid agencies have thus far delivered. As Tom Munnecke, head of Uplift Academy and a pioneer in new philanthropy, put it to a British newspaper: "Instead of having to go to one big, centralized bureaucracy such as the Red Cross or Oxfam, we can now go to the edge and take control."[35] At the edge, donors forged in Silicon Valley–style venture capitalism apply a broad range of tools from that milieu to vet projects, while would-be recipients make their proposals in the knowledge that they are competing with peers around the world. The boards and program officers of the big foundations and bureaucrats of large aid agencies have seen their influence lessened—whether by the new tools that aim to disintermediate them or by the celebrity activists, such as U2 frontman Bono or Senegalese singer Youssou N'Dour, who have used global media and communications platforms to advance their own views and priorities.

That said, the lines are not completely rigid, and the traditional players are capable of adapting—or at least trying to adapt. The Rockefeller Foundation, for example, is one of the original investors in the venture-philanthropy Acumen Fund. Desai and Kharas note that many major official agencies are splitting into specialized units in order to improve focus and reduce waste. Steps like these only confirm that the future of philanthropy is going to be more fragmented than in the past. Would Rockefeller, Carnegie, and their cohorts object? Not necessarily. "Rockefeller viewed his philanthropy through the lens of his business," Acumen Fund founder Jacqueline Novogratz told *Forbes*. "It was highly centralized, it was top-down, it was based on experts and it was big picture." Today a new class of entrepreneurs, finance and technology workers who forged their wealth in the networked economy, are simply applying their own business worldview to philanthropy, as Novogratz put it, "from the bottom-up of the market."[36] Andrew Carnegie favored "scientific philanthropy." It is logical enough that as the "science" of business has pointed away from large centralized corporations to the advantage of small, fast, and networked new players, philanthropy would follow in the same way.

MEDIA: EVERYONE REPORTS, EVERYONE DECIDES

Around the world and especially in the most Internet-intense markets, the sources and repositories of the news were—and are—in a constant state of flux. The rapid and relentless digitization of information and communication has led to cohabitation on the same platforms by different types of content (news, analysis, opinion, commercial, propaganda), emanating from different kinds of providers (news organizations, advertisers, advocates, individuals). Once-separate media with their own technological requirements and business cultures are converging: radio and newspapers now operate as much online as in their original format, and derive more and more of their revenue that way.

News consumers have watched their favorite newspaper attempt to preserve advertising and develop new revenue streams, find the right design and figure out the balance between free and paid Web content, staff bureaus in other cities and countries, allocate personnel between print and online operations, and so forth. Many have failed. In the United States, for example, an average of fifteen papers, or just about 1 percent of the industry, vanished each year from 2006 to 2011. In terms of circulation and advertising revenues, the US newspaper industry has shrunk 43 percent since 2000.[37] Television viewers have seen their favorite shows made available on-demand and online through partnerships with preferred video companies. Radio listeners can now choose to get their music from satellite stations, or through new tailored services such as Spotify and Pandora. News addicts can seek out coverage from one or another source, letting Google or Yahoo filter it through their news aggregators, or perhaps letting their Facebook and Twitter contacts do the sorting, relying on whatever links those people see fit to share.

The implications of these developments, while much debated, are less clear. Journalists understandably spend considerable time fretting over the future of their profession; but where is power in the media, and in what direction is it shifting? The answer depends a great deal—perhaps more than in any other field—on where one looks for clues.

On the one hand, evidence abounds to support the argument that a small number of major firms control a very large share of global media. One count of dominant firms in the US media market placed their number at 50 in 1983, decreasing to 23 in 1990, six in 2000, and five thereafter.[38] Certainly media mergers accelerated in the United States after 1990, and regulatory changes lifting bans on certain kinds of cross-platform media holdings helped spur this along. More recently, the purchase of the Dow Jones company, owners of the *Wall Street Journal,* by Rupert Murdoch's News Corp added to the heft of one of the seven top-tier international multi-media corporations identified by the Spanish sociologist and renowned media scholar Manuel Castells: Time Warner, Disney, News Corp, Bertelsmann, NBC, CBS, and Viacom.[39]

Whatever its effects on democracy, acquisition and consolidation in the media industry have yielded what might charitably be called mixed results as a business strategy. When Time Warner spun off AOL about a decade after its infamous merger, AOL's value was a fraction of the price reflected in the original $175 billion merger. And that result is not an exception: according to one analysis, from 2000 to 2009, the largest media conglomerates together wrote down more than $200 billion in assets. And these companies' poor stock performance relative to indexes such as the S&P predates the business destruction precipitated by the Internet. Media companies have a history of predominantly achieving growth through acquisition, but revenue growth has not necessarily translated into better stock performance and a certain kind of market power.[40]

On the other hand, power in the media business these days is increasingly wielded by technology firms and content-deliverers of one type or another. Castells, for example, adds to the top-tier list Google, Microsoft, Yahoo!, and Apple—all of them technology firms that have made significant moves into media of one kind or another—to form a snapshot of the "global core" of media operations today. Facebook should surely also be on it, especially after its 2012 initial public offering worth more than $100 billion. Indeed, by 2015, Facebook is expected to account for one out of every five digital display ads sold.[41] Even in 2011, five technology companies (not including Apple and Amazon) accounted for 68 percent of all online ad revenue. The relations that exist between these giants are not solely cutthroat and competitive, in that they also involve case-by-case collaboration through local joint ventures in various countries and regions, content or platform development, distribution and advertising deals, and sometimes membership on one another's boards of directors.[42]

But does this mean power is concentrated—or more concentrated than before—in the media industry? First, the comparison is hard to establish since changing technology keeps shifting the boundaries of the media industry. Second, even if merger activity seems to have bred consolidation in some countries and formed some major international media empires, the choice of media in any given country is more abundant today than it was a few decades ago. Until the 1970s or 1980s, the state controlled most or all television and radio not only in developing countries and the Eastern bloc but also in much of Western Europe. Third, the consumer experience via the Internet has expanded the range of choices. The *New York Times,* for example, offers local news coverage for Chicago; the *Guardian,* based in London, has become a popular news site in the United States; the *National,* published in Abu Dhabi, features highbrow culture coverage that draws its writers—and its audience—from well outside its local market. As the journalist Michael Kinsley observed in 2010, "Every English-language paper published anywhere in the world is now in competition with every other."[43] Finally, any argument that the media is more concentrated now than in the past should not forget that the American Big Three TV networks, the Associated Press news agency, and numerous other players long held dominant positions in their respective segments, and that is no longer the case.

But the nature of the media, with their appeal to our curiosity and belief systems, is such that their power lies as much in authority (of its writers and sources) and influence (on our views and decisions) as it does in business organization and company revenues. The newspaper considered "of record" in its national market—the *New York Times, Le Monde, El País*—is rarely the one with the largest circulation or revenue. Tabloids usually enjoy the largest readership. A subtle hierarchy places certain media outlets ahead of others with respect to credibility and prestige. Now, not only is that hierarchy under threat but the boundaries of journalism as a profession have fallen, as one after another upstart venture has shown itself able to compete with, if not surpass, established journalistic outlets. The Huffington Post, for example, which used to be derided by mainstream media as a rip-off aggregator, has beefed up its reporting staff and won the Pulitzer Prize for national reporting in 2012. Widespread digital and cellphone cameras and video recorders have catapulted "citizen journalism" to the forefront, with ordinary people competing with paparazzi for celebrity shots (which online brokers then market to the tabloids) or supplying raw evidence of police brutality or early images of a natural disaster. (It should be noted, however, that David Wood, the Pulitzer Prize–winner at The Huffington Post, has decades of reporting experience.) Meanwhile, the ease of publishing on the Internet has turned blogs on everything from electoral politics to fiscal policy, rock music, and business travel into credible and revenue-earning specialty sources that often outperform beat reporters and magazine analysts.

Consider the case of statistics geek Nate Silver, who applied the skills he honed crunching baseball numbers to the 2008 and 2012 US presidential campaigns on his site fivethirtyeight.com. Using his own model to aggregate polling data, Silver was able to predict the outcome of the Super Tuesday primaries between Barack Obama and Hillary Clinton; he went on to predict Obama's defeat of John McCain as early as March 2008, and his detailed predictions on Election Night got forty-nine out of fifty states right, and in the 2012 elections also predicted accurately the results. In the past, someone like Silver might have had a hard time being heard, for lack of an outlet. Instead, fivethirtyeight.com rose to cult status during the campaign, compelling TV channels to invite Silver onto some of their panels, and was licensed by the *New York Times* in 2010.

As different platforms converge, blogger-turned-analyst is just one of many mutations that have unsettled the traditional media work hierarchies. In addition to hiring more reporters, The Huffington Post in 2011 opened its own twenty-four-hour online news channel and announced in June 2012 that it would start a separate online magazine available only through the Apple Store.[44] It has expanded internationally, launching operations in Spain, Italy, and France.

Meanwhile, newspapers and magazines have launched blogs and brought on board big-name independent bloggers. In Britain, for example, the major newspapers (*Guardian, The Times, Daily Telegraph*) have formed stables of dozens of online opinion and argument writers. Few traits or functions are exclusive to one type of media organization. News, opinion, and entertainment are all fair game; print, audio, and video outlets are increasingly working in one another's medium; and the combination of easy access to both content creation and distribution tools has torn down the barriers surrounding both the profession of journalism and the scope and specialization of any news organization.

So, less power for traditional news outlets even as the media industry grows more commercial and entertainment-driven? Not necessarily. In 2012, for example, the Nieman Journalism Lab profiled three European newspaper companies that are successfully pursuing different strategies to thrive in the digital age: Sanoma, Finland's largest news company, has pioneered new ways to profitably convert its print subscribers to digital access; Norway's Schibsted, the world's eighth-biggest news company, operates in twenty-eight countries and gets more than a third of its revenues from digital offerings, or about three times as much as the average newspaper; Switzerland's Zeitung Online is experimenting with "hyperlocalism," winning readers by ignoring stories about President Obama and world affairs in favor of those about the town mayor and canton politics.

The rise of small, outsider, and citizen journalism and social networking in the media may prove complementary to some of the existing players. Among the new forces are also independent investigative groups with nonprofit funding such as ProPublica, an "independent, nonprofit newsroom" (to use its own descriptor) whose partnerships with established newspapers in the United States have already begun to win awards (in ProPublica's case, a 2011 Pulitzer Prize). And one example of clever harnessing of social media by a major newspaper came in October 2009, when the *Guardian* got around a court injunction that prevented it from reporting a question raised in the House of Commons with the assistance of a timely tweet by its editor, Alan Rusbridger. The case concerned the oil trading firm Trafigura, which was implicated in a toxic-waste scandal in West Africa and whose lawyers had secured the injunction. "*Guardian* prevented from reporting parliament for unreportable reasons," Rusbridger posted, sparking an overnight flurry of online chatter that blew open the topic. In an industry experiencing as thorough a state of flux and technological revolution as the media are, the rise and relevance of all manner of small, decentralized participants are undeniable, but the traditional players may yet have the last word.[45] The growing popularity of mobile devices, for example, has led not only to a spike in news consumption but also to a flight to quality, as consumers prefer apps and home pages of established news organizations with a reputation for objectivity.[46]

This chapter has focused on churches, unions, philanthropies, and the media. But it could just as well have been devoted to the power shifts in the academy, where online learning, for-profit schools, and growing global competition are intensifying the struggle to attract students and research funding and to stay on top of the pecking order for prestige. It could have explored the decay of power in scientific innovation, which has become more a global than a national enterprise, with collaborators across borders and emerging norms for greater sharing of data and knowledge. Or it could have zeroed in on museums, which have had to contend not only with new competitors—the establishment of world-league museums in far-flung places like Tasmania and Qatar, for example—and groundbreaking methods of cultural interaction but also with the increasing assertiveness of empowered developing countries seeking to retrieve their cultural patrimony. Or it could have highlighted sports, old franchises given new life by innovative methods and nouveau riche owners, or new national juggernauts seeking to translate their surging gross domestic products into a greater haul of Olympic gold or thriving entertainment industries.

No realm has been left untouched by the More, Mobility, and Mentality revolutions. And none is immune to the shifts that have made power easier to get, harder to use, and more difficult to hold on to. In religion, philanthropies, and media—the arenas of conflict and competition for our souls, hearts, and brains—we see not only the interplay of new forces but also the fragmentation and polarization that are remaking our societies at all levels. We have more choices open to us in these areas than ever before.

But this raises the question of what happens when the mosaic of faith shatters into a thousand, a million jagged pieces. When the quest for common good devolves into bespoke kindness designed to advance a particular cause for a particular person. Or when citizens forsake all the news that's fit to print for only the news they want to hear. All of these amount to a challenge to efforts at collective action. And from climate change to rising inequality, the enormous challenges that we face demand collective action and a new shared way of thinking about the accretion and use of power. We will consider both shortly—after we examine, in the next chapter, whether this brave new world is really here to stay after all, and whether the decay of power has more benefits or more costs for society.

CHAPTER TEN

THE DECAY OF POWER

Is the Glass Half-Full or Half-Empty?

I AM AWARE THAT I AM ARGUING THAT POWER IS DECAYING EVEN AS headlines regularly point to the contrary. Some governments are becoming larger. Within countries, wealth and income are indeed becoming more concentrated. The middle class in rich countries is shrinking, and a tiny set of people is accumulating unimaginable riches. Groups and individuals with huge wealth use it to gain inordinate political influence. In the United States, a billionaire casino owner, hedge fund managers, and real estate tycoons blatantly use their money to fund "Super-PACs" that advance narrow agendas or promote candidates who will defend their business interests. In Russia, China, and many other places, oligarchs in cahoots with government officials call the shots—figuratively and literally. Powerful media moguls use their influence to extend their media power to presidential palaces. The "99 percent" feel swindled, impoverished, and exploited by the rich and powerful 1 percent.

How, then, can it be true that power is decaying, spreading, and becoming more ephemeral? Or that the powerful are under siege? Because, as these pages have shown, the powerful today are more constrained than in the past, their hold on power is far less secure than that of their predecessors, and their tenures are shorter.

Vladimir Putin, for example, surely has enormous power, but he is increasingly embattled and his range of options has narrowed since his first term as Russia's president and, subsequently, as prime minister. Similarly, it appeared that the few bankers who came out on top after the 2008 financial crisis would rule the global financial system for a long time; yet, less than four years later, several of them had lost their jobs while others were besieged by the discovery of their price rigging (Barclays), hidden trading losses (JPMorganChase), money laundering (HSBC), illicit dealings with Iran (Standard Chartered), insider trading by one of their board members (Goldman Sachs), and so on. These events did not extinguish the economic might of the large banks, and the banking lobby continues to wield enormous political clout. But some top executives have lost power, and the banks are surely more constrained in what they can do. Only the most naïve or blindly arrogant CEOs—and not just bankers—feel that their jobs are safe. Economic inequality—long tolerated and in some countries even celebrated—is becoming the focus of debate in many countries. From the United States and Europe to the streets of the Arab world or even China, the peaceful—or at least silent—coexistence with inequality is ending.

And as we have seen in previous chapters, many other arenas of human endeavor once dominated by traditional power players are now contested battlefields where entrenched incumbents are regularly challenged and, with growing regularity, ousted.

This is good news.

CELEBRATING THE DECAY OF POWER

The undeniably positive consequences of the decay of power include freer societies, more elections and options for voters, new platforms for organizing communities, more ideas and possibilities, more investment and trade, and more competition among firms and thus more options for consumers. None of these consequences is universal, and we can find disheartening exceptions in each case, but the larger trend is demonstrably clear.

In politics, for example, the rise in political freedoms is obvious; authoritarianism is in retreat. Of course, the democratic boom is far from complete. Some countries (think China, Saudi Arabia, North Korea, Cuba, Belarus) have yet to experience it or, like Russia, are doing so only in partial, frustrating measure. Yet the forces that undermine authoritarianism are still at work in the public squares that have come to symbolize the Arab Spring and even in the streets of Tehran, on China's websites and increasingly in the streets of its cities, and in other societies governed by repressive regimes bent on controlling their people. We now see more and more scholarly articles with titles such as "Why China Will Democratize," claiming that the autocratic days of the giant nation are numbered, and predictions of the end of the Chinese Communist Party's grip on power are multiplying.[1]

And why not? Why should China be an exception? For much of the rest of the world, political power has grown consistently less concentrated. In recent decades, an unprecedented number of political parties and factions have credibly competed for electoral power, and governments in office have been more prone than ever before to fall or to change. Fewer influential political scientists are likely to argue, as some did in Asia as recently as the 1990s, the merits of political order and controlled transitions, or to caution that some countries are not robust and cohesive enough for sudden democratic opening.[2] Back in the 1970s, the celebrated Harvard scholar Samuel Huntington could point to numerous countries coming out of colonial rule or going through rapid social change and link the pace and scope of these changes to a pattern of violence, riots, insurrections, or coups. "Authority has to exist before it can be limited," Huntington wrote, "and it is authority that is in scarce supply in those modernizing countries where government is at the mercy of alienated intellectuals, rambunctious colonels, and rioting students."[3] Such views are hard to locate today, except maybe in the doctrine and official press of the Chinese Communist Party or among those who fear that the demise of Middle Eastern dictators is destined to bring to power even more repressive and obscurantist dictatorships. And we know that during transitions to democracy, nations often undergo political convulsions that make them hard to govern, thus feeding nostalgia for their old authoritarian order.

Economic globalization adds yet more reasons to celebrate the decay of power among traditional megaplayers. Small, faraway companies now strip market share from corporations that have been household names; startups pioneer new business models that send corporate giants reeling. As we saw in Chapter 8, in a telling example of the effects on power of the More, Mobility, and Mentality revolutions, venture capital investment models have spread from Silicon Valley to many other nations, energizing latent entrepreneurial skills in once-unlikely hubs of business innovation. And new multinationals have emerged from countries that until recently no world-class company viewed as breeding grounds of potential competitors.

We know that shifts in the pecking order of companies are as old as the modern market economy, and that a profound link between innovation and "creative destruction" is at the heart of capitalism's vitality. Yet, the massive global changes we now see go further.[4] They could not have happened without the decay of power.

At the core here is something that is hard not to like: just as the decay of power in politics has undermined authoritarian regimes, in business it has curtailed monopolies and oligopolies while giving consumers more choices, lower prices, and better quality. Classical economics and liberal political thought are premised on the idea that monopolies are almost always undesirable. Even areas where monopolies were once thought unavoidable, such as the provision of water and electricity, can now be opened to competition. Those coming of age today may have a hard time imagining a situation when all telephone companies around the world were monopolies, often owned by the state and frequently incapable of delivering decent service. Yet that is how it was not long ago. Today, telephony is fiercely contested, and no company feels safe or permanent regardless of its size and resources. Our distaste for monopoly extends to oligopolies and cartels. So the more the decay of power prevents small groups of large firms from exerting abusive market power, the more we are predisposed to celebrate it.

WHAT'S NOT TO LIKE? THE DANGERS OF DECAY

But celebrating the benefits of the decay of power should not lead us to ignore that a glass that is half-full is also half-empty. The decay of power also entails dangers.

It is one of the fundamental reasons why governments are increasingly incapable of making the decisions needed to deal with their country's problems or why groups of leading nations are becoming increasingly slower and less effective at tackling international problems.

The decay of power also is one of the forces driving the profusion of myriad criminal, terrorist, or otherwise malevolent nonstate actors. For them, frontiers are irrelevant and governments are an increasingly ineffectual hindrance that they attack, undermine, or ignore.[5]

In addition, the dilution of power has facilitated the rise of extremist politics—whether separatist, xenophobic, and sectarian—in established democracies and fledgling political systems.

It has nurtured all manner of improvised groups, companies, and media outlets that evade traditional scrutiny and whose sponsors hide in the cacophony of the Web. It has also created more opportunities for business fraud and commercial deceit.

It often takes high-profile cases and news headlines about individuals and organizations to give us a glimpse of the bigger problem. Yet each of these individual players is vulnerable to the decay of its power. That doesn't mean that we should not worry about them, of course—competition in criminality hardly redeems it. But we should remember that the Taliban, Al Qaeda, and Zetas, the Mexican drug cartel, have their own splinters, off-shoots, and mutations; that the threat from a unified China is different from the threat posed by a China that is itself going through a rapid and weakening dilution of power among regions, interest groups, and competing factions within the Communist Party; and so on.

Ultimately, the players will change, overtaken by their own rivals or mutating from within. In many instances, the tools they use to exert their power are here to stay; in other cases, new players will become powerful through their invention of new tools to gain power. The power enjoyed by Facebook or Google resides in new technologies that others don't have. Al Qaeda derived its power from its new and murderous ways of "doing business."

Moreover, the sheer scale of the More, Mobility, and Mentality revolutions has simultaneously made our problems bigger and more complex and weakened our mechanisms for addressing them. Consider the threat of climate change: even as the rise from poverty of China and India has lifted the lives of billions, it has also accelerated their greenhouse gas emissions dramatically. China overtook the United States as the single largest emitter of greenhouse gases in 2006, and India that year was ranked fourth. Any effort to reduce carbon emissions in one country must take into account the actions of the other—not least because as environmental policies and carbon pricing mechanisms in developed countries take hold, companies have responded by shifting their carbon-intensive production offshore. From arms exports and Internet-domain conventions to fisheries and agricultural trade, just about every subject for international negotiation now involves more demands from a growing number of stakeholders. As a result, we are increasingly unable to take action that goes beyond the lowest common denominator and actually makes a dent in the problem at hand. Having a more diverse and inclusive group of actors at the table (the erstwhile "weak") and reducing the number of decisions arbitrarily imposed on the world by a few powerful players are worth applauding, but the heightened difficulty of getting things done is not.

POLITICAL PARALYSIS AS
COLLATERAL DAMAGE OF THE DECAY OF POWER

That paralysis has become acutely evident in the United States. As politics has become more polarized, the defects of a system overloaded with checks and balances have become more apparent. Francis Fukuyama calls this system a "vetocracy." He writes: "Americans take great pride in a constitution that limits executive power through a series of checks and balances. But those checks have metastasized. And now America is a vetocracy. When this system is combined with ideologized parties, . . . the result is paralysis. . . . If we are to get out of our present paralysis we need not only strong leadership, but changes in institutional rules."[6]

Economist Peter Orszag witnessed the workings of vetocracy and its nefarious consequences. Writing in 2011, he reflected on what he had just witnessed as one of the top economic policymakers in the United States: "During my recent stint in the Obama administration as director of the Office of Management and Budget, it was clear to me that the country's political polarization was growing worse—harming Washington's ability to do the basic, necessary work of governing. . . . Radical as it sounds we need to counter the gridlock of our political institutions by making them a bit less democratic. I know that such ideas carry risk. And I have arrived at these proposals reluctantly: they come more from frustration than from inspiration. But we need to confront the fact that a polarized, gridlocked government is doing real harm to our country. And we have to find some way out of it."

Orszag is hardly a radical with autocratic tendencies. In fact, his proposals are essentially technocratic reforms: he favors boosting fiscal automatic stabilizers (the tax and spending provisions that automatically expand when the economy slows down and contract when the economy grows), backstop rules (events that are triggered when Congress does not act, thus changing the default mode from inaction to action), and relying more on expert commissions empowered to work and operate with rules that shield them from partisan pressures.[7]

While the foregoing examples are based on the recent experience of the United States, most democracies are also suffering from this combination of acute political polarization and an institutional design that makes it very hard for the government to make timely and effective decisions. Remember that, as noted in Chapter 5, of the world's thirty-four wealthiest democracies, in 2012 only four had a president or prime minister whose party also had a majority in parliament. And like the United States, other countries are not lacking in creative ideas to reform their system of checks and balances and enable the government to break out of the policy paralysis and improve the quality of the policies it adopts. But these advances are not occurring. Not in the United States and not elsewhere. Not even the crushing pressures produced by the economic crisis in Europe have enabled leaders to secure the power they need to react quickly and effectively. In fact, the contrary happened: as the economic crisis fueled even more political polarization and fragmentation, it further weakened both those in power and those who opposed them. No one seemed to have the ability to make the changes that were desperately needed.

The end of power, indeed.

RUINOUS COMPETITION

There is a concept in economics called ruinous competition. It refers to circumstances in which the prices charged by firms in a given industry become too low to cover the cost of production. Firms do this when they want to get rid of inventories quickly, or when their goal is not to maximize profits in the short term but to bankrupt one or more rivals. These rivals then react in kind. When this situation becomes more than just a temporary surge in overly aggressive business tactics, it risks undermining the industry as a whole. Certain conditions make ruinous competition more likely. It happens, for instance, when there is a great deal of surplus capacity—idle factories and equipment, or warehouses full of overstock—and businesses keep lowering prices just to keep things running. In a sense, ruinous competition is a perverse mutation of the ideal competition that economists hold so dear.

Ruinous competition is a good metaphor to illustrate what can go wrong with the diffusion of power and its attendant decay. When power is harder to use and to keep and spreads to a larger and ever-shifting cast of small players, forms of competition and interaction that are detrimental to the social good are more likely to arise, threatening the health of economies, the vitality of cultures, the stability of nations, and even world peace.

In political philosophy, the analogous idea is encapsulated in the classic contrast between two extremes: tyranny and anarchy. When overly concentrated, power produces tyranny. At the opposite end, the more fragmented and diluted power becomes, the greater the risk of anarchy—a state in which there is no order. Both of these extremes are rare: even the most tyrannical system has cracks, and in the most anarchic situation, a modicum of order and a power structure eventually obtains and chaos abates. But the central message here is that the excessive dilution of power and the inability of leading actors to lead are as dangerous as the excessive concentration of power in a few hands.

The excessive decay of power, whereby every significant actor can veto the initiative of others but no one of them has the power to impose its will, is as much a risk to a nation's political system and society or to any community or even a family as it is to the system of nations. When power becomes so constrained, paralysis ensues and stability, predictability, safety, and material prosperity suffer.

BE CAREFUL WHAT YOU WISH FOR: OVERDOSING ON CHECKS AND BALANCES

The ways to maintain order in an environment where power is dispersed, fleeting, and decaying are manifold. Among them are federalism, political alliances and coalitions, international organizations, internationally accepted (and imposed) rules and norms, checks and balances between branches of government, and moral or ideological ties under banners like Christendom, Islam, social democracy, or socialism. They are all answers to an old problem, one that dates back to the Greek city-states. But today's decay of power has yet to give birth to its own institutional responses: innovations in organizing public life that can allow us to enjoy the fulfillment and personal autonomy that hyper-diffuse power promises while staving off its very real, very dangerous threats.

To imagine the effects of the decay of power on the social good, consider a graph shaped as an inverted U-curve. It plots the decay of power—concentrated at the left, diffuse at the right—against widely desired values such as political and social stability, reliable public institutions, and economic vitality.

FIGURE 10.1. THE DECAY OF POWER: INVERTED U-CURVE

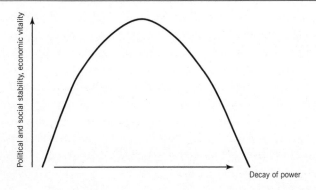

The horizontal axis, which tracks the decay of power, starts with a situation (at the extreme left, near the origin of the axis) of maximum concentration and control of power in a few hands. This is the place where tyranny, monopolies, and forms of tight control in political and economic life that deliver inadequate levels of social well-being are located. At the other extreme in that horizontal axis, power is hyper-diffuse and diluted. There, the collapse of order brings anarchy and the situation becomes as socially undesirable as that at the other extreme, where concentration is high and political and economic monopolies are the norm.

The challenge is to find ways to inhabit the middle of the curve in a time of massive and rapid change. Our tolerance—how broad a band in the middle of a curve we are prepared to accept—will vary. In economic life, both monopoly and ruinous hyper-competition are sub-optimal, but the stakes are usually not life and death; ultimately we can live with a broad range of situations, even if we want improvement. When politics becomes so scattered that it nurtures extremisms and violence, the stakes are more urgent. When the world's military order gets so scattered that pirates, terrorists, militias, criminal cartels, and rogue states can defy the armies of powerful nations, the stakes could not be higher.

Our horizon is crowded with great issues such as nuclear proliferation and climate change that simply cannot be resolved if the world system becomes increasingly destabilized, riddled by fractures, and hampered by a steady decline in its capacity for collective action. The decay of power is complicating such issues—especially as more countries pursue nuclear programs or gain the ability to invent sophisticated cyber-attack worms and target opponents at home and abroad. The weaker power of the dominant actors is complicating the search for solutions as well; we no longer have one or two superpowers that can simply enforce their terms on the rest of the world.

Collective efforts such as maintaining peace, deterring terrorism, coordinating economic policies to stimulate global growth, fighting disease, stopping climate change, allocating scarce resources, fighting money laundering and fraud, and protecting endangered species are global public goods. In other words, they are the kinds of results that benefit everyone, including those who did nothing to help bring them about. This sets up the classic dilemma that social scientists call the collective action problem.[8] No single player is able to bring about the changes on its own, yet all players have an incentive to wait around—expending no resources—until someone else does the work for them. In the end the change is never achieved, even though everyone stood to benefit from it.

The decay of power exacerbates the collective action problem. It is already happening in the international arena, as more and more "small" countries veto, foot-drag, demand special consideration, or generally undermine the efforts of the "big" nations in one area after another. Meanwhile, the big nations themselves have more channels available to work at cross-purposes. The twentieth-century response to the demand for global public goods was to create international organizations, from the United Nations and all its specialized agencies to the World Bank, IMF, and regional groups. But too often now these institutions are merely scrambling to keep pace with the booming demands and evolving threats in the areas they are supposed to oversee.

One response is for a coalition of powerful nations ("coalition of the willing") to bypass international organizations and take action directly, as the United States and others did in Iraq. Yet even that possibility is affected by the decay of power: first, because other nations are increasingly able to resist or interfere with any such coalition's plans, but also because political coalitions tend to be more and more fractured, and public opinion less and less committed and patient, even within these leading countries. Wave after wave of the dilution of power—and not just in politics—comes crashing in to make the problem more complicated. The same country whose government and military is trying to bring about change in some faraway place, leading a coalition of nations in that effort, may also harbor foundations and charities that direct money and information to its opponents and host the computer servers that relay their point of view and mobilize new adherents. As the scope grows for small players to make investments, lead campaigns, donate money, and start media outlets that give them power, the benefits—pluralism, democracy, initiative, a sense of meaning—also create new obstacles to confronting crises, finding purpose, and getting things done.

FIVE RISKS

No matter the arena, the decay of power generates risks that could lower social welfare and individual quality of life in the short term and prompt a backlash or even a disaster down the line. Beyond the political paralysis and the other negative consequences we've examined, there are five concrete effects of the decay of power that pose significant risks.

Disorder

Hobbes and the other classical political philosophers said it from the beginning, and their insight—recall Chapter 1—remains true. For many individuals the acquisition of power is—or seems to be—an innate urge. But in the construction of societies, power is a solution to the problem of disorder. We consent to the power of the state because it is supposed to guarantee the minimum level of stability and predictability we need to lead fulfilling lives. Rules from business regulation, libel laws, and ballot access to international treaties all aim to calm the unpredictability of life and ward off the risk of chaotic disorder, even anarchy.

What we concede to these institutions—and the people who lead them—and what we demand that they deliver in return have changed over time and among societies as human values and expectations evolve. The More, Mobility, and Mentality revolutions have led billions to expect and demand more. And we have better tools for accountability. Yet the core promise of power—that it produce order—remains the heart of our consent. The decay of power discussed in this book threatens that promise in a way that political rivalry, business competition, conflict among nations, and even world wars in the twentieth-century sense did not. The implications are obvious: while few societies become and remain anarchic for long periods, it is not that hard for a society to become paralyzed by too high a level of power decay. This can turn even advanced and mature democracies into stagnant entities incapable of responding to the challenges and demands of the twenty-first century. As noted, Europe's inability to respond in a timely and effective way to its devastating economic crisis offers a painful example of the corroding effects of the end of power. With even more perilous consequences, so does our inability to act decisively to limit the emissions of greenhouse gases that are warming our planet.

The De-skilling and Loss of Knowledge

Centralized and hierarchical organizations held sway for more than a century for a reason. Political parties, large corporations, churches, foundations, bureaucracies, militaries, prestigious universities, and cultural institutions accumulate experience, practices, and knowledge within their walls; they archive their successes and inculcate habits, culture, and operational routines in their employees or members. None of this transfers into a world of diffuse power without some—or a lot of—loss. The possibility that political parties can be replaced by ad-hoc "movements," temporary electoral coalitions, or even single-issue, nongovernmental organizations (the "greens," "pirates," "small-government") is appealing to the millions of voters everywhere who are fed up with the corruption, ideological stagnation, and disappointing government performance of many political parties. But while the flaws of most parties are often unquestionable, their demise implies the disappearance of important reservoirs of highly specific knowledge that are not easy to replicate by the alluring newcomers— many of which tend to be what Swiss historian Jacob Burckhardt called "terrible simplifiers," the demagogues who seek power by exploiting the ire and frustration of the population and making appealing but "terribly simplified" and, ultimately, deceitful promises.[9]

The same holds for the experience of large firms as employers and investors. Micro-enterprises, pop-up stores, venture funds, social networks, and the like have a hard time replicating a large firm's accumulated intellectual capital. The radical decentralization of knowledge—from Wikipedia to open-source software development to MIT course material available free online—is one of the most exciting trends in the dispersion of power. But the ability of these new sources of knowledge to match internal R&D or preserve institutional memory is inconsistent at best. Our individual choices about education and employment are not necessarily better or more sustainable in an environment where power is too diffuse. Excessive institutional fragmentation can be as bad for creating and wisely using knowledge as are the stifling environments that obtain when power is overly concentrated.

The Banalization of Social Movements

Social and political causes today have "followers" who "like" them in the ether of digital media. On social media platforms, hordes of Facebook friends or Twitter followers can create the illusion that a group promoting a particular cause is indeed a powerful force. In some cases that may be true. While the role played by Facebook and Twitter in the Arab Spring might have been overstated, there is no doubt that social media did boost the capabilities of the antigovernment forces.

But that is not the most common experience. For most people in the world, Web-based social or political activism represents little more than the touching of a button. Perhaps, a bit more meaningfully, they will make a small donation—for instance, $5 to the Red Cross after an earthquake or another natural disaster—by sending a text message to a designated phone number. That is not insignificant, but it doesn't constitute the kind of risk-taking activism that propelled so many of the great social movements. Author Evgeny Morozov calls this new, low-involvement and low-impact participation "slacktivism." It is, he says, "the ideal type of activism for a lazy generation: why bother with sit-ins and the risk of arrest, police brutality, or torture if one can be as loud campaigning in the virtual space?" The problem with slacktivism, he argues, is not so much that it is made up of tiny low-risk contributions—after all, each of these is genuine in some way; rather, there is a risk that the obsession with online petitions, numbers of followers, and "likes" will divert potential supporters and take resources away from organizations doing the higher-risk and higher-reward work: "Are the publicity gains . . . worth the organizational losses?"[10] As echoed by Malcolm Gladwell, this emerging counterpoint to the fetishization of social media illustrates the danger of irrelevance created by the decay of power.[11] The ability to endorse a cause, start a petition, or even do something more concrete such as set up one's own online storefront on Amazon or eBay, or send money to a selected recipient a world or a neighborhood away, is on one level liberating and individually fulfilling. Yet the proliferation of small players and short-term initiatives brings the risk that actual, forceful, coalitions directed toward specific social goals become impossible to orchestrate. Call it the collective action problem gone subatomic.

Boosting Impatience and Shortening Attention Spans

While millions of online activists may raise the social visibility of myriad issues, they also create a level of "noise" and distraction that makes it very hard for any single cause to retain popular attention and support long enough to gain substantial and permanent strength. Hyper-competition can be as deleterious to civic and political activism as for private companies faced with a profusion of competitors that forces each one of them into small size and limited power.

Moreover, the more tenuous the grasp on power of leaders, institutions, or organizations—in other words, the more inherently slippery power becomes—the more likely they are to be governed by short-term incentives and fears, and the fewer their incentives to plan for the longer term. Government leaders elected for increasingly shorter periods, corporate leaders with their eyes on the next quarterly results, generals aware that the success of armed interventions depends more than ever on the support of a fickle public that is less tolerant of casualties—all of these are examples of how time compression constrains the options of the powerful.

At the individual level a paradox of the decay of power is that it may give us more tools for living in the moment, even as it compresses the horizon of our choices. This is happening at the same time that it becomes crystal clear that most of our domestic or international problems are immune to quick fixes and that their solution and alleviation require sustained and consistent efforts. Patience may be the scarcest resource of all in a world where the decay of power continues unabated.

Alienation

Power and its institutions have been with us for so long, and the barriers to power traditionally so high, that we have composed the meaning of our lives—our choices about what to do, what to accept, what to challenge— within these parameters. Big changes with uncertain consequences often breed alienation—the estrangement or distancing of people from each other, or from what used to matter to them, or, in extreme cases, even a certain separation from their own sense of self, the identity that defined them in their own eyes. Think about what happens when a company is sold, merged, or restructured, or when contending theological interpretations lead to splits within a church or when profound alterations in the political order redistribute power in a country. Changes in the power structure, the traditional hierarchy, predictable norms, and well-known rules inevitably lead to disorientation and heightened anxiety. They may even lead to *anomie,* which is the breakdown of social bonds between an individual and the community. The French sociologist Émile Durkheim described anomie as "a rule that is a lack of rule."[12]

The bombardment of technology; the explosion of digital communication and online opinion, distraction, and noise; the decline of automatic acceptance of traditional authorities (president, judge, boss, elder, parent, priest, police officer, teacher) feed a disequilibrium with broad and poorly understood consequences. What are the social, political, and economic consequences of the fact that, in 1950, fewer than 10 percent of American households consisted of only one person whereas by 2010 that number had climbed to nearly 27 percent? Families are also power structures and there, too, power is decaying: those who have it (usually the parents, men, and older members) nowadays face more constraints. What does it tell us about trust in society that numerous social science studies have documented a decreased number of confidants among citizens in developed countries, as well as a corresponding rise in feelings of loneliness?[13]

IF THERE IS A MOUNTING RISK TO DEMOCRACY AND LIBERAL SOCIETIES in the twenty-first century, it is less likely to come from a conventional, modern threat (China) or a premodern one (Radical Islam) than from within societies where alienation has set in. As examples, consider the rise of movements that express or exploit social anger—from the new far-right and far-left parties in Europe and Russia to the Tea Party movement in the United States. On the one hand, each of these growing movements is a manifestation of the decay of power, as they owe their influence to the decline of the barriers that sheltered incumbents. On the other, the inchoate rage they express results in large part from alienation as the traditional markers of order and economic security have come down. And their search for a compass in the past—for instance, in nostalgia for the Soviet Union, eighteenth-century readings of the American constitution advocated by characters dressed in period costume, Osama bin Laden's exhortations about the restoration of the Caliphate, and Hugo Chavez's paeans to Simon Bolivar—reveals just how much the decay of power, if we fail to adjust to it and move it toward the social good, may backfire and turn destructive.

CHAPTER ELEVEN

POWER IS DECAYING

So What? What to Do?

THE FIRST AND PERHAPS MOST IMPORTANT IMPLICATION OF THIS book is the urgent need to change the way we think and talk about power.

One way to start is to refocus the conversation about how power is changing, what its sources are, who has it, and who is losing it and why. While we cannot anticipate the many changes that flow from the decay of power, we *can* adopt a mindset that will provide maximum flexibility, enabling us to plan better for the future and minimize the effects of the risks just mentioned.

It is important to recognize that the effects of the decay of power on the future now commonly envisioned by scholars, opinion makers, and political leaders have been just as discombobulating as in every other field.

Consider how fragmented and incomplete so much of the prevailing discourse has become. Take international politics, for example, and more specifically the debates about which country will dominate the twenty-first century: The United States or China? The emerging markets? No one? In the business world, one school of critics points to consolidation, oligarchy, and the cementing of power by a global corporate—and especially financial—elite, while an equally fervent set of views points to hyper-competition and the disruptive effects of new technologies and business models. Similarly, trends in global religion are either grounds for deep concern over fundamentalism and intolerance or healthy signs of social participation that can help advance moderation and liberty and peaceful coexistence.

All these arguments—and their opposites—crowd the shelves in book-stores, the opinion pages of newspapers worldwide, and of course, more stridently, our television screens and social media. And none of them are wrong. Or rather, advocates of each one can marshal a set of facts and evidence to make their own plausible and thought-provoking case.

Indeed, it's striking how little consensus exists about the direction of change in our world and what threats we need to anticipate as a result—let alone how to deal with them. For all the flood of data and opinions available today, we lack a reliable compass: a clear framework to help make sense of changes taking place in all these realms that are more and more connected. Any road map for the future will fall short if it lacks a better understanding of the ways in which power is changing and their consequences.

The implications of the decay of power are momentous and manifold. But it will be impossible to distill them and integrate them into the world-view and the mindsets of decision makers—in people's homes, in presidential palaces, or in boardrooms—unless we create a different conversation that takes into account what is happening to power.

And the first step in changing the conversation about power is to get off the elevator.

GET OFF THE ELEVATOR

Much talk about power today is still fundamentally traditional—and thus often dangerously antiquated. Exhibit A is the continued prevalence of elevator thinking: the obsession with who is going up and who is coming down—which country, city, industry, company, political leader, business potentate, religious patriarch, or pundit is gaining power and which, or who, is losing it. Elevator thinking is deeply rooted in the instinct to rank and to proclaim *Number One.* It is the allure of the sports league table, or the horse race.

You can, of course, rank competitors at any given time by their assets, power, and achievements. At the global level, states do compete with each other, after all, and factors such as a country's economic output, its network of military installations and resources, population, landmass, manufacturing prowess, and so on offer metrics for measuring and ranking. But the picture they offer is ephemeral—a snapshot with ever shorter exposure—and, worse, it is misleading. The more we fixate on rankings, the more we risk ignoring or underestimating how much the decay of power is weakening all the competing parties, not just the ones in apparent decline but also the ones on the rise.

Many Chinese writers and scholars are bullish on China's rise; likewise Indians, Russians, and Brazilians for their respective countries. Europeans are consumed by their continent's increasing marginalization in the world's geopolitical chess game. But the bulk of elevator conversation comes from the United States, where analysts tirelessly argue whether the decline of the country is terminal, treatable, transient, or indeed an illusion. Others make more nuanced arguments about the "rise of the rest" and the passage to a world where geopolitics is "multipolar."[1]

Other books that analyze the diluting effects on power caused by the proliferation of new countries capable of influencing global outcomes also do so without getting off the elevator or transcending the perspective that uses the nation-state as chief protagonist and the main unit of analysis. Charles Kupchan, a respected international relations theorist, argues that "the western order will not be displaced by a new great power or dominant political model. The twenty-first century will not belong to America, China, Asia, or anyone else. It will be no one's world. For the first time in history, the world will be interdependent—but without a center of gravity or global guardian."[2] This is also the view of author and business consultant Ian Bremmer, who called it "G-Zero: a world order in which no country or durable alliance of countries can meet the challenges of global leadership."[3] And both of these authors echo Zbigniew Brzezinski's assertion that "we have entered a post-hegemonic era," meaning that in the years ahead no country will be able to call the shots in global politics as much as some of the great powers did in the past.[4]

It is hard to disagree with any of this, and in Chapter 5 we examined the many forces that conspire against the permanent dominance of any single nation-state. But keeping our lens focused on the nation-state— even when arguing that none of them will dominate world affairs—can blur our view of the other forces reshaping international affairs: the decay of power in domestic politics, business, and the rest.

Whether the United States is a hegemon, an indispensable power, or an empire at sunset, and whether China or some other rival stands to take its place, may be a debate that consumes international relations. But its terms are not adapted to a world where power is decaying—where unprecedented forms of fracturing are under way within each of these countries and across systems of trade, investment, migration, and culture. Identifying who is up and who is down is less important than understanding what is going on *inside* those nations, political movements, corporations, and religions that are on the elevator. Who is up and who is down will matter ever less in a world in which those who get to the top don't stay there for long and are able to do less and less with the power they have while there.

MAKE LIFE HARDER
FOR THE "TERRIBLE SIMPLIFIERS"

A second important implication of this analysis is our heightened vulnerability to bad ideas and bad leaders. In short, once we have gotten off the elevator, we need to get skeptical, especially toward the latter-day version of Burckhardt's "terrible simplifiers."

The decay of power creates fertile soil for demagogic challengers who exploit disappointments with incumbents, promise change, and take advantage of the bewildering noise created by the proliferation of actors, voices, and proposals. The confusion created by changes that come too fast, that are too disruptive and undercut old certainties and ways of doing things—all by-products of the More, Mobility, and Mentality revolutions— offer great opportunities for leaders with bad ideas. Top bankers who championed toxic financial instruments as creative solutions, US politicians who promise to eliminate the fiscal deficit without raising taxes, and, at the other extreme, the French president François Hollande's decision to levy an extraordinary 75 percent tax on the income of the rich are only a few examples. Information technology evangelists, those who believe that technological "fixes" alone will solve hitherto intractable human problems, also tend to overstate their claims and end up being "terrible simplifiers."

These dangerous demagogues can be found in all of the areas discussed in these pages: the entrepreneurs and thinkers who argued that Internet companies with minimal assets and meager or no revenues deserved higher valuations than "old economy" companies with steady cash flows and vast assets, the strategists who promised that invading Iraq would be a "cakewalk" and the invaders would be welcomed as liberators or that the war would "pay for itself" thanks to Iraq's oil revenues. Osama bin Laden and Al Qaeda, the Taliban, and other murderous movements also depend on the terrible simplifications that they successfully manage to popularize. The promises and assumptions of the "Bolivarian Revolution" inspired by Hugo Chavez or, at the opposite extreme, those of the US Tea Party are also rooted in terrible simplifications immune to the lessons of experience and, for that matter, to data and scientific evidence.

Of course, demagogues, charlatans, and snake-oil peddlers are nothing new; history is replete with the stories of those who have gained power and whose stay at the top had terrible consequences. What *is* new is an environment where it has become far easier for newcomers—including those with toxic ideas—to acquire power.

Being on the lookout for the terrible simplifiers and denying them the influence they seek has always been necessary. And strengthening our ability—individual and collective, intellectual and political—to detect them in our midst is even more of a priority in a world undergoing rapid, bewildering change. That starts with embracing the reality of the decay of power and, again, changing our conversation to reflect it. Not just in the corridors of presidential palaces, corporate headquarters, and university boardrooms but even more so in encounters around watercoolers in offices, in casual conversations among friends, and at the dinner table at home.

These conversations are the indispensable ingredients of a political climate that is less welcoming to the terrible simplifiers. For as Francis Fukuyama correctly argues, to eradicate the vetocracy that is paralyzing the system, "political reform must first and foremost be driven by popular, grassroots mobilization."[5] This, in turn, requires focusing the conversation on how to contain the negative aspects of the decay of power and move us to the positive sloping side of the inverted U-curve. For this to happen, we need something that is very difficult: an increased disposition in democratic societies to give more power to those who govern us. And that is impossible unless we trust them more. Which is of course even more difficult. But also indispensable.

Bring Trust Back

Although the decay of power affects all realms of organized human activity, the consequences in some are more ominous than in others. The lessened ability of business executives to impose their will or retain power is less problematic than when that happens to elected leaders who are paralyzed by the vetocracy.

And at the international level the level of paralysis is even more ominous. Global problems are multiplying while the capacity of the international community to contain them is stagnant or dwindling. In other words, the inability of some business executives to make things happen threatens us all less than when national and international leaders are, like Gulliver, immobilized by thousands of small "micropowers" that tie them down.

When was the last time you heard that a large number of countries agreed to a major international accord on a pressing issue? Not in more than a decade and, for some important issues, that span of inaction stretches to even two or three. The inability of European nations—which ironically had already adopted shared governing arrangements—to act together in the face of a crippling economic crisis is as revealing of this paralysis as is the inability of the world to do something to curb the emissions of greenhouse gases that are warming the planet. Or the inability to stop massacres like those that erupted in Syria in 2012.

The pattern—and the emergency—is clear: Since the early 1990s, as the effects of globalization and the More, Mobility, and Mentality revolutions spread around the world, the need for effective multicountry collaboration has soared. But the capacity of the world to respond to these new needs has not kept pace. Critical multilateral talks have failed, deadlines have been missed, financial commitments and promises have not been honored, execution has stalled. International collective action has fallen far short of what was offered and, more importantly, needed.[6] These failures represent not only the now almost chronic lack of international consensus but, indeed, another important manifestation of the decay of power.

And what has all this to do with the need to restore trust?

The failure of political leaders to effectively collaborate with other nations is related to their weakness at home. Governments with weak or nonexistent mandates are unable to strike international deals as these often require commitments, compromises, concessions, and even sacrifices that their publics won't allow them to make. The implication is not that we need to give blank checks and unrestrained power to those who govern us: we know that power without controls, accountability, and countervailing forces is dangerous and unacceptable. But we also need to recognize that when our society operates on the declining side of the inverted U-curve, additional constraints to the power of those in government end up hurting us. Restoring trust is essential to relax these controls and bring them to the side of the inverted U-curve in which society benefits. The exploding number and complexity of the checks and balances that restrain the power of those who run democratic governments are direct results of the decline of trust. In some countries, this decline has become a permanent trend. Recall the observation of Carnegie's President Jessica Mathews, who was quoted in Chapter 4 in the context of the Mentality revolution: "[In the United States] anyone under the age of forty has lived their entire life in a country the majority of whose citizens do not trust their own national government to do what they think is right."[7]

There are, of course, many good reasons not to trust politicians and, in general, those in power: not only their mendacity and corruption but also the frequent underperformance of governments when compared with our expectations as voters. Moreover, we are all better informed, and heightened media scrutiny is prone to highlight the misdeeds, mistakes, and inadequacies of governments. As a result, the low levels of trust in government that are now common have become chronic.

This needs to change. We need to restore trust in government and in our political leaders. For this to happen will require profound changes in the way political parties organize and operate and in how they screen, monitor, hold accountable, and promote—or demote—their leaders. Adapting political parties to the twenty-first century is a priority.

STRENGTHEN POLITICAL PARTIES: THE LESSONS FROM OCCUPY WALL STREET AND AL QAEDA

In most democracies, parties continue to be the principal political organizations and still retain substantial power. But beneath the surface, they are as fragmented, weakened, and polarized as the overall political system in which they are embedded. In fact, today, most old-line political parties are unable to muster the power they once had. An illustrative example is the hostile takeover of the Republican Party by the Tea Party and the internal divisions the latter has unleashed in what was once one of the world's most powerful political machines. Similarly crippling factional conflicts are visible in political parties around the world.

By any reckoning, since the 1990s political parties have had a bad stretch. In most countries, opinion surveys show that their prestige and value in the eyes of the very people they serve are declining and, in some cases, have plummeted to an all-time low.[8]

The end of the Cold War and, more specifically, the collapse of communism as an inspirational idea blurred the ideological lines that gave many parties their unique identity. As electoral platforms became indistinguishable, the personalities of candidates became the main, and often the only, differentiating factor. To win elections, political parties relied less on the popular appeal of their ideals and ideas and more on marketing techniques, the media prowess of candidates, and, of course, the money they could raise. Naturally, the same scandals that tarnish individual politicians also affect the political organizations to which they belong. Again, freer media and more independent parliaments and judiciaries ensured that corrupt practices once carefully hidden or silently tolerated became painfully visible and obviously criminal, thus degrading the "brand" of the political party. The public tarnishing was also fueled by political parties that could no longer distinguish themselves ideologically from their opponents and relied on corruption accusations and scandals to define political rivals in the minds of voters. It is impossible to ascertain whether political corruption actually increased in the past decades, but it certainly has been more publicized than ever.

Meanwhile, whereas political parties struggled, social movements and nongovernmental organizations (NGOs) thrived. Even murderous terrorist organizations like Al Qaeda (which in many important ways are also NGOs) went global and had a good run in the 1990s. As the ties between political parties and their electorates weakened, those between NGOs and their supporters became tighter. As the public standing of politicians and political parties continued its secular decline, the prestige and influence of NGOs grew. Trust in NGOs grew as fast as trust in political parties dwindled. Their ability to recruit young and highly motivated activists willing to sacrifice for the organization and its cause is an organizational skill that has become more common among NGOs than among political parties.

As NGOs pursued their single issues with monomaniacal zeal, political parties chased a multitude of different, even contradictory, goals and seemed monomaniacal only in their pursuit of campaign contributions. In countries where political parties remained banned or stifled, NGOs became the only channel of political and social activism. In most other nations, NGOs grew rapidly because they were less tainted by corruption, often belonged to a larger international network, and generally had clearer ideals, a less hierarchical structure, and a closer relationship with their members. NGOs also had the advantage of having a clear mission. Whether dedicated to protecting human rights, saving the environment, lessening poverty, or controlling population growth, members rarely lost sight of what their organizations stood for. All of these factors led new cohorts of political activists, who in the past would have gravitated toward political parties, to tend instead toward NGOs.

The growth of NGOs is, on balance, a welcome trend. What is far less welcome, and indeed ought to be reversed, is the erosion in the public standing of political parties, which in many countries—Italy, Russia, Venezuela, and so on—has led to their virtual disappearance and replacement with ad hoc electoral machines.

The key to parties' resurgence and increased effectiveness is to regain the ability to inspire, energize, and mobilize people—especially the young—who would otherwise disdain politics altogether, or channel whatever political energy they have through single-issue organizations or even fringe groups.

Political parties must therefore be willing to adapt their structures and methods to a more networked world. Just as relatively flat, less hierarchical structures have enabled NGOs to be more nimble, adaptable, and more attuned to the needs and expectations of their members, so they might also help political parties reach new members, become more agile, advance their agendas, and hopefully become better at fighting the terrible simplifiers that seek power inside and outside the party.

NGOs gain the trust of their supporters by making their members feel they are having a direct impact, that their efforts are indispensable, that their leaders are accountable, transparent, and not beholden to dark or unknown interests. Political parties need to elicit these same feelings from larger segments of society and to be capable of enlisting members beyond their narrow, traditional base of stalwart activists.

Only then will they be able to recover the kind of power they need to govern us well.

INCREASE POLITICAL PARTICIPATION

Easier said than done. Who has the time? And the patience to attend all the meetings and group activities that come with the involvement in any collective undertaking—especially a political party? These and other good reasons explain why only rarely do most people get actively involved in political parties or social causes in ways that go beyond the giving of an occasional donation or attending a meeting or a rally once in a very long while. Under normal circumstances, political involvement and social activism are for minorities.

But in recent years we have been surprised by sudden surges of interest in public affairs, the mobilization of vast numbers of usually uninterested, even apathetic citizens, and the engagement of tens of thousands in political activities that are more demanding (and in some countries more dangerous) than attending a political party's meeting.

In the United States, for example, Barack Obama and his presidential campaign in 2008 were able to motivate large numbers of political neophytes and young people who would not normally be interested or engaged in one of the two parties' electoral activities. Beyond the background and race of the candidate, a lot more happened in the 2008 campaign that was also unprecedented: from the innovations in social media used to target political advertising to specific voters, to the use and recruitment of volunteers, to the novel approaches to fundraising. The surprises inherent in the sudden surge of political activism by hitherto-inert groups did not stop with the political newcomers to the Obama campaign. Energized or, rather, infuriated by the financial crises and the perception of unfairness in the distribution of the burdens of the crisis, the Occupy Wall Street movement and its thousands of equivalents in cities around the world also stunned governments and political parties that scrambled to understand its nature and functioning while searching for ways to tap the political energy of these largely spontaneous movements.

The most surprising and consequential manifestation of this broader activist trend started with an upheaval in a small town in Tunisia in December 2010. It led to the toppling of the government there and ultimately to the contagious wave of protests and demonstrations throughout the Middle East that became the Arab Spring. Millions of once passive—and repressed—citizens became political actors willing to make extreme sacrifices that included not just risking their own lives but even putting their families in danger. In contrast to the "Occupy" movements, which so far have been unable to convert political energy into political power, in the Arab Spring the political awakening did lead to important power shifts.

Thus, whereas under normal circumstances political participation is for small groups of engaged activists, in other instances, such as revolutions, political activism becomes the obsessive focus of entire societies. But revolutions are too costly, their outcome is too uncertain, and progress is not their guaranteed result. Therefore, the challenge is to avoid costly and risky revolutions while creating and channeling the political energy latent in all societies to effect desirable changes. The best way to do that is through more competitive political parties.

Rethinking political parties, modernizing their recruiting methods, and retooling their organization and operations can boost their allure and make them more worthy of the trust of the societies they wish to govern. Ideally, they could also become more effective laboratories of political innovation.

Only when we restore trust in the political system at home—and thus endow our leaders with the capacity to contain the decay of power and enable them to make hard decisions and avoid gridlock—will we be able to tackle the most pressing global challenges. And for this we need stronger, more modern, and more democratic political parties that stimulate and facilitate participation.

THE COMING SURGE OF POLITICAL INNOVATIONS

Restoring trust, reinventing political parties, finding new ways in which average citizens can meaningfully participate in the political process, creating new mechanisms of effective governance, limiting the worst impacts of checks and balances while averting excessive concentrations of unaccountable power, and enhancing the capacity of nation-states to work together should be the central political goals of our time.

Without these changes, sustained progress in fighting the threats at home and abroad that conspire against our security and prosperity will be impossible.

In this era of revolutionary change, where almost nothing we do or experience in our daily lives has been left unaffected, one critical area remains surprisingly untouched: the way we govern ourselves, our communities, nations, and the international system. Or the ways in which we as individuals engage in the political process. Ideologies have come and gone, political parties have risen and fallen, and some government practices have been improved by reforms and information technology. Electoral campaigns now rely on more sophisticated methods of persuasion—and, of course, more people than ever are governed by a leader they have elected and not by a dictator. While welcome, these changes pale in comparison with the extraordinary transformations in communications, medicine, business, and war.

In short, disruptive innovation has not arrived in politics, government, and political participation.

But it will. We are on the verge of a revolutionary wave of positive political and institutional innovations. As this book has shown, power is changing in so many arenas that it will be impossible to avoid important transformations in the way humanity organizes itself to make the decisions it needs to survive and progress. This kind of surge in radical and positive innovations in government has happened before. Greek democracy and the wave of political innovations unleashed by the French Revolution are just two of the best-known examples. We're overdue for another. As the historian Henry Steele Commager asserted about the eighteenth century:

We invented practically every major political institution which we have, and we have invented none since. We invented the political party and democracy and representative government. We invented the first independent judiciary in history. . . . We invented judicial review. We invented the superiority of the civil over the military power. We invented freedom of religion, freedom of speech, the Bill of Rights—well, we could go on and on. . . . Quite a heritage. But what have we invented since of comparable importance?[9]

After World War II, we did experience another surge of political innovations designed to avert another global conflict. That led to the creation of the United Nations, and to a plethora of specialized international agencies such as the World Bank and the International Monetary Fund that changed the world's institutional landscape.

ANOTHER, EVEN MORE SWEEPING, WAVE OF INNOVATIONS IS BUILDING, one that promises to change the world as much as the technological revolutions of the last two decades did. It will not be top-down, orderly, or quick, the product of summits or meetings, but messy, sprawling, and in fits and starts. Yet it is inevitable. Driven by the transformation in the acquisition, use, and retention of power, humanity must, and will, find new ways of governing itself.

APPENDIX

Democracy and Political Power: Main Trends During the Postwar Period

Note to readers: This appendix—prepared by Mario Chacón, PhD, Yale University—applies particularly to Chapter 5.

MEASURING THE EVOLUTION OF DEMOCRACY AND DICTATORSHIP

I start by taking a look at how the number of democratic regimes has changed over the last four decades. To determine which countries are democracies and which ones are not, I have used two taxonomies widely employed in the academic literature.

The first taxonomy of regimes is the one provided in the *Freedom in the World* survey conducted by Freedom House (2008). In this survey, regimes are classified as "not free," "partially free," and "free." Each country is classified depending on a scale that measures political rights and civil liberties. The subcategories measured in the scale are freedom of electoral processes, political pluralism, functioning of government, freedom of expression and belief, associational and organizational freedom, rule of law, and personal rights. For purposes of the analysis, I categorize "free" countries as full democracies, and "not free" and "partially free" countries as nondemocratic.

The second source I used is the regime classification of Przeworski et al. (2000), which is based on a minimalist definition of democracy similar to the one proposed by Schumpeter (1964). In this classification, a "democracy" is a regime in which the government is selected through contested elections. Thus, in this classification free and fair contestation is the fundamental facet in any democratic regime (see Dahl 1971 for a similar approach). Using these two classifications, I have calculated the percentage of all independent regimes in the world that are classified as "democratic" (as opposed to "nondemocratic") in any given year.

245

Figure A.1 shows the evolution of democratic regimes worldwide since 1972.*

FIGURE A.1. PERCENTAGE OF DEMOCRATIC REGIMES: 1972–2008

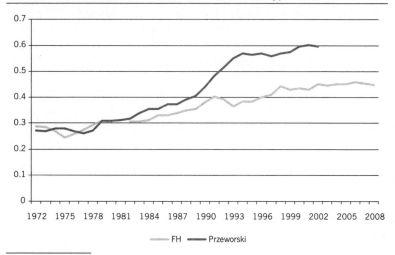

SOURCE: Adapted from Freedom House Index.

As shown in Figure A.1, the percentage of democracies across the world has increased significantly in the last four decades. According to Freedom House, in 1972 a little more than 28 percent of the 140 independent regimes observed in the world were democratic. Thirty years later, in 2002, this figure was 45 percent. This global increase in the number of democracies is confirmed by Przeworski's data. In this classification, between 1972 and 2002 the percentage of democracies increased from 27 percent in 1972 to 59 percent in 2002. The differences between the two measures are to be expected given that the conditions for democracy used by Freedom House are somewhat stricter than the ones used by Przeworski and his co-authors. Yet, we can conclude from this first approximation that there has been an overall positive trend in the number of democratic regimes around the world in the past three decades.

Are there regional differences in the evolution of democratic regimes? If the factors causing drastic regime changes are clustered across space, we should observe regional patterns in the evolution of democratic regimes. These regional patterns are closely related to the idea of "waves of democratization" described originally by

*The start point of 1972 corresponds to data availability. The Freedom House Index covers the period from 1972 to 2008.

Huntington (1991). To explore this possibility, in Figures A.2 and A.3 I show the evolution of democratic regimes (as a percentage of all the regimes) in Latin America, sub-Saharan Africa, the ex-Soviet bloc, North Africa, and the Middle East.*

As shown in these two figures, many Latin American and ex-Soviet countries experienced a democratic transition during the period from 1975 to 1995. These transitions occurred mostly in the late 1970s for Latin America and in the early 1990s for the ex-Soviet bloc (following the fall of the Berlin wall in 1989). In 2008, 54 and 48 percent of the Latin American and ex-Soviet countries, respectively, are classified as free (democratic) by Freedom House. There is also a positive trend in democratization in sub-Saharan Africa, although it is less steep than the trend for Latin America. The Arab countries of North Africa and the Middle East are remarkably stable, and fewer than 10 percent of them are classified as democracies throughout these years. These patterns are confirmed by Przeworski's data, which are graphically represented in Figure A.3.

These trends, of course, do not yet capture the effect of the Arab Spring on the political regimes in North Africa and the Middle East.

FIGURE A.2. REGIONAL TRENDS (FREEDOM HOUSE 2010)

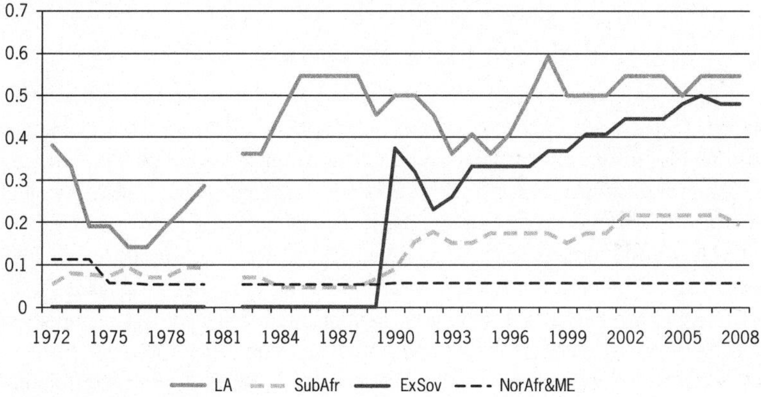

SOURCE: Adapted from Freedom House, *Freedom in the World: Political Rights and Civil Liberties 1970–2008* (New York: Freedom House, 2010).

The OECD countries are not shown because these countries did not experience any radical regime change during the period in question. Given that all of these countries were democratic at the beginning of the period studied, their evolution is characterized by a stable (consolidated) democracy.

---

*The regional classification is the one used by the World Bank.

FIGURE A.3. REGIONAL TRENDS IN DEMOCRACY (PRZEWORSKI ET AL., 2000)

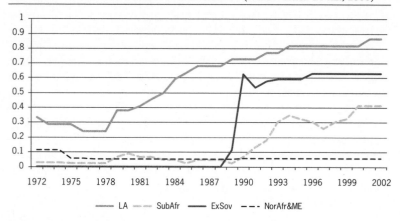

SOURCE: Adapted from A. Przeworski, M. Alvarez, J. A. Cheibub, and F. Limongi. 2000. *Democracy and Development: Political Institutions and Well-Being in the World, 1950–1990*, Cambridge University Press, New York.

MINOR REFORMS AND LIBERALIZATIONS

The figures presented thus far focus on radical political transformations in which a political regime becomes (or ceases) to be a democracy. These numbers may hide smaller movements toward democracy in many countries that did not experience a full transition. Minor reforms may induce important changes in the distribution of political power and human rights. For instance, many nondemocratic regimes introduced and allowed electoral competition to elect the legislature and high executive positions. Even if most of the elections in regimes considered fully democratic are not completely fair, minor liberalization may signal important changes in the distribution of power. Moreover, many transitions occur gradually, so the initiation of electoral competition may be indicative of future democratizations.

To explore minor reforms, I have employed the *Polity Score* developed in the Polity Project of Marshall and Jaggers (2004). This measure is a continuous approximation that allows us to capture smaller regime changes, whether or not they end in democratization. Specifically, the Polity Score is a 20-point scale (ranging from –20, for a full autocracy, to 20, the score of a full democracy) measuring various facets of democracy and autocracy. The components of the scale include competitiveness and openness of the executive recruitment, constraint on the executive, and competitiveness of political participation. Figure A.4 presents the evolution of the world average Polity Score.

FIGURE A.4. EVOLUTION OF DEMOCRACY: 1970–2008

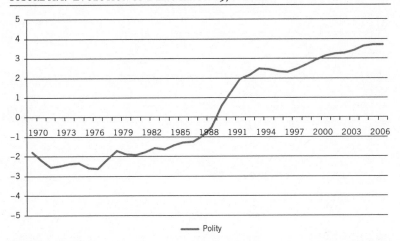

SOURCE: Adapted from Monty Marshall, K. Jaggers, and T. R. Gurr, 2010. Polity IV Project, "Political Regime Characteristics and Transitions, 1800–2010," http://www.systemicpeace.org /polity4.htm.

Figure A.4 is fully consistent with Figure A.1. In 1972, the world average was –1.76 for 130 countries; in 2007, it was 3.69 for 159 countries.* Arguably an even more interesting exercise is to examine region-specific trends using the Polity Score. Figure A.5 presents the same world average disaggregated by region. (Note that the countries of East Asia and the Pacific are also included here.) Figure A.5 is analogous to Figures A.2 and A.3, but instead of radical reforms it shows average movements in the democracy scores by region, regardless of whether or not these regimes have become (or stopped being) democratic.

As illustrated in Figure A.5, the positive trends in the Polity Score over the last four decades, which indicate that countries are becoming more democratic over time, are global. This figure also indicates that the pace of democratic improvement differs across regions. The Latin American and the ex-Soviet countries exhibit the greatest improvements in their democracy scores, the East Asian and the Pacific countries and sub-Saharan Africa exhibit significant improvements, and the North African and the Middle Eastern countries exhibit the least improvements. All three trends are more pronounced during the post-1990 period than during the pre-1990 period.

---

*The Polity project excludes countries with less than 100,000 inhabitants.

FIGURE A.5. REGIONAL TRENDS IN DEMOCRACY: POLITY SCORE

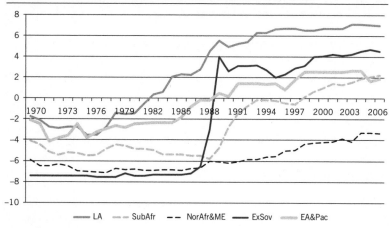

SOURCE: Adapted from Monty Marshall, K. Jaggers, and T. R. Gurr, 2010. Polity IV Project, "Political Regime Characteristics and Transitions, 1800–2010," http://www.systemicpeace.org /polity4.htm.

PROXIES OF LIBERALIZATION AND DEMOCRATIZATION

The above indicators are based on qualitative characteristics of the regimes observed, whereas in this section I have focused on characteristics that are directly related to political liberalization (or to democratization). First, I looked at the level of political competition. For many political theorists, the level and the type of political competition are the fundamental features of any democratic regime (see Dahl 1971). A simple approximation to the level of competition is to examine the party composition of legislatures across regimes. In one-party regimes like China or Cuba, the incumbent party monopolizes all seats in the legislature and the opposition's candidates are not allowed to run at the national level. The number of seats held by opposition parties in the legislature could be a good proxy for how competitive and democratic the electoral process is. Moreover, the introduction of party competition in the legislature (as opposed to the executive) is generally the first step in a full-scale democratization. For instance, the Mexican transition of 2000 started in the early 1980s, when the ruling party, the Partido Revolucionario Institucional (PRI), allowed for meaningful congressional elections and reserved a certain number of seats for opposition parties in the lower chamber.

Next, as a proxy for competitiveness I calculated the percentage of seats in parliament held by all minority parties and independents, as in Vanhanen (2002). In cases where the legislature composition is not available, I used the vote share of

all the small parties, also as in Vanhanen (2002). Formally, the measure of political competitiveness (PC) is given by the following equation:

$$PC = (100 - \%SeatsMajorityParty)/100$$

In this operationalization, political competition ranges from 0 cases in which
the government party controls all seats in the legislature to values close to 1, cases
in which the dominant party is very small. Thus, low (high) values of PC are associated with less (more) competition. For simplicity, countries in which there is no
elected legislature in any given year are coded as 0. Note that these numbers are
available for the entire postwar period so that we can see both the medium- and
long-term trends. Figure A.6 presents the world average, and Figure A.7 presents
the regional averages.

As we can see from these figures, the immediate postwar years and the entire
Cold War period are associated with an overall decline in political competition.
This trend continues until the late 1970s. Then, in the 1980s, it reverses and we observe an increase in the global average of our variable: political competition. This
positive trend in the post-1970s is consistent with Figures A.1 through A.4. Clearly,
democratization tends to promote party competition and political divisions (aris-
ing from opposition groups) in the legislature.

FIGURE A.6. POLITICAL COMPETITION, WORLD AVERAGE: POSTWAR PERIOD

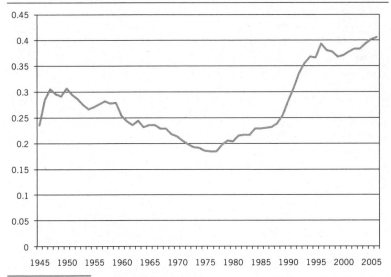

SOURCE: Adapted from Tatu Vanhanen. 2002. "Measures of Democratization 1999–2000." Unpublished manuscript.

Figure A.7 gives us an even better understanding about the general decline in political competition during the 1945–1975 period. Here, I show the averages for the same regions as those highlighted in Figures A.2 and A.3—Latin America, sub-Saharan Africa, North Africa, and the Middle East—as well as the average for the Organisation for Economic Co-operation and Development (OECD) countries.* This graph shows that the global decline in political competition was caused by a sharp decline in the developing world. While the OECD competition remained stable, Latin America and Africa experienced a wave of authoritarianism in the period between 1945 and 1975. However, the positive tendency in political competition in these countries during the post-1970s is consistent with the positive trends in democracy presented in the previous section.

FIGURE A.7. POLITICAL COMPETITION, REGIONAL AVERAGES: POSTWAR PERIOD

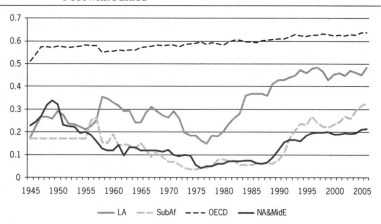

SOURCE: Adapted from Monty Marshall, K. Jaggers, and T. R. Gurr, 2010. Polity IV Project, "Political Regime Characteristics and Transitions, 1800–2010," http://www.systemicpeace.org /polity4.htm.

*For purposes of this analysis I included only the original OECD countries. Mexico, Chile, Turkey, Korea, the Czech Republic, and Poland are not included in the OECD group.

References

Dahl, Robert A. 1971. *Polyarchy: Participation and Opposition*. New Haven: Yale University Press.

Freedom House. 2010. *Freedom in the World: Political Rights and Civil Liberties 2010*. New York: Freedom House.

Huntington, Samuel P. 1991. *The Third Wave: Democratization in the Late Twentieth Century*. Normal: University of Oklahoma Press.

Marshall, Monty G., K. Jaggers, and T. R. Gurr, 2010. "Political Regime Characteristics and Transitions, 1800–2010." Polity IV Project, http://www.systemic peace.org/polity4.htm.

Przeworski, A., M. Alvarez, J. A. Cheibub, and F. Limongi. 2000. *Democracy and Development: Political Institutions and Well-Being in the World, 1950–1990*. New York: Cambridge University Press.

Schumpeter, Joseph. 1964. *Capitalism, Socialism, and Democracy*. New York: Harper & Brothers.

Vanhanen, Tatu. 2002. "Measures of Democratization 1999–2000." Unpublished manuscript. University of Tampere, Finland.

Acknowledgments

I BEGAN TO WRITE THIS BOOK SHORTLY AFTER JUNE 7, 2006. THAT was the day when I published a column in *Foreign Policy* magazine titled "Megaplayers Vs. Micropowers." The column's central message was that the trend "where players can rapidly accumulate immense power, where the power of traditional megaplayers is successfully challenged, and where power is both ephemeral and harder to exercise, is evident in every facet of human life. In fact, it is one of the defining and not yet fully understood characteristics of our time." The column was well received and I was thus encouraged to expand it into a book. It only took me seven years to convert that intention into this book. . . . Yes, I am a slow writer.

But that is not the only reason why it took so long. I also had many distractions. Until 2010, I was the editor-in-chief of *Foreign Policy* magazine, a demanding job that slowed down my book writing but also gave me a wealth of opportunities to test, expand, and refine my ideas on how power is changing. Interacting with the authors who wrote for the magazine and with its brilliant staff was a constant source of inspiration, information, and intellectual challenge. They took me where I could not have gone on my own, and for that, I am very grateful.

The person who deserves most of the credit for helping me develop the ideas in this book is Siddhartha Mitter. His support, suggestions, and overall contribution to the book are immeasurable. Siddhartha's talent is only exceeded by his generosity. James Gibney, the first editor I hired at *FP*, and one of the best editors I know, was also instrumental in pushing me to clarify my thinking and forcing me to render my thoughts in the clearest possible language. I am very fortunate to have had the help of these two extraordinary colleagues and dear friends.

Jessica Mathews, the president of the Carnegie Endowment for International Peace, read and commented in great detail on several drafts of the manuscript and was a constant source of ideas, criticism, and guidance. Her 1997 article, "Power Shift," continues to be the seminal work that influences all of us who write about power and its contemporary changes. Jessica also gave me the time to finish the book at Carnegie, my professional home since the early 1990s. I am deeply indebted to her and to the Carnegie Endowment.

I am also grateful to Phil Bennett, Jose Manuel Calvo, Matt Burrows, Uri Dadush, Frank Fukuyama, Paul Laudicina, Soli Ozel, and Stephen Walt, who read the entire manuscript and gave me detailed comments that made the book vastly better. And to Strobe Talbott, a longtime, generous friend who is now the president of the Brookings Institution, and who not only found the time to read several drafts of the entire manuscript but also spent hours helping me refine the implications of the decay of power.

Thanks are due to those who over the long period of this book's gestation gave me their time, shared their insights, critiqued my ideas, and in some cases, read and commented on early drafts of individual chapters: Mort Abramowitz, Jacques Attali, Ricardo Avila, Carlo de Benedetti, Paul Balaran, Andrew Burt, Fernando Henrique Cardoso, Tom Carver, Elkyn Chaparro, Lourdes Cue, Wesley Clark, Tom Friedman, Lou Goodman, Victor Halberstadt, Ivan Krastev, Steven Kull, Ricardo Lagos, Sebastian Mallaby, Luis Alberto Moreno, Evgeny Morozov, Dick O'Neill, Minxin Pei, Maite Rico, Gianni Riotta, Klaus Schwab, Javier Solana, George Soros, Larry Summers, Gerver Torres, Martin Wolf, Robert Wright, Ernesto Zedillo, and Bob Zoellick.

A special note of thanks goes to Professor Mario Chacón of New York University, who prepared the appendix, a detailed analysis of empirical data showing the manifestations of the decay of power in national politics worldwide.

I had superb research assistants throughout the period I worked on this book. I'd like to thank Josh Keating, Bennett Stancil, and Shimelse Ali for their help in making the book as strong as possible.

Those who think that the internet and search engines have made libraries obsolete have not had the experience of working with the staff of the Carnegie Endowment's library. Kathleen Higgs, Christopher Scott, and Keigh Hammond not only helped me find the sources and data I needed but often also alerted me to material that I did not know existed and in some instances proved critical in shaping my thinking. Thank you!

I owe a very special debt of gratitude to Melissa Betheil. She doubled as my executive assistant and researcher, performing with grace and intelligence what often seemed an impossible balancing act. Lara Ballou also helped me manage my diverse activities with kindness and effectiveness. A couple of years ago, Lara joined Marina Spindler in running The Group of Fifty, an organization over which I preside and which would have consumed far more of my time were it not for Marina and Lara's efforts. My thanks to these three indispensable colleagues.

I am very fortunate to have as my agent and as my editor two of the top professionals in the business. Rafe Sagalyn, my longtime literary agent, gently but firmly helped me to define more precisely the book I wanted to write and then found the right publisher and editor for such a book. Tim Bartlett, at Basic Books, who has edited many of the most significant recent works on power and its mutations, took a strong interest in this project and spent an inordinate amount of time reading, commenting on, and editing my drafts. I am immensely grateful to both of them. At Basic Books, Tim's assistants Sarah Rosenthal and Kaitlyn Zafonte were tremendously helpful. Sandra Beris and Christine J. Arden of Basic's production team provided splendid editorial support. And Michele Jacob, Basic's publicity director, and Caitlyn Graf, my publicist, were early and enthusiastic supporters of the book. I thank everyone on the team at Basic for getting behind the book.

I also want to recognize and express my thanks to Luis Alberto Moreno, Nelson Ortiz, Roberto Rimeris, and Alberto Slezynger. They know why.

My biggest thank-you, however, goes to my wife Susana, and to our children Adriana, Claudia, and Andres, a group now reinforced by Jonathan and Andrew. They give me the love, strength, and unconditional support that makes everything worthwhile. That is why this book is dedicated to them.

Moisés Naím
Washington, DC
March 2013

NOTES

CHAPTER ONE

1. Dylan Loeb McClain, "Masters of the Game and Leaders by Example," *New York Times,* November 12, 2011.

2. "The title of Grandmaster has been used since 1838, but gained greater currency in the early twentieth century, when tournaments were sometimes designated grandmaster events, e.g. Ostend 1907, San Sebastian 1912." The World Chess Federation (*Federation Internationale des Echecs,* known as FIDE from its French acronym) introduced the formal title "International Grandmaster" in 1950. The meaning of this term has changed during the history of chess. In the early twentieth it referred to someone who "might sensibly be considered as a challenger for the world championship, but eighty years later some to whom the world champion could give odds bear that name" (*"World Championship" Oxford Companion to Chess,* p. 450; Hooper and Whyld, *Oxford Companion to Chess,* p. 156).

3. Robson, *Chess Child: The Story of Ray Robson, America's Youngest Grandmaster.*

4. James Black, quoted in Michael Preston, "12-Year-Old Brooklyn Chess Champ Eyes Bold Move: Becoming Youngest Grandmaster Ever," *Daily News,* June 2, 2011.

5. D. T. Max, "The Prince's Gambit," *The New Yorker,* March 21, 2011, http://www.newyorker.com/reporting/2011/03/21/110321fa_fact_max.

6. Mig Greengard, quoted in ibid.

7. Edward Tenner, "Rook Dreams," *The Atlantic,* December 2008.

8. Max, "The Prince's Gambit."

9. Ivan Arreguín-Toft, "How the Weak Win Wars: A Theory of Asymmetric Conflict," *International Security* 26, no. 1 (2001): 93–128; Ivan Arreguín-Toft, "How a Superpower Can End Up Losing to the Little Guys," *Nieman Watchdog,* March 23, 2007, www.niemanwatchdog.org. On the impact of IEDs, see Tom Vanden Brook, "IED Attacks in Afghanistan Set Record," *USA Today,* January 25, 2012.

10. Martin Wolf, "Egypt Has History on Its Side," *Financial Times,* February 15, 2011. The updated figure for 2011 is from the Polity IV Project's *Global Report 2011,* which was compiled at George Mason University (Wolf's original source).

11. Emmanuel Saez, "Striking It Richer: The Evolution of Top Incomes in the United States (Updated with 2009 and 2010 Estimates)," March 2, 2012, http://elsa.berkeley.edu/~saez/saez-UStopincomes-2010.pdf.

12. Robert Frank, "The Wild Ride of the 1%," *Wall Street Journal,* October 22, 2011.

13. The sources for the facts and statistics cited here on business and managerial turnover can be found in the endnotes to Chapter 8.

14. ArcelorMittal's Web address is www.arcelormittal.com.

15. See my *Illicit: How Smugglers, Traffickers and Copycats Are Hijacking the Global Economy.*

16. Todd Gitlin, *Occupy Nation: The Roots, the Spirit, and the Promise of Occupy Wall Street* (New York: HarperCollins, 2012).

17. Joseph Marks, "TechRoundup," *Government Executive,* November 2011, p. 43.

18. Aday et al., "New Media and Conflict After the Arab Spring," p. 21.

19. Machiavelli, *The Prince,* ch. 3, http://www.constitution.org/mac/prince03.htm.

20. Hobbes, *Leviathan,* ch. 11, http://www.bartleby.com/34/5/11.html.

21. Nietzsche, *Thus Spake Zarathustra,* ch. 34, http://nietzsche.thefreelibrary.com/Thus-Spake-Zarathustra/36–1; see also Meacham, "The Story of Power," *Newsweek,* December 20, 2008.

22. Dahl, "The Concept of Power"; see also Zimmerling, "The Concept of Power," ch. 1. Another more academic definition was offered in 2005 by two leading scholars, Michael Barnett and Raymond Duvall: "Power is the production in and through social relations, of effects that shape the capacities of actors to determine their circumstances and fate." Based on this definition, they propose a taxonomy of power: compulsory, institutional, structural, and productive. See Barnett and Duvall, "Power in International Politics."

23. Hobbes, *Leviathan,* ch. 13, http://www.bartleby.com/34/5/13.html.

Chapter Two

1. For a detailed discussion, see MacMillan, *Strategy Formulation: Political Concepts,* particularly ch. 2.

2. The other two channels of power—coercion and reward—actually alter the situation.

3. At the theoretical level, finding a precise definition of barriers to entry has led to considerable hair-splitting among economists. One approach defines barriers to entry as factors that enable firms that are already in the market to command prices that are higher than unfettered competition would produce, yet without inducing new competitors to enter. Another approach identifies barriers to entry as any costs that a new competitor faces prior to entering the market, yet that firms already in the market do not face. In other words, the distinction is between a *protected price advantage* for firms already in the market and a *supplementary cost,* such as an entry fee, for would-be competitors. Other economists

have more complex definitions still, but nothing in these debates takes away from the core insight that barriers to entry are essential to understanding the dynamics of a marketplace and the use of market power to maximize long-term profits. (For further discussion of this issue, see Demsetz, "Barriers to Entry.")

4. On barriers to entry in politics, see Kaza, "The Economics of Political Competition."

CHAPTER THREE

1. LaFeber, *The Cambridge History of American Foreign Relations, Volume 2: The American Search for Opportunity, 1865–1913,* p. 186.

2. Adams, *The Education of Henry Adams: An Autobiography,* p. 500.

3. Chandler, *The Visible Hand: The Managerial Revolution in American Business;* see also Chandler, *Scale and Scope: The Dynamics of Industrial Capitalism.*

4. Lewis et al., *Personal Capitalism and Corporate Governance: British Manufacturing in the First Half of the Twentieth Century.* See also Micklethwait and Wooldridge, *The Company: A Short History of a Revolutionary Idea.*

5. Alan Wolfe, "The Visitor," *The New Republic,* April 21, 2011.

6. See "Max Weber" entry in *Concise Oxford Dictionary of Politics,* p. 558.

7. See "Max Weber" entry in *Encyclopaedia Britannica,* Vol. 12, p. 546.

8. Wolfgang Mommsen, "Max Weber in America," *American Scholar,* June 22, 2000.

9. Marianne Weber, *Max Weber: A Biography* (New York: Transaction Books, 1988).

10. Scaff, *Max Weber in America,* pp. 41–42.

11. Mommsen, "Max Weber in America."

12. Weber, *Economy and Society: An Outline of Interpretive Sociology.*

13. Scaff, *Max Weber in America,* p. 45.

14. Ibid., p. 45.

15. Weber, *Economy and Society: An Outline of Interpretive Sociology,* p. 973.

16. Weber, "Unequalled Models," in *Essays on Sociology,* p. 215.

17. Weber, "Politics as a Vocation," in *Economy and Society,* p. 223.

18. McNeill, *The Pursuit of Power,* p. 317.

19. The information in this paragraph is drawn from Zunz, *Philanthropy in America: A History.*

20. Coase, "The Nature of the Firm." The author describes his motivation for this research in his Nobel Prize lecture, which is available online at http://www.nobelprize.org/nobel_prizes/economics/laureates/1991/coase-lecture.html.

21. A more modern rendition of the transaction cost approach was offered by Coase's student Oliver Williamson in his important book *Markets and Hierarchies: Analysis and Antitrust Implications.* Williamson was awarded the Nobel Prize in Economics in 2009.

22. Leebaert, *The Fifty-Year Wound: The True Price of America's Cold War Victory,* p. xiii.

23. Sloan, *My Years with General Motors.*

24. Howe, "This Age of Conformity"; Riesman, Glazer, and Denney, *The Lonely Crowd: A Study of the Changing American Character.*

25. Marx and Engels, *The Communist Manifesto.*

26. Mills, *White Collar: The American Middle Classes.*

27. Mills, *The Power Elite.*

28. Eisenhower's speech is available online at http://www.h-net.org/~hst306 /documents/indust.html.

29. Domhoff, *Who Rules America? Challenges to Corporate and Class Dominance.*

30. Christopher Lasch, "The Revolt of the Elites: Have They Canceled Their Allegiance to America?" *Harper's,* November 1994.

31. Klein's talk is available online at http://fora.tv/2008/10/20/Naomi_Klein _and_Joseph_Stiglitz_on_Economic_Power#fullprogram.

32. Simon Johnson, "The Quiet Coup," *Atlantic,* May 2009, http://www.the atlantic.com/magazine/archive/2009/05/the-quiet-coup/7364/. See also Johnson and Kwak, *13 Bankers.*

CHAPTER FOUR

1. Interview with Javier Solana, Washington, DC, May 2012.

2. Larkin, *Collected Poems.*

3. William Odom, "NATO's Expansion: Why the Critics Are Wrong," *National Interest,* Spring 1995, p. 44.

4. Charles Kenny, "Best. Decade. Ever," *Foreign Policy,* September–October 2010, http://www.foreignpolicy.com/articles/2010/08/16/best_decade_ever.

5. Xavier Sala-i-Martin and Maxim Pinkovskiy, "African Poverty Is Falling . . . Much Faster Than You Think!," NBER Working Paper No. 15775, February 2010.

6. Interview with Homi Kharas, Washington, DC, February 2012.

7. The results of this OECD survey and other relevant reports can be found at www.globalworksfoundation.org/Documents/fact465.science_000.pdf.

8. Brzezinski, *Strategic Vision: America and the Crisis of Global Power.*

9. Jason DeParle, "Global Migration: A World Ever More on the Move," *New York Times,* June 26, 2010.

10. Jorge G. Castañeda and Douglas S. Massey, "Do-It-Yourself Immigration Reform," *New York Times,* June 1, 2012.

11. The figures on remittances are quoted from the World Bank Development Indicators Database (2011 edition).

12. Dean Yang, "Migrant Remittances," in *Journal of Economic Perspectives* 25, no. 3 (Summer 2011), pp. 129–152 at p. 130.

13. Richard Dobbs, "Megacities," *Foreign Policy,* September–October 2010, http://www.foreignpolicy.com/articles/2010/08/16/prime_numbers_megacities.

14. The National Intelligence Council, Office of the Director of National Intelligence, "Global Trends 2030: Alternative Worlds" (Washington, DC, 2012).

15. Saxenian, *The New Argonauts: Regional Advantage in a Global Economy.*

16. The figures on tourist arrivals are from the World Bank's World Development Indicators Database (2011 edition).

17. World Bank, "World Development Report 2009: Reshaping Economic Geography" (2009).

18. The figures on foreign exchange are from the Bank for International Settlements: Statistical Report (2011), http://www.bis.org/publ/rpfxf10t.htm.

19. "Somali Mobile Phone Firms Thrive Despite Chaos," Reuters, November 3, 2009.

20. These data are taken from the World Bank's World Development Indicators Database (multiple years) and the International Telecommunications Union indicators database.

21. Ibid.

22. Ibid.

23. Data provided by Facebook, Twitter, and Skype.

24. Long Distance Post, "The History of Prepaid Phone Cards," http://www.ldpost.com/telecom-articles/.

25. Ericsson (telecom company), *Traffic and Market Report,* June 2012.

26. Huntington, *Political Order in Changing Societies.*

27. Al-Munajjed et al., "Divorce in Gulf Cooperation Council Countries: Risks and Implications," Booz and Co, 2010.

28. National Intelligence Council, Office of the Director of National Intelligence, "Global Trends 2030: Alternative Worlds" (Washington DC, 2012), p. 12.

29. Frey, *Diversity Explosion: How New Racial Demographics Are Remaking America.*

30. William Frey, "A Boomlet of Change," *Washington Post,* June 10, 2012.

31. Inglehart and Welzel, *Modernization, Cultural Change and Democracy.*

32. Pharr and Putnam, *Disaffected Democracies: What's Troubling the Trilateral Countries.* For a discussion of this issue as it applies to the United States, see also Mann and Ornstein, *It's Even Worse Than ⁇ Looks: How the American Constitutional System Collided with the New Politics of Extremism.*

33. Mathews, "Saving America."

34. For Gallup survey data on public confidence in sixteen institutions between 1936 and 2012, see http://www.gallup.com/poll/1597/Confidence-Institutions.aspx?utm_source=email-a-friend&utm_medium=email&utm_campaign=sharing&utm_content=morelink. For Gallup survey data on labor unions, see http://www.gallup.com/poll/12751/Labor-Unions.aspx?utm_source=email-a-friend&utm_medium=email&utm_campaign=sharing&utm_content=morelink. For Gallup survey data on Congress, see http://www.gallup.com/poll/1600/Congress-Public.aspx?utm_source=email-a-friend&utm_medium=email&utm_campaign=sharing&utm_content=morelink. And for Gallup survey data on government, see http://www.gallup.com/poll/27286/Government.aspx?utm_source=email-a-friend&utm_medium=email&utm_campaign=sharing&utm_content=morelink.

35. "Americans' Approval of the Supreme Court is Down in a New Poll," *New York Times,* June 8, 2012.

36. Pew Global's Web address is http://www.pewglobal.org/.

37. Norris, *Critical Citizens: Global Support for Democratic Government.*

38. "European Commission," *Eurobarometer,* http://ec.europa.eu/public_opinion /archives/eb/eb76/eb76_first_en.pdf.

39. Shelley Singh, "India Accounts for 51% of Global IT-BPO Outsourcing: Survey," *Times of India,* April 28, 2012, http://timesofindia.indiatimes.com/tech /news/outsourcing/India-accounts-for-51-of-global-IT-BPO-outsourcing-Survey /articleshow/12909972.cms.

40. Nadeem, *Dead Ringers: How Outsourcing Is Changing the Way Indians Understand Themselves.*

41. Dhar, "More Indian Women Postponing Motherhood."

42. Schumpeter, "The Historical Approach to the Analysis of Business Cycles," in *Essays: On Entrepreneurs, Innovations, Business Cycles, and the Evolution of Capitalism,* p. 349.

CHAPTER FIVE

1. This passage was originally part of a speech given at Munich University in 1918. See Weber, *Essays in Sociology,* p. 78.

2. Ronald Brownstein, "The Age of Volatility," *The National Journal,* October 29, 2011.

3. Interview with Minxin Pei, Washington, DC, June 2012.

4. Interview with Lena Hjelm-Wallén, Brussels, May 2011.

5. Tiririca, quoted in "Ex-clown Elected to Brazil Congress Must Prove He Can Read and Write," November 11, 2010, http://www.abc.net.au/news/2010-10 -05/brazilian-clown-elected-to-congress/2285224.

6. Beppe Severgnini, "The Chirruping Allure of Italy's Jiminy Cricket," *Financial Times,* June 4, 2012.

7. Greg Sargent, "Sharron Angle Floated Possibility of Armed Insurrection," *Washington Post,* June 15, 2010, http://voices.washingtonpost.com/plum-line/2010 /06/sharron_angle_floated_possibil.html.

8. This figure is quoted from Matt Golder, "Democratic Electoral Systems Around the World, 1946–2000," *Electoral Studies* (2004), https://files.nyu.edu /mrg217/public/es_long.pdf. In the same publication, see also Figures 5.1 and 5.2, which show the proliferation of sovereign states, the decline of dictatorships, and the rise of democracies.

9. See Marshall et al., "Political Regime Characteristics and Transitions, 1800–2010" (2010), Polity IV Project, available online at http://www.systemicpeace .org/polity/polity4.htm.

10. Larry Diamond, "The Democratic Rollback," *Foreign Affairs,* March-April 2008; see also Larry Diamond, "Can the Whole World Become Democratic? Democracy, Development and International Politics," PhD thesis, University of California at Irvine, April 17, 2003.

11. Golder, "Democratic Electoral Systems Around the World, 1946–2000." As of 2004, Golder had identified Brunei and the United Arab Emirates, both of which

held parliamentary elections in 2011. The Election Guide website run by IFES has no record of elections in Brunei.

12. Dalton and Gray, "Expanding the Electoral Marketplace."

13. Golder, "Democratic Electoral Systems Around the World, 1946–2000."

14. Interview with Bill Sweeney, Washington, DC, June 2012.

15. This figure is based on my own calculations.

16. For a statistical analysis and more details, see the appendix to this chapter at the end of the book.

17. In prior elections, Richard Nixon, Lyndon Johnson, Franklin D. Roosevelt, and Warren Harding won the presidency with a larger margin than Ronald Reagan's in 1984.

18. Updated information is available in BBC News, "Belgium Swears in New Government Headed by Elio Di Rupo," December 6, 2011, http://www.bbc.co.uk /news/world-europe-16042750.

19. Narud and Valen, "Coalition Membership and Electoral Performance."

20. Damgaard, "Cabinet Termination."

21. Wil Longbottom, "Shiver Me Timbers! Pirate Party Wins 15 Seats in Berlin Parliamentary Elections," *Daily Mail*, September 19, 2011, http://www.dailymail .co.uk/news/article-2039073/Pirate-Party-wins-15-seats-Berlin-parliamentary -elections.html.

22. Richard Chirgwin, "Pirate Party Takes Mayor's Chair in Swiss City: Welcome to Eichberg, Pirate Politics Capital of the World," *The Register* (UK), September 23, 2012, http://www.theregister.co.uk/2012/09/23/pirate_wins_eichberg _election/.

23. The concept of the "selectorate" is from Bueno de Mesquita et al., *The Logic of Political Survival*.

24. Kenig, "The Democratization of Party Leaders' Selection Methods: Canada in Comparative Perspective."

25. Carey and Polga-Hecimovich, "Primary Elections and Candidate Strength in Latin America."

26. Joel M. Gora, quoted in Eggen, "Financing Comes Full Circle After Watergate."

27. Kane, "Super PAC Targets Incumbents of Any Stripe,"

28. Blake, "Anti-Incumbent Super PAC's Funds Dry Up."

29. See Ansell and Gingrich, "Trends in Decentralization."

30. Stein, "Fiscal Decentralization and Government Size in Latin America."

31. Aristovnik, "Fiscal Decentralization in Eastern Europe: A Twenty-Year Perspective."

32. Stephen J. Kobrin, "Back to the Future: Neo-medievalism and the Postmodern Digital World Economy," *Journal of International Affairs*, Vol. 51, No. 2 (Spring 1998): 361–386.

33. Pilling, "India's Bumble Bee Defies Gravity."

34. Goldstein and Rotich, "Digitally Networked Technology in Kenya's 2007– 2008 Post-Election Crisis."

35. Niknejad, "How to Cover a Paranoid Regime from Your Laptop."

36. Friedman, *The Lexus and the Olive Tree*, pp. 101–111; emphasis added.

37. Elinor Mills, "Old-Time Hacktivists: Anonymous, You've Crossed the Line," *CNet,* March 30, 2012, http://news.cnet.com/8301–27080_3–57406793–245/old -time-hacktivists-anonymous-youve-crossed-the-line.

38. Diamond and Plattner, *Liberation Technology: Social Media and the Struggle for Democracy,* p. xi.

39. Interview with Lena Hjelm-Wallén, Brussels, May 2011.

40. Interview with Ricardo Lagos, Santiago, November 2012.

CHAPTER SIX

1. Shan Carter and Amanda Cox, "One 9/11 Tally: $3.3 Trillion," *New York Times,* September 8, 2011; Tim Fernholtz and Jim Tankersley, "The Cost of bin Laden: $3 Trillion over 15 Years," *National Journal,* May 6, 2011.

2. "Soldier Killed, 3 Missing After Navy Vessel Hit Off Beirut Coast," *Haaretz,* June 15, 2006.

3. One Earth Future Foundation, *The Economic Cost of Somali Piracy, 2011* (Boulder, CO: 2012).

4. John Arquilla, *Insurgents, Raiders and Bandits: How Masters of Irregular Warfare Have Shaped Our World,* pp. xv–xvi.

5. Runyon, *On Broadway,* p. 87.

6. As quoted by Winston Churchill in *The Second World War,* p. 105.

7. "United States Department of Defense Fiscal Year 2012 Budget Request," February 2012, http://comptroller.defense.gov/defbudget/fy2012/FY2012_Budget _Request_Overview_Book.pdf.

8. Edward Luce, "The Mirage of Obama's Defense Cuts," *Financial Times,* January 30, 2012.

9. All of the investments made in military hardware under the Reagan administration will phase out over the 2010s and 2020s. Some in the Navy are arguing against carriers; if this position wins the debate, the United States might have less than eleven carriers in a decade or two.

10. Human Security Report Project (HSRP), *Human Security Report 2009/2010: The Causes of Peace and The Shrinking Costs of War,* December 2, 2010, http:// www.hsrgroup.org/human-security-reports/20092010/overview.aspx.

11. Ibid.

12. Ibid.

13. The event described in the text (based on "Amputations Soared Among US Troops in 2011," http://news.antiwar.com/2012/02/09/amputations-soared-among -us-troops-in-2011/) is backed up by this particular chart from Pentagon: http:// timemilitary.files.wordpress.com/2012/01/amp-chart.png. The IED casualty figure comes from the Brookings Afghanistan index.

14. ICC International Maritime Bureau (IMB), Piracy & Armed Robbery News & Figures, http://www.icc-ccs.org/piracy-reporting-centre/piracynewsafigures.

15. Damon Poeter, "Report: Massive Chamber of Commerce Hack Originated in China," *PC Magazine,* December 21, 2011, http://www.pcmag.com/article2 /0,2817,2397920,00.asp.

16. Ann Scott Tyson, "US to Raise 'Irregular War' Capabilities," *Washington Post,* December 4, 2008; US Department of Defense, *Quadrennial Defense Review,* February 2010, http://www.defense.gov/qdr/.

17. Thomas Mahnken, quoted in Andrew Burt, "America's Waning Military Edge," *Yale Journal of International Affairs,* March 2012, http://yalejournal.org /wp-content/uploads/2012/04/Op-ed-Andrew-Burt.pdf.

18. Mao Zedong, "The Relation of Guerrilla Hostilities to Regular Operations," http://www.marxists.org/reference/archive/mao/works/1937/guerrilla-warfare /ch01.htm.

19. Global Security, "Second Chechnya War—1999–2006," http://www.global security.org/military/world/war/chechnya2.htm.

20. William Lynn, quoted in Burt, "America's Waning Military Edge."

21. Ivan Arreguín-Toft, "How the Weak Win Wars: A Theory of Asymmetric Conflict," *International Security* 26, no. 1 (2001): 93–128; Ivan Arreguín-Toft, "How a Superpower Can End Up Losing to the Little Guys," *Nieman Watchdog,* March 23, 2007, www.niemanwatchdog.org.

22. Marc Hecker and Thomas Rid, "Jihadistes de tous les pays, dispersez-vous," *Politique Internationale* 123 (2009): fn 1.

23. John Arquilla, "The New Rules of Engagement," *Foreign Policy,* February–March 2010.

24. Rod Nordland, "War's Risks Shift to Contractors," *New York Times,* February 12, 2012.

25. Singer, *Wired for War: The Robotics Revolution and Conflict in the Twenty-First Century,* p. 18.

26. Lind et al., "The Changing Face of War."

27. Amos Harel and Avi Issacharoff, "A New Kind of War," *Foreign Policy,* January 20, 2010.

28. Singer, *Wired for War.*

29. Sutherland, *Modern Warfare, Intelligence and Deterrence,* p. 101.

30. Scott Wilson, "Drones Cast a Pall of Fear," *Washington Post,* December 4, 2011.

31. Francis Fukuyama, "The End of Mystery: Why We All Need a Drone of Our Own," *Financial Times,* February 25, 2012.

32. Christian Caryl, "America's IED Nightmare," *Foreign Policy,* December 4, 2009; Thom Shanker, "Makeshift Bombs Spread Beyond Afghanistan, Iraq," *New York Times,* October 29, 2009.

33. Tom Vanden Brook, "IED Attacks in Afghanistan Set Record," *USA Today,* January 25, 2012, http://www.usatoday.com/news/world/story/2012–01–25/IEDs -afghanistan/52795302/1.

34. Jarret Brachman, "Al Qaeda's Armies of One," *Foreign Policy,* January 22, 2010; Reuel Marc Gerecht, "The Meaning of Al Qaeda's Double Agent," *Wall Street Journal,* January 7, 2010.

35. Amos Yadlin, quoted in Amir Oren, "IDF Dependence on Technology Spawns Whole New Battlefield," *Haaretz,* January 3, 2010.

36. Kaplan, *The Coming Anarchy: Shattering the Dreams of the Post–Cold War.*

37. Chua, *World on Fire: How Exporting Free Market Democracy Breeds Ethnic Hatred and Global Instability.*

38. Hecker and Rid, *War 2.0: Irregular Warfare in the Information Age.*

39. Ann Scott Tyson, "New Pentagon Policy Says 'Irregular Warfare' Will Get Same Attention as Traditional Combat," *Washington Post,* December 4, 2008.

40. Tony Capaccio, "Pentagon Bolstering Commandos After Success in Killing Bin Laden," *Bloomberg News,* February 9, 2012.

41. "The Changing Character of War," ch. 7 in Institute for National Strategic Studies, *Global Strategic Assessment 2009,* p. 148.

42. David E. Johnson et al., "Preparing and Training for the Full Spectrum of Military Challenges: Insights from the Experience of China, France, the United Kingdom, India and Israel," National Defense Research Institute, 2009.

43. John Arquilla interview in "Cyber War!," *Frontline,* April 24, 2003, www .pbs.org.

44. Amir Oren, "IDF Dependence on Technology Spawns Whole New Battle-field," *Haaretz,* January 3, 2010.

45. John Arquilla, "The New Rules of Engagement," *Foreign Policy,* February–March 2010.

46. Joseph S. Nye, Jr., "Is Military Power Becoming Obsolete?" *Project Syndicate,* January 13, 2010.

47. "Q and A: Mexico's Drug-Related Violence," *BBC News,* March 30, 2012, http://www.bbc.co.uk/news/world-latin-america-10681249.

48. Thomas Rid, "Cracks in the Jihad," *The Wilson Quarterly,* Winter 2010.

49. Hecker and Rid, "Jihadistes de tous les pays, dispersez-vous!"

CHAPTER SEVEN

1. Peter Hartcher, "Tipping Point from West to Rest Just Passed," *Sidney Morning Herald,* April 17, 2012.

2. Comments to Hartcher's column dated April 17, 2012.

3. "Secret US Embassy Cables Revealed," Al Jazeera, November 29, 2010.

4. Interview with Jessica Mathews, Washington, September 2012.

5. Interview with Zbigniew Brzezinski, Washington, May 2012.

6. Murphy, *Are We Rome? The Fall of an Empire and the Fate of America.*

7. "Bin-Laden's Death One of Top News Stories of 21th Century," *Global Language Monitor,* May 6, 2011, http://www.languagemonitor.com/top-news/bin -ladens-death-one-of-top-news-stories-of-21th-century/.

8. Robert Fogel, "123,000,000,000,000," *Foreign Policy,* January–February 2010; see also Dadush, *Juggernaut.*

9. Joe Leahy and Stefan Wagstyl, "Brazil Becomes Sixth Biggest Economy," *Financial Times,* March 7, 2012, p. 4.

10. Kindleberger, *The World in Depression, 1929–1939;* see also Milner, "International Political Economy: Beyond Hegemonic Stability," *Foreign Policy,* Spring 1998.

11. William C. Wohlforth, "The Stability of a Unipolar World," *International Security* 24, no. 1 (1999): 5–41.

12. See Nye, *Bound to Lead: The Changing Nature of American Power,* and Nye, *Soft Power: The Means to Success in World Politics.* In 2011, Nye published another book on the subject titled *The Future of Power.*

13. Patrick, "Multilateralism and Its Discontents: The Causes and Consequences of U.S. Ambivalence."

14. United States Department of State, *Treaties in Force: A List of Treaties and Other International Agreements of the United States in Force on January 1, 2012.*

15. Peter Liberman, "What to Read on American Primacy," *Foreign Affairs,* March 12, 2009; see also Stephen Brooks and WilliamWohlforth, "Hard Times for Soft Balancing," *International Security* 30, no. 1 (Summer 2005): 72–108.

16. Ferguson, *Colossus.*

17. Robert Kagan, "The End of the End of History," *New Republic,* April 23, 2008.

18. Robert A. Pape, "Soft Balancing Against the United States," *International Security* 30, no. 1 (Summer 2005): 7–45; on soft balancing, see also Stephen Brooks and William Wohlforth, "Hard Times for Soft Balancing," *International Security* 30, no. 1 (Summer 2005): 72–108.

19. Zakaria, *The Post-American World.*

20. Randall L. Schweller, "Ennui Becomes Us," *The National Interest,* January–February 2010.

21. Douglas M. Gibler, *International Military Alliances from 1648 to 2008.*

22. On the ISAF, see Anna Mulrine, "In Afghanistan, the NATO-led Force Is 'Underresourced' for the Fight Against the Taliban: When It Comes to Combat, It Is a Coalition of the Willing and Not-So-Willing," *U.S. News,* June 5, 2008.

23. "Spanish Court says Venezuela Helped ETA, FARC," Reuters, March 1, 2010.

24. "Small Arms Report by the UN Secretary General, 2011," http://www.iansa.org/resource/2011/04/small-arms-report-by-the-un-secretary-general-2011.

25. For data on India and Brazil, see "Aid Architecture: An Overview of the Main Trends in Official Development Assistance Flows," World Bank, May 2008.

26. Homi Kharas, "Development Assistance in the 21st Century"; see also Waltz and Ramachandran, "Brave New World: A Literature Review of Emerging Donors and the Changing Nature of Foreign Assistance."

27. Kharas, "Development Assistance in the 21st Century."

28. Ibid.

29. "Aid Architecture: An Overview of the Main Trends in Official Development Assistance Flows"; see also Homi Kharas, "Trends and Issues in Development Aid."

30. The sources for the data on south-south investment can be found in Chapter 8.

31. For further information about the Pew Global Attitudes Project, see http://www.pewglobal.org/.

32. Kathrin Hille, "Beijing Makes Voice Heard in US," *Financial Times,* February 14, 2012.

33. Joshua Kurlantzick, "China's Charm: Implications of Chinese Soft Power," CEIP Policy Brief No. 47, June 2006; Kurlantzick, "Chinese Soft Power in Southeast

Asia," *The Globalist,* July 7, 2007; Loro Horta, "China in Africa: Soft Power, Hard Results," Yale Global Online, November 13, 2009; Joshua Eisenman and Joshua Kurlantzick, "China's Africa Strategy," *Current History,* May 2006.

34. Tharoor, "India's Bollywood Power"; see also Tharoor, "Indian Strategic Power: 'Soft.'"

35. "India Projecting Its Soft Power Globally: ICCR Chief," *Deccan Herald* (New Delhi), October 7, 2011.

36. Ibsen Martinez, "Romancing the Globe," *Foreign Policy,* November 10, 2005; on the Korea example, see Akshita Nanda, "Korean Wave Now a Tsunami," *Straits Times,* December 13, 2009.

37. The Anholt-GfK Roper Nation Brands Index (2012), http://www.gfkamerica .com/newsroom/press_releases/single_sites/008787/index.en.html.

38. Sam Dagher, Charles Levinson, and Margaret Coker, "Tiny Kingdom's Huge Role in Libya Draws Concern," *Wall Street Journal,* October 17, 2011.

39. Georgina Adam, "Energy—and Ambition to Match," *Financial Times,* March 10, 2012.

40. Global Security Forum, "Changing Patterns in the Use of the Veto in The Security Council," June 2012, http://www.globalpolicy.org/images/pdfs/Tables_and _Charts/Changing_Patterns_in_the_Use_of_the_Veto_as_of_March_16_2012.pdf.

41. "Copenhagen Summit Ends in Blood, Sweat and Recrimination," *The Telegraph,* December 20, 2009.

42. Joshua Chaffin and Pilita Clark, "Poland Vetoes EU's Emissions Plan," *Financial Times,* March 10–11, 2012.

43. Elmer Plischke, "American Ambassadors—An Obsolete Species? Some Alternatives to Traditional Diplomatic Representation," *World Affairs* 147, no. 1 (Summer 1984): 2–23.

44. Josef Korbel, "The Decline of Diplomacy: Have Traditional Methods Proved Unworkable in the Modern Era? *Worldview,* April 1962.

45. Moisés Naím, "Democracy's Dangerous Impostors," *Washington Post,* April 21, 2007; Naím, "What Is a GONGO?" *Foreign Policy,* April 18, 2007.

46. Another example concerns Transdniestria; see "Disinformation," *Economist,* August 3, 2006.

47. Cited by Naím, "Democracy's Dangerous Impostors."

48. On ALBA, see Joel Hirst, "The Bolivarian Alliance of the Americas," *Council on Foreign Relations,* December 2010.

49. Joe Leahy and James Lamont, "BRICS to Debate Creation of Common Bank," *Financial Times,* March 2012.

50. On minilateralism, see Moisés Naím, "Minilateralism: The Magic Number to Get Real International Action," *Foreign Policy,* July–August 2009. For Stephen Walt's response, see "On Minilateralism," Foreignpolicy.com, Tuesday, June 23, 2009, http://walt.foreignpolicy.com/posts/2009/06/23/on_minilateralism.

CHAPTER EIGHT

1. Interview with Paolo Scaroni, Barcelona, June 2010.

2. Data for bank concentration are quoted from *Bloomberg*'s Financial Database (retrieved August 2012).

3. Jeremy Kahn, "Virgin Banker," *Bloomberg Markets,* May 2012.

4. James Mackintosh, "Top 10 Hedge Funds Eclipse Banks with Profits of 28bn for Clients," *Financial Times,* March 2, 2011.

5. Mark Gongloff, "Jamie Dimon Complains More, As JPMorgan Chase Losses Eclipse $30 Billion," The Huffington Post, May 21, 2012.

6. Bob Moon, "Kodak Files for Bankruptcy," *Marketplace* (NPR), January 19, 2012, http://www.marketplace.org/topics/business/kodak-files-bankruptcy; Lilla Zuil, "AIG's Title as World's Largest Insurer Gone Forever," *Insurance Journal,* April 29, 2009.

7. Carola Frydman and Raven E. Sacks, "Executive Compensation: A New View from a Long-Term Perspective, 1936–2005," FEDS Working Paper No. 2007–35, July 6, 2007.

8. John Challenger's comments were reported by Gary Strauss and Laura Petrecca in "CEOs Stumble over Ethics Violations, Mismanagement," *USA TODAY,* May 15, 2012, and the percentage of CEOs ousted before retirement is from a Conference Board survey cited by David Weidner in "Why Your CEO Could Be in Trouble," *Wall Street Journal,* September 15, 2011.

9. Nat Stoddard, "Expect Heavy CEO Turnover Very Soon," *Forbes,* December 16, 2009.

10. Per-Ola Karlsson and Gary L. Neilson, "CEO Succession 2011: The New CEO's First Year," Booz and Company special report in *Strategy+Business,* No. 67 (Summer 2012); see also Booz, Allen, and Hamilton, "CEO Succession 2005: The Crest of the Wave," *Strategy+Business,* No. 43 (Summer 2005).

11. Robert Samuelson, "The Fears Under Our Prosperity," *Washington Post,* February 16, 2006, citing the work of Diego Comin and Thomas Philippon, "The Rise in Firm-Level Volatility: Causes and Consequences," *NBER Macroeconomics Annual* 20 (2005): 167–201 (published by University of Chicago Press), http://www.jstor.org/stable/3585419.

12. "The World's Biggest Companies," *Forbes,* April 18, 2012, http://www.forbes.com/sites/scottdecarlo/2012/04/18/the-worlds-biggest-companies/, and http://www.forbes.com/global2000/.

13. Lynn, *Cornered: The New Monopoly Capitalism and the Economics of Destruction;* Lynn and Longman, "Who Broke America's Jobs Machine?"

14. Ghemawat, *World 3.0: Global Prosperity and How to Achieve It,* p. 91.

15. Peter Wells, "Whatever Happened to Industrial Concentration?," AutomotiveWorld.com, April 19, 2010; John Kay, "Survival of the Fittest, Not the Fattest," *Financial Times,* March 27, 2003; John Kay, "Where Size Is Not Everything," *Financial Times,* March 3, 1999.

16. John Lippert, Alan Ohnsman, and Rose Kim, "How Hyundai Scares the Competition," *Bloomberg Markets,* April 2012, p. 28.

17. Ghemawat, *World 3.0: Global Prosperity and How to Achieve It,* p. 95.

18. "Brand Rehab," *Economist,* April 8, 2010; Oxford Metrica, *Reputation Review,* 2010, www.oxfordmetrica.com/.

19. Luisa Kroll, "Forbes World's Billionaires 2012," *Forbes,* March 7, 2012, http://www.forbes.com/sites/luisakroll/2012/03/07/forbes-worlds-billionaires-2012/.

20. Ibid.

21. Rajeshni Naidu-Ghelani, "Chinese Billionaires Lost a Third of Wealth in Past Year, Study Shows," CNBC.com, September 17, 2012, http://www.cnbc.com /id/49057268/Chinese_Billionaires_Lost_a_Third_of_Wealth_in_Past_Year_Study _Shows.

22. Coase, "The Nature of the Firm."

23. This is a straightforward index but it does not capture, for instance, whether there are major differences in market share within this subset—that is, whether one or two firms are especially dominant. The Herfindahl-Hirschman Index, named after the economists Orris C. Herfindahl and Albert O. Hirschman, partially remedies this measurement flaw by giving extra weight to the biggest players. The US Department of Justice, for instance, uses this index to help determine whether antitrust action is warranted in a given field. For further discussion of this issue, see Hirschman, "The Paternity of an Index."

24. Scott L. Baier and Jeffrey H. Bergstrand, "The Growth of World Trade: Tariffs, Transport Costs, and Income Similarity," *Journal of International Economics* 53, no. 1 (February 2001): 1–27.

25. Economic and Social Commission for Asia and the Pacific *Monograph Series on Managing Globalization: Regional Shipping and Port Development Strategies* (Container Traffic Forecast), 2011.

26. David Goldman, "Microsoft's $6 Billion Whoopsie," CNNMoney, July 12, 2012, http://money.cnn.com/2012/07/02/technology/microsoft-aquantive/index .htm.

27. Thom and Greif, "Intangible Assets in the Valuation Process: A Small Business Acquisition Study"; Galbreath, "Twenty-First Century Management Rules: The Management of Relationships as Intangible Assets."

28. Interview with Lorenzo Zambrano, Monterrey, Mexico, 2011.

29. See The Gap Inc. and Inditex annual reports from 2007 to 2011.

30. Data obtained from Zara's corporate website: http://www.inditex.com/en /who_we_are/timeline.

31. "Zara: Taking the Lead in Fast-Fashion," *Businessweek,* April 4, 2006.

32. "Retail: Zara Bridges Gap to Become World's Biggest Fashion Retailer," *Guardian,* August 11, 2008.

33. John Helyar and Mehul Srivastava, "Outsourcing: A Passage Out of India," *Bloomberg Businessweek,* March 19–25, 2012, pp. 36–37.

34. Ben Sills, Natalie Obiko Pearson, and Stefan Nicola, "Power to the People," *Bloomberg Markets,* May 2012, p. 51.

35. Koeppel, *Banana: The Fate of the Fruit That Changed the World;* see also the company's website (http://chiquita.com/Our-Company/The-Chiquita-Story.aspx) as well as the Chiquita Brands entry at the Funding Universe website (http://www .fundinguniverse.com/company-histories/Chiquita-Brands-International-Inc -Company-History.html).

36. Interbrand, "Brand Valuation: The Financial Value of Brands," *Brand Papers*, http://www.brandchannel.com/papers_review.asp?sp_id=357; see also John Gapper, "Companies Feel Benefit of Intangibles," *Financial Times*, April 23, 2007.

37. Interbrand, "Best Global Brands 2011," *Brand Papers*, http://www.inter brand.com/en/best-global-brands/best-global-brands-2008/best-global-brands -2011.aspx.

38. Saxenian, "Venture Capital in the 'Periphery': The New Argonauts, Global Search and Local Institution Building"; Saxenian, "The Age of the Agile"; Saxenian, "The International Mobility of Entrepreneurs and Regional Upgrading in India and China.

39. John Maraganore, quoted in Glen Harris, "Bio-Europe 2007: As Big Pharma Model Falters, Biotech Rides to the Rescue," *Bioworld Today*, November 13, 2007.

40. Kerry A. Dolan, "The Drug Research War," *Forbes*, May 28, 2004; "Big Pharma Isn't Dead, But Long Live Small Pharma," *Pharmaceutical Executive Europe*, July 8, 2009; Patricia M. Danzon, "Economics of the Pharmaceutical Industry," *NBER Reporter*, Fall 2006.

41. Quinn Norton, "The Rise of Backyard Biotech," *The Atlantic*, June 2011, p. 32.

42. Henry W. Chesbrough, "The Era of Open Innovation," *MIT Sloan Management Review*, April 15, 2003.

43. Michael Stanko et al., "Outsourcing Innovation," *MIT Sloan Management Review*, November 30, 2009; James Brian Quinn, "Outsourcing Innovation: The New Engine of Growth," *MIT Sloan Management Review*, July 15, 2000.

44. "Outsourcing Innovation," *Businessweek*, March 21, 2005.

45. "Outsourcing Drug Discovery Market Experiencing Continued Growth, Says New Report," *M2 Presswire*, July 4, 2008.

46. Christensen, *The Innovator's Dilemma: When New Technologies Cause Great Firms to Fail*, p. xi.

47. Ibid., p. 233.

48. These data are quoted from "Data on Trade and Import Barriers" at www .worldbank.org.

49. The World Bank, "Doing Business 2011"; see also www.doingbusiness.org.

50. Priyanka Akhouri, "Mexico's Cinepolis Targets 40 Screens in India This Year," *Financial Express* (India), January 1, 2010.

51. Interview with Alejandro Ramirez, Cartagena, Colombia, January 2012.

52. World Bank Group, "'South-South' FDI and Political Risk Insurance: Challenges and Opportunities," *MIGA Perspectives*, January 2008.

53. According to *UNCTAD: World Investment Report 2012*: "Flows to developed countries increased by 21 per cent, to $748 billion. In developing countries FDI increased by 11 per cent, reaching a record $684 billion. FDI in the transition economies increased by 25 per cent to $92 billion. Developing and transition economies respectively accounted for 45 per cent and 6 per cent of global FDI. UNCTAD's projections show these countries maintaining their high levels of investment over the next three years" (p. xi).

54. Aykut and Goldstein, "Developing Country Multinationals: South-South Investment Comes of Age"; "South-South Investment," www.unctad.org; Peter Gammeltoft, "Emerging Multinationals: Outward FDI from the BRICS Countries," *International Journal of Technology and Globalization* 4, no. 1 (2008): 5–22.

55. Interview with Antoine van Agtmael, Washington, DC, May 2012.

56. "Mexico's CEMEX to Take Over Rinker," Associated Press, June 8, 2007.

57. Clifford Kraus, "Latin American Companies Make Big US Gains," *New York Times,* May 2, 2007; Frank Ahrens and Simone Baribeau, "Bud's Belgian Buyout," *Washington Post,* July 15, 2008; Peter Marsh, "Mittal Fatigue," *Financial Times,* October 30, 2008.

58. Graham Bowley, "Rivals Pose Threat to New York Stock Exchange," *New York Times,* October 14, 2009; Jacob Bunge, "BATS Exchange Overtakes Direct Edge in February US Stock Trade," *Dow Jones Newswires,* March 2, 2010.

59. "Shining a Light on Dark Pools," *The Independent,* May 22, 2010.

60. Nina Mehta, "Dark Pools Win Record Stock Volume as NYSE Trading Slows to 1990 Levels," *Bloomberg News,* February 29, 2012.

61. Venkatachalam Shunmugam, "Financial Markets Regulation: The Tipping Point," May 18, 2010, www.voxeu.org.

62. Institutional Investor, *Hedge Fund 100* (2012).

63. *Bloomberg Markets,* February 2012, p. 36.

64. Gary Weiss, "The Man Who Made Too Much," Portfolio.com, January 7, 2009.

65. Mallaby, *More Money Than God,* pp. 377–378.

66. James Mackintosh, "Dalio Takes Hedge Crown from Soros," *Financial Times,* February 28, 2012.

67. Ibid.

CHAPTER NINE

1. "Latin America Evangelism Is 'Stealing' Catholic Flock," *Hispanic News,* April 16, 2005.

2. Diego Cevallos, "Catholic Church Losing Followers in Droves," IPS news agency, October 21, 2004.

3. Indira Lakshmanan, "Evangelism Is Luring Latin America's Catholics," *Boston Globe,* May 8, 2005; "Hola, Luther," *Economist,* November 6, 2008; Carlos G. Cano, "Lutero avanza en America Latina," *El País,* July 30, 2010.

4. Hanna Rosin, "Did Christianity Cause the Crash?" *The Atlantic,* December 2009.

5. Pew Forum on Religion and Public Life, "Spirit and Power: A 10-Country Survey of Pentecostals," October 2006.

6. Edir Macedo, quoted in Tom Phillips, "Solomon's Temple in Brazil Would Put Christ the Redeemer in the Shade," *Guardian,* July 21, 2010.

7. Alexei Barrionuevo, "Fight Nights and Reggae Pack Brazilian Churches," *New York Times,* September 15, 2009.

8. Richard Cimino, "Nigeria: Pentecostal Boom—Healing or Reflecting a Failing State?" *Religion Watch,* March 1, 2010.

9. Pew Forum on Religion and Public Life, "Global Christianity: A Report on the Size and Distribution of the World's Christian Population," December 2011.

10. Ibid.

11. Pew Forum on Religion and Public Life, "Faith on the Move: The Religious Affiliation of International Migrants," March 2012.

12. Larry Rohter, "As Pope Heads to Brazil, a Rival Theology Persists," *New York Times,* May 7, 2007.

13. Diego Cevallos, "Catholic Church Losing Followers in Droves," IPS news agency, October 21, 2004; see also "In Latin America, Catholics Down, Church's Credibility Up," Catholic News Service, June 23, 2005.

14. "The Battle for Latin America's Soul," *Time,* June 24, 2001.

15. Allen, *The Future Church,* p. 397.

16. "Pentecostals Find Fertile Ground in Latin America," BBC Radio 4 Crossing Continents, bbc.co.uk.

17. Indira Lakshmanan, "Evangelism Is Luring Latin America's Catholics," *Boston Globe,* May 8, 2005.

18. On the rise and advantage of evangelicals, see André Corten, "Explosion des pentecôtismes africains et latino-américains," *Le Monde Diplomatique,* December 2001; and Peter Berger, "Pentecostalism: Protestant Ethic or Cargo Cult?" *The American Interest,* July 29, 2010.

19. Alexander Smoltczyk, "The Voice of Egypt's Muslim Brotherhood," *Spiegel,* February 15, 2011; see also John Esposito and Ibrahim Kalin, "The 500 Most Influential Muslims in the World in 2009," Edmund A. Walsh School of Foreign Service, Georgetown University. (Sheikh Dr. Yusuf al Qaradawi, head of the International Union of Muslim Scholars, is ninth on the list.)

20. Harold Meyerson, "When Unions Disappear," *Washington Post,* June 13, 2012.

21. For data in trends in union membership in Europe, see Sonia McKay, "Union Membership and Density Levels in Decline," *EIROnline,* Eurofound Document ID No. EU0603029I 01–09–2006 (download at http://www.eurofound .europa.eu/eiro/2006/03/articles/eu0603029i.htm), and J. Visser, "Union Membership Statistics in 24 Countries," *Monthly Labor Review* 129, no. 1 (January 2006), http://www.bls.gov/opub/mlr/2006/01/art3abs.htm.

22. Alasdair Roberts, "Can Occupy Wall Street Replace the Labor Movement?" *Bloomberg,* May 1, 2012.

23. For further information on Stern, see Harold Meyerson, "Andy Stern: A Union Maverick Clocks Out," *Washington Post,* April 14, 2010.

24. Steven Greenhouse, "Janitors' Union, Recently Organized, Strikes in Houston," *New York Times,* November 3, 2006.

25. On China's labor movement, see David Barboza and Keith Bradsher, "In China, Labor Movement Enabled by Technology," *New York Times,* June 16, 2010, and Edward Wong, "As China Aids Labor, Unrest Is Still Rising," *New York Times,* June 20, 2010.

26. Richard Sullivan, "Organizing Workers in the Space Between Unions," American Sociological Association paper, January 17, 2008.

27. OECD, "Development Aid: Total Official and Private Flows Net Disbursements at Current Prices and Exchange Rates" (Table 5), Paris, April 4, 2012, http://www.oecd-ilibrary.org/development/development-aid-total-official-and-private-flows_20743866-table5.

28. Giving USA Foundation, *Giving USA 2011: The Annual Report on Philanthropy for the Year 2010,* www.givingusareports.org.

29. These numbers are quoted from annual reports of the Foundation Center, available online at www.foundationcenter.org/findfunders/.

30. James M. Ferris and Hilary J. Harmssen, *California Foundations: 1999–2009: Growth Amid Adversity,* The Center on Philanthropy and Public Policy, University of Southern California.

31. Again, see Foundation Center at http://foundationcenter.org/findfunders/.

32. Mauro de Lorenzo and Apoorva Shah, "Entrepreneurial Philanthropy in the Developing World," AEI Online, American Enterprise Institute, December 12, 2007; Michael Jarvis and Jeremy M Goldberg, "Business and Philanthropy: The Blurring of Boundaries," Business and Development Discussion Papers 9, World Bank Institute, Fall 2008.

33. Raj M. Desai and Homi Kharas, "Do Philanthropic Citizens Behave Like Governments? Internet-Based Platforms and the Diffusion of International Private Aid," Wolfensohn Center for Development at Brookings, Working Paper 12, October 2009.

34. Moyo, *Dead Aid.*

35. Tom Munnecke has also weighed in on the subject of "micro-philanthropy": see Tom Munnecke and Heather Wood Ion, "Towards a Model of Micro-Philanthropy," May 21, 2002, givingspace.org.

36. Jacqueline Novogratz, quoted in Richard C Morais, "The New Activist Givers," *Forbes,* June 1, 2007, http://www.forbes.com/2007/06/01/philanthropy-wealth-foundation-pf-philo-in_rm_0601philanthropy_inl.html.

37. Pew Research Center, "State of the News Media 2012," March 19, 2012.

38. Bagdikian, *The New Media Monopoly.*

39. Amelia H. Arsenault and Manuel Castells, "The Structure and Dynamics of Global Multi-Media Business Networks," *International Journal of Communication* 2 (2008): 707–748.

40. Bruce C. Greenwald, Jonathan A. Knee, and Ava Seave, "The Moguls' New Clothes," *The Atlantic,* October 2009.

41. Pew Research Center, "State of the News Media 2012," March 19, 2012.

42. Arsenault and Castells, "The Structure and Dynamics of Global Multi-Media Business Networks."

43. Michael Kinsley, "All the News That's Fit to Pay For," *The Economist: The World in 2010,* December 2010, p. 50.

44. Christine Haughney, "Huffington Post Introduces Its Online Magazine," *New York Times,* June 12, 2012.

45. "The Trafigura Fiasco Tears Up the Textbook," *Guardian,* October 14, 2009; "Twitterers Thwart Effort to Gag Newspaper," *Time,* October 13, 2009.

46. Pew Research Center, "State of the News Media 2012," March 19, 2012.

Chapter Ten

1. Yu Liu and DingDing Chen, "Why China Will Democratize," *The Washington Quarterly* (Winter 2012): 41–62; interview with Professor Minxin Pei, Washington, DC, June 15, 2012.

2. Fareed Zakaria offered the best synthesis on this subject in his 2003 book *The Future of Freedom: Illiberal Democracy at Home and Abroad.*

3. Huntington, *Political Order in Changing Societies,* p. 8.

4. The title of Thomas Friedman's best seller *The World Is Flat* captures how pervasive this change has been: how the diffusion of power has drastically altered the world's business and commercial landscape. Friedman also eloquently points to the political consequences of these changes (see especially pages 371–414).

5. I document the ascent of a new breed of transnational criminal networks and their substantial consequences for the global order, and our daily lives, in *Illicit: How Smugglers, Traffickers and Copycats are Hijacking the Global Economy.* And I discuss the effects of the international financial crisis in global crime and the growing criminalization of governments in "Mafia States: Organized Crime Takes Office," *Foreign Affairs,* May–June 2012.

6. Francis Fukuyama, "Oh for a Democratic Dictatorship and Not a Vetocracy," *Financial Times,* November 22, 2011.

7. Peter Orszag, "Too Much of a Good Thing: Why We Need Less Democracy," *The New Republic,* October 6, 2011, pp. 11–12.

8. Olson, *The Logic of Collective Action: Public Goods and the Theory of Groups.*

9. Burckhardt, *The Greeks and Greek Civilization.*

10. Morozov, "The Brave New World of Slacktivism," *Foreign Policy,* May 19, 2009, http://neteffect.foreignpolicy.com/posts/2009/05/19/the_brave_new_world _of_slacktivism; see also Morozov's *The Net Delusion: The Dark Side of Internet Freedom.*

11. Malcolm Gladwell, "Small Change: Why the Revolution Will Not Be Tweeted," *The New Yorker,* October 4, 2010, http://www.newyorker.com/reporting/2010/10/04 /101004fa_fact_gladwell.

12. Émile Durkheim, *Suicide* (New York: Free Press, 1951; first published in 1897).

13. Stephen Marche, "Is Facebook Making Us Lonely?," *The Atlantic,* May 2012.

Chapter Eleven

1. Several influential authors argue that despite the proliferation of other powers in the international scene, the United States will continue to play the leading role because of various attributes: its military reach combined with a lack of territorial ambition (Robert D. Kaplan's *Monsoon*), its combination of "soft" and "smart"

power (Joseph Nye's *The Future of Power*), and its internal vibrancy and evolution through enterprise, immigration, and free speech (as a different Robert Kaplan argues in *The World America Made*). Conversely, Fareed Zakaria, author of *The Post-American World,* maintains that America is no longer the supreme power even though it still commands leadership in a multipolar world, thanks to its top rankings as having one of the most competitive economies, having the largest numbers of the world's best universities, and other unique assets. Why? In part because its current crop of politicians might not be up to making good on its promise. (See also Fareed Zakaria, "The Rise of the Rest," *Newsweek,* May 12, 2008.)

2. Kupchan, *No One's World: The West, the Rising Rest, and the Coming Global Turn.*

3. Bremmer, *Every Nation for Itself: Winners and Losers in a G-Zero World,* p. 1.

4. Brzezinski, *Strategic Vision: America and the Crisis of Global Power.*

5. Francis Fukuyama, "Oh for a Democratic Dictatorship and Not a Vetocracy," *Financial Times,* November 22, 2011.

6. The most recent multilateral initiative successfully endorsed by a large number of countries was in 2000, when 192 nations signed the United Nations Millennium Declaration, an ambitious set of eight goals ranging from halving the world's extreme poverty to halting the spread of HIV/AIDS and providing universal primary education—all by 2015. The last trade agreement that included many nations dates back to 1994, when 123 countries gathered to negotiate the creation of the World Trade Organization and agreed on a new set of rules for international trade. Since then, all other attempts to reach a global trade deal have crashed. The same is true with multilateral efforts to curb nuclear proliferation: the last significant international nonproliferation agreement was in 1995, when 185 countries agreed to permanently adopt an existing nonproliferation treaty. In the decade and a half since, multilateral initiatives have not only failed but India, Pakistan, and North Korea have demonstrated their certain status as nuclear powers. On the environment, the Kyoto Protocol, a global deal aimed at reducing greenhouse gas emissions, has been ratified by 184 countries since it was adopted in 1997, but the United States, the world's second-largest air polluter after China, has not done so, and many of the signatories have missed their targets. For further discussion of these issues, see my article "Minilateralism: The Magic Number to Get Real International Action," *Foreign Policy,* July–August 2009.

7. Mathews, "Saving America."

8. Gallup Inc., *The World Poll* (multiple years); Pew Research Center, http://pewresearch.org/topics/publicopinion/, Program on International Policy Attitudes, University of Maryland; Eurobarometer, http://ec.europa.eu/public_opinion/index_en.htm; LatinoBarometro, http://www.latinobarometro.org/latino/latinobarometro.jsp.

9. Henry Steele Commager, quoted in Moyers, *A World of Ideas: Conversations with Thoughtful Men and Women About American Life Today and the Ideas Shaping Our Future,* p. 232.

BIBLIOGRAPHY

Note to readers: Full citations of newspaper and other articles not reflected in the list below are provided in the chapter endnotes.

Adams, Henry. *The Education of Henry Adams: An Autobiography.* Boston: Houghton Mifflin, 1918.

Aday, Sean, Henry Farrell, Marc Lynch, John Sides, and Deen Freelon. "New Media and Conflict After the Arab Spring." *Peaceworks,* no. 80 (2012).

Allen, John L., Jr. *The Future Church.* New York: Doubleday, 2009.

Al-Munajjed, Mona et al. "Divorce in Gulf Cooperation Council Countries: Risks and Implications." *Strategy+Business,* Booz and Co., November 2010.

Ansell, Christopher, and Jane Gingrich. "Trends in Decentralization." In Bruce Cain et al., eds., *Democracy Transformed? Expanding Political Opportunities in Advanced Industrial Democracies.* New York: Oxford University Press, 2003.

Aristovnik, Aleksander. "Fiscal Decentralization in Eastern Europe: A Twenty-Year Perspective." MRPA Paper 39316, University Library of Munich (2012).

Arquilla, John. *Insurgents, Raiders and Bandits: How Masters of Irregular Warfare Have Shaped Our World.* Lanham, MD: Ivan R. Dee, 2011.

Arreguín-Toft, Ivan. "How a Superpower Can End Up Losing to the Little Guys." *Nieman Watchdog,* March 2007.

———. "How the Weak Win Wars: A Theory of Asymmetric Conflict." *International Security* 26, no. 1 (2001).

Arsenault, Amelia H., and Manuel Castells. "The Structure and Dynamics of Global Multi-Media Business Networks." *International Journal of Communication* 2 (2008).

Aykut, Dilek, and Andrea Goldstein. "Developing Country Multinationals: South-South Investment Comes of Age." In David O'Connor and Mónica Kjöllerström, eds., *Industrial Development for the 21st Century.* New York: Zed Books, 2008.

Bagdikian, Ben H. *The New Media Monopoly.* Boston, MA: Beacon Press, 2004.

Baier, Scott L., and Jeffrey H. Bergstrand. "The Growth of World Trade: Tariffs, Transport Costs, and Income Similarity." *Journal of International Economics* 53, no. 1 (2001).

Barnett, Michael, and Raymond Duvall. "Power in International Politics." *International Organization* 59 (Winter 2005).

Bremmer, Ian. *Every Nation for Itself: Winners and Losers in a G-Zero World.* New York: Portfolio Penguin, 2012.

Brzezinski, Zbigniew. *Strategic Vision: America and the Crisis of Global Power.* New York: Basic Books, 2012.

Bueno de Mesquita, Bruce, Alastair Smith, Randolph M. Siverson, and James D. Morrow. *The Logic of Political Survival.* Cambridge, MA: MIT Press, 2003.

Burckhardt, Jacob. *The Greeks and Greek Civilization.* New York: St. Martin's Griffin, 1999.

Burr, Barry. "Rise in CEO Turnover." *Pensions and Investments,* October 15, 2007.

Burt, Andrew. "America's Waning Military Edge." *Yale Journal of International Affairs,* March 2012.

Carey, John M., and John Polga-Hecimovich. "Primary Elections and Candidate Strength in Latin America." *The Journal of Politics* 68, no. 3 (2006).

Chandler, Alfred P. *Scale and Scope: The Dynamics of Industrial Capitalism.* Cambridge, MA: Harvard University Press, 1990.

———. *The Visible Hand: The Managerial Revolution in American Business.* Cambridge, MA: Harvard University Press, 1977.

Chesbrough, Henry W. "The Era of Open Innovation." *MIT Sloan Management Review,* April 2003.

Christensen, Clayton. *The Innovator's Dilemma: When New Technologies Cause Great Firms to Fail.* Cambridge, MA: Harvard Business Review Press, 1997.

Chua, Amy. *World on Fire: How Exporting Free Market Democracy Breeds Ethnic Hatred and Global Instability.* New York: Anchor, 2004.

Churchill, Winston. *The Second World War.* London: Mariner Books, 1948.

Coase, Ronald H. "The Nature of the Firm." *Economica* 4, no. 16 (1937).

Comin, Diego, and Thomas Philippon. "The Rise in Firm-Level Volatility: Causes and Consequences." *NBER Macroeconomics Annual* 20 (2005).

Cronin, Patrick M. *Global Strategic Assessment 2009: America's Security Role in a Changing World.* Washington, DC: Published for the Institute for National Strategic Studies by the National Defense University Press, 2009.

Dadush, Uri. *Juggernaut.* Washington, DC: Carnegie Endowment, 2011.

Dahl, Robert A. "The Concept of Power." *Behaviorial Science* 2, no. 3 (1957).

Dalton, Russell, and Mark Gray. "Expanding the Electoral Marketplace." In Bruce Cain et al., eds., *Democracy Transformed? Expanding Political Opportunities in Advanced Industrial Democracies.* New York: Oxford University Press, 2003.

Damgaard, Erik. "Cabinet Termination." In Kaare Strom, Wolfgang C. Muller, and Torbjörn Bergman, eds., *Cabinets and Coalition Bargaining: The Democratic Life Cycle in Western Europe.* New York: Oxford University Press, 2010.

de Lorenzo, Mauro, and Apoorva Shah. "Entrepreneurial Philanthropy in the Developing World." American Enterprise Institute (2007).

Demsetz, Harold. "Barriers to Entry." UCLA Department of Economics Discussion, Paper No. 192, January 1981.

Desai, Raj M., and Homi Kharas. "Do Philanthropic Citizens Behave Like Governments? Internet-Based Platforms and the Diffusion of International Private Aid." Washington, DC: Wolfensohn Center for Development Working Papers, October 2009.

Dhar, Sujoy. "More Indian Women Postponing Motherhood." InterPress Service, May 28, 2012.

Diamond, Larry. "Can the Whole World Become Democratic? Democracy, Development and International Politics." UC Irvine: Center for the Study of Democracy, April 2003.

Diamond, Larry, and Marc F. Plattner. *Liberation Technology: Social Media and the Struggle for Democracy.* Baltimore: Johns Hopkins University Press, 2012.

Domhoff, G. William. *Who Rules America? Challenges to Corporate and Class Dominance.* New York: McGraw-Hill, 2009.

Economic and Social Commission for Asia and the Pacific. *Monograph Series on Managing Globalization: Regional Shipping and Port Development Strategies* (Container Traffic Forecast), 2011.

Eisenman, Joshua, and Joshua Kurlantzick. "China's Africa Strategy." *Current History,* May 2006.

Ferguson, Niall. *Colossus.* New York: Penguin Books, 2004.

Ferris, James M., and Hilary J. Harmssen. "California Foundations: 1999–2009—Growth Amid Adversity." The Center on Philanthropy and Public Policy, University of Southern California (2012).

Freedom House. *Freedom in the World: Political Rights and Civil Liberties 1970–2008.* New York: Freedom House, 2010.

Frey, William H. *Diversity Explosion: How New Racial Demographics Are Remaking America.* Washington, DC: Brookings Institution Press, 2013.

Friedman, Thomas. *The Lexus and the Olive Tree.* New York: Anchor Books, 2000.

———. *The World Is Flat: A Brief History of the Twenty-First Century.* New York: Farrar, Straus & Giroux, 2005.

Frydman, Carola, and Raven E. Sacks. "Executive Compensation: A New View from a Long-Term Perspective, 1936–2005," FEDS Working Paper No. 2007-35, July 2007.

Galbreath, Jeremy. "Twenty-First Century Management Rules: The Management of Relationships as Intangible Assets." *Management Decision* 40, no. 2 (2002).

Gammeltoft, Peter. "Emerging Multinationals: Outward FDI from the BRICS Countries." *International Journal of Technology and Globalization* 4, no. 1 (2008).

Ghemawat, Pankaj. *World 3.0: Global Prosperity and How to Achieve It.* Boston, MA: Harvard Business Review Press, 2011.

Gibler, Douglas M. *International Military Alliances from 1648 to 2008.* Washington, DC: Congressional Quarterly Press, 2010.

Gitlin, Todd. *Occupy Nation: The Roots, the Spirit, and the Promise of Occupy Wall Street.* New York: HarperCollins, 2012.

Golder, Matt. "Democratic Electoral Systems Around the World." *Electoral Studies* (2004).

Goldstein, Joshua, and Juliana Rotich. "Digitally Networked Technology in Kenya's 2007–2008 Post-Election Crisis." Berkman Center Research Publication, September 2008.

"Growth in United Nations Membership, 1945–Present," http://www.un.org/en/members/growth.shtml

Habbel, Rolf, Paul Kocourek, and Chuck Lucier. "CEO Succession 2005: The Crest of the Wave." *Strategy+Business,* Booz and Co., May 2006.

Hecker, Marc, and Thomas Rid. "Jihadistes de tous les pays, dispersez-vous." *Politique internationale* 123 (2009).

———. *War 2.0: Irregular Warfare in the Information Age.* New York: Praeger Security International, 1999.

Hirschman, Albert O. "The Paternity of an Index." *American Economic Review* 54, no. 5 (1964).

Hobbes, Thomas. *Leviathan.* London: Penguin, 1988.

Hooper, David, and Kenneth Whyld. *Oxford Companion to Chess.* New York and Oxford: Oxford University Press, 1992.

Horta, Loro. "China in Africa: Soft Power, Hard Results." Yale Global Online, November 13, 2009.

Howe, Irving. "This Age of Conformity." *Partisan Review* 21, no. 1 (1954).

Huntington, Samuel. *Political Order in Changing Societies.* New Haven: Yale University Press, 1968.

Inglehart, Ronald, and Christian Welzel. *Modernization, Cultural Change and Democracy.* New York and Cambridge: Cambridge University Press, 2005.

Interbrand. "Best Global Brands 2011." *Brand Papers,* 2011.

———. "Brand Valuation: The Financial Value of Brands." *Brand Papers,* 2011.

Jarvis, Michael, and Jeremy M. Goldberg. "Business and Philanthropy: The Blurring of Boundaries." *Business and Development,* Discussion Paper No. 9 (2008).

Johnson, David E., et al., "Preparing and Training for the Full Spectrum of Military Challenges: Insights from the Experience of China, France, the United Kingdom, India and Israel." National Defense Research Institute (2009).

Johnson, Simon, and James Kwak. *13 Bankers: The Wall Street Takeover and the Next Financial Meltdown.* New York: Pantheon, 2010.

Kaplan, Robert. *The World America Made.* New York: Knopf, 2012.

Kaplan, Robert D. *Monsoon: The Indian Ocean and the Future of American Power.* New York: Random House, 2011.

———. *The Coming Anarchy: Shattering the Dreams of the Post–Cold War.* New York: Vintage, 2001.

Kaplan, Steven N., and Bernadette A. Minton. "How Has CEO Turnover Changed? Increasingly Performance Sensitive Boards and Increasingly Uneasy CEOS." NBER Working Paper 12465, August 2006.

Karlsson, Per-Ola, and Gary L. Neilson. "CEO Succession 2011: The New CEO's First Year." *Strategy+Business,* Booz and Co., Summer 2012.

Kaza, Greg. "The Economics of Political Competition." *NRO Financial,* December 17, 2004.

Kenig, Ofer. "The Democratization of Party Leaders' Selection Methods: Canada in Comparative Perspective." Canadian Political Science Association conference paper, May 2009.

Kharas, Homi. "Development Assistance in the 21st Century." Contribution to the VIII Salamanca Forum: The Fight Against Hunger and Poverty, July 2–4, 2009.

———. "Trends and Issues in Development Aid." Washington, DC: Brookings Institution, November 2007.

Kindleberger, Charles P. *The World in Depression, 1929–1939.* Berkeley: University of California Press, 1973.

Koeppel, Dan. *Banana: The Fate of the Fruit That Changed the World.* New York: Plume Publishing, 2008.

Korbel, Josef. "The Decline of Democracy." *Worldview,* April 1962.

Kupchan, Charles A. *No One's World: The West, the Rising Rest, and the Coming Global Turn.* New York: Oxford University Press, 2012.

Kurlantzick, Joshua. "China's Charm: Implications of Chinese Soft Power." Carnegie Endowment for International Peace Policy Brief 47, June 2006.

———. "Chinese Soft Power in Southeast Asia." *The Globalist,* July 2007.

LaFeber, Walter. *The Cambridge History of American Foreign Relations, Vol. 2: The American Search for Opportunity, 1865–1913.* Cambridge, MA: Cambridge University Press, 1995.

Larkin, Philip. "Annus Mirabilis." *Collected Poems.* New York: Farrar, Straus & Giroux, 1988.

Leebaert, Derek. *The Fifty-Year Wound: The True Price of America's Cold War Victory.* Boston: Little, Brown and Company, 2002.

Lewis, Myrddin John, Roger Lloyd-Jones, Josephine Maltby, and Mark Matthews. *Personal Capitalism and Corporate Governance: British Manufacturing in the First Half of the Twentieth Century.* Surrey, UK: Ashgate Farnham, 2011.

Lind, William S., Keith Nightengale, John F. Schmitt, Joseph W. Sutton, and Gary I. Wilson. "The Changing Face of War: Into the Fourth Generation." *Marine Corps Gazette* (1989).

Lynn, Barry. *Cornered: The New Monopoly Capitalism and the Economics of Destruction.* New York: Wiley, 2010.

Lynn, Barry, and Phillip Longman. "Who Broke America's Jobs Machine?" *Washington Monthly,* March–April 2010.

Machiavelli, Niccolo. *The Prince.* New York: Bantam Books, 1984.

MacMillan, Ian. *Strategy Formulation: Political Concepts.* St. Paul, MN: West Publishing, 1978.

Mallaby, Sebastian. *More Money Than God.* New York: Penguin, 2010.

Mann, Thomas, and Norman Ornstein. *It's Even Worse Than It Looks: How The American Constitutional System Collided with the New Politics of Extremism.* New York: Basic Books, 2012.

Marshall, Monty G., Keith Jaggers, and Ted Robert Gurr. "Political Regime Characteristics and Transitions, 1800–2010" (2010), Polity IV Project, http://www.systemicpeace.org/polity/polity4.htm.

Marx, Karl, and Friedrich Engels. *The Communist Manifesto.* New York: Verso, reprint edition 1998.

Mathews, Jessica. "Saving America." Thomas Jefferson Foundation Medal Lecture in Citizen Leadership, University of Virginia, April 13, 2012.

McLean, Iain, and Alistair McMillan. *The Concise Oxford Dictionary of Politics.* Oxford: Oxford University Press, 2009.

McNeill, William H. *The Pursuit of Power.* Chicago: University of Chicago Press, 1982.

Micklethwait, John, and Adrian Wooldridge. *The Company: A Short History of a Revolutionary Idea.* New York: Random House, 2003.

Mills, C. Wright. *The Power Elite.* Oxford and New York: Oxford University Press, 2000.

———. *White Collar: The American Middle Classes.* New York: Oxford University Press, 2002.

Mommsen, Wolfgang. "Max Weber in America." *American Scholar,* June 22, 2000.

Morozov, Evgeny. *The Net Delusion: The Dark Side of Internet Freedom.* New York: PublicAffairs, 2011.

Moyers, Bill. *A World of Ideas: Conversations with Thoughtful Men and Women About American Life Today and the Ideas Shaping Our Future.* New York: Doubleday, 1989.

Moyo, Dambisa. *Dead Aid: Why Aid Is Not Working and How There Is a Better Way for Africa.* New York: Farrar, Straus & Giroux, 2009.

Murphy, Cullen. *Are We Rome? The Fall of an Empire and the Fate of America.* Boston: Mariner Books, 2007.

Nadeem, Shehzad. *Dead Ringers: How Outsourcing Is Changing the Way Indians Understand Themselves.* Princeton: Princeton University Press, 2011.

Naím, Moisés. *Illicit: How Smugglers, Traffickers and Copycats Are Hijacking the Global Economy.* New York: Doubleday, 2005.

Narud, Hanne Marthe, and Henry Valen. "Coalition Membership and Electoral Performance." In Kaare Strom, Wolfgang C. Muller, and Torbjörn Bergman, eds., *Cabinets and Coalition Bargaining: The Democratic Life Cycle in Western Europe.* New York: Oxford University Press, 2010.

National Intelligence Council, Office of the Director of Central Intelligence, *Global Trends 2030: Alternative Worlds.* Washington, DC (2012).

Nietzsche, Friedrich. *Thus Spake Zarathustra.* Mineola: Dover Publications, 1999.

Norris, Pippa, ed. *Critical Citizens: Global Support for Democratic Government.* Oxford: Oxford University Press, 1999.

Nye, Joseph S., Jr. *Bound To Lead: The Changing Nature of American Power.* New York: Basic Books, 1991.

———. *The Future of Power.* New York: PublicAffairs, 2011.

———. *Soft Power: The Means to Success in World Politics.* New York: PublicAffairs, 2005.

Olson, Mancur. *The Logic of Collective Action: Public Goods and the Theory of Groups.* Cambridge, MA: Harvard University Press, 1971.

Pape, Robert A. "Soft Balancing Against the United States." *International Security* 30, no. 1 (2005).

Patrick, Stewart. "Multilateralism and Its Discontents: The Causes and Consequences of U.S. Ambivalence." In Stewart Patrick and Shepard Forman, eds., *Multilateralism and U.S. Foreign Policy.* Boulder, CO: Lynne Reiner, 2001.

Pew Research Center. "State of the News Media 2012." March 19, 2012.

Pharr, Susan, and Robert Putnam. *Disaffected Democracies: What's Troubling the Trilateral Countries.* Princeton: Princeton University Press, 2000.

Quinn, James Brian. "Outsourcing Innovation: The New Engine of Growth." *MIT Sloan Management Review,* July 15, 2000.

Reynolds, Glenn. *An Army of Davids: How Markets and Technology Empower Ordinary People to Beat Big Media, Big Government, and Other Goliaths.* New York: Thomas Nelson, 2006.

Rid, Thomas. "Cracks in the Jihad." *The Wilson Quarterly,* Winter 2010.

Riesman, David, Nathan Glazer, and Reuel Denney. *The Lonely Crowd: A Study of the Changing American Character.* New Haven: Yale University Press, 1950.

Robson, Gary. *Chess Child: The Story of Ray Robson, America's Youngest Grandmaster.* Seminole, FL: Nipa Hut Press, 2010.

Runyon, Damon. *On Broadway.* New York: Picador, 1975.

Saez, Emmanuel, "Striking It Richer: The Evolution of Top Incomes in the United States." Berkeley: University of California Press, March 2012.

Sala-i-Martin, Xavier, and Maxim Pinkovskiy. "African Poverty Is Falling . . . Much Faster Than You Think!" NBER Working Paper No. 15775, February 2010.

Saxenian, AnnaLee. "The Age of the Agile." In S. Passow and M. Runnbeck, eds., *What's Next? Strategic Views on Foreign Direct Investment.* Jönköping, Sweden: ISA and UNCTAD, 2005.

———. *The New Argonauts: Regional Advantage in a Global Economy.* Cambridge, MA: Harvard University Press, 2006.

———. "The International Mobility of Entrepreneurs and Regional Upgrading in India and China." In Andrés Solimano, ed., *The International Mobility of Talent: Types, Causes, and Development Impact.* Oxford: Oxford University Press, 2008.

———. "Venture Capital in the 'Periphery': The New Argonauts, Global Search and Local Institution Building." *Economic Geography* 84, no. 4 (2008).

Scaff, Lawrence A. *Max Weber in America.* Princeton: Princeton University Press, 2011.

Schumpeter, J. A. *Essays: On Entrepreneurs, Innovations, Business Cycles, and the Evolution of Capitalism.* New Brunswick and London: Transaction Books, 1949.

Shirky, Clay. *Here Comes Everybody: The Power of Organizing Without Organization.* New York: Penguin Books, 2009.

Singer, P. W. *Wired for War: The Robotics Revolution and Conflict in the Twenty-First Century.* London and New York: Penguin, 2011.

Sloan, Alfred. *My Years with General Motors.* New York: Doubleday, 1963.

Stanko, Michael, et al. "Outsourcing Innovation." *MIT Sloan Management Review,* November 30, 2009.

Stein, Ernesto. "Fiscal Decentralization and Government Size in Latin America." *Inter-American Development Bank,* January 1998.

Sullivan, Richard. "Organizing Workers in the Space Between Unions." American Sociological Association, January 17, 2008.

Sutherland, Benjamin, ed. *Modern Warfare, Intelligence and Deterrence.* London: Profile Books, 2011.

Tharoor, Sashi. "Indian Strategic Power: 'Soft.'" *Global Brief,* May 13, 2009.

———. "India's Bollywood Power." *Project Syndicate,* January 16, 2008.

Thom, Randall, and Toni Greif. "Intangible Assets in the Valuation Process: A Small Business Acquisition Study." *Journal of Academy of Business and Economics,* April 1, 2008.

United Nations Conference on Trade and Development (UNCTAD). *World Investment Report 2012.*

United Nations Secretary General. *Small Arms Report,* 2011.

United States Department of Defense. *Fiscal Year 2012 Budget Request,* February 2012.

United States Department of State. *Treaties in Force: A List of Treaties and Other International Agreements of the United States in Force,* January 1, 2012.

Waltz, Julie, and Vijaya Ramachandran. "Brave New World: A Literature Review of Emerging Donors and the Changing Nature of Foreign Assistance." *Center for Global Development,* Working Paper No. 273, November 2011.

Weber, Marianne. *Max Weber: A Biography.* New York: Transaction Books, 1988.

———. *Essays in Sociology,* 5th ed. Oxon, UK: Routledge, 1970.

———. *Economy and Society: An Outline of Interpretive Sociology.* Berkeley: University of California Press, 1978.

Weber, Max. *The Vocation Lectures: Science as a Vocation, Politics as a Vocation.* Indianapolis: Hackett Publishing Company, 2004.

Williamson, Oliver. *Markets and Hierarchies: Analysis and Antitrust Implications.* New York: The Free Press, 1975.

Wohlforth, William C. "The Stability of a Unipolar World." *International Security* 24, no. 1 (1999).

World Bank. "Aid Architecture: An Overview of the Main Trends in Official Development Assistance Flows." International Development Association, Resource Mobilization, February 2007.

———. "Doing Business," 2011.

———. "South-South FDI and Political Risk Insurance: Challenges and Opportunities." *MIGA Perspectives,* January 2008.

———. "World Development Indicators Database," 2011.

———. "World Development Report 2009: Reshaping Economic Geography," (2009).

"World Championship" Oxford Companion to Chess. New York and Oxford: Oxford University Press, 1992.

Yang, Dean. "Migrant Remittances." *Journal of Economic Perspectives* 25, no. 3 (Summer 2011).

Zakaria, Fareed. *The Future of Freedom: Illiberal Democracy at Home and Abroad.* New York: W. W. Norton, 2003.

———. *The Post-American World: Release 2.0.* New York: W. W Norton, 2012.

Zedong, Mao. "The Relation of Guerrilla Hostilities to Regular Operations." *On Guerrilla Warfare.* Champaign: First Illinois Paperback, 2000.

Zimmerling, Ruth. *Influence and Power: Variations on a Messy Theme.* New York: Springer Verlag, 2005.

Zuil, Lilla. "AIG's Title as World's Largest Insurer Gone Forever." *Insurance Journal,* April 29, 2009.

Zunz, Olivier. *Philanthropy in America: A History.* Princeton: Princeton University Press, 2012.

INDEX